BECOMING
ODYSSA

Adventures on
the Appalachian Trail

JENNIFER PHARR DAVIS

BEAUFORT BOOKS • NEW YORK

Library of Congress Cataloging-in-Publication Data

Davis, Jennifer Pharr.

Becoming odyssa : epic adventures on the Appalachian Trail / Jennifer Pharr Davis.

p. cm.

ISBN 978-08253-0568-9 (alk. paper)

1. Hiking—Appalachian Trail. 2. Appalachian Trail—Description and travel. 3. Davis, Jennifer Pharr—Travel—Appalachian Trail. I. Title.

GV199.42.A68D38 2010
796.510974—dc22
2010028097

For inquiries about volume orders, please contact:
Beaufort Books
27 West 20th Street, Suite 1102
New York, NY 10011
sales@beaufortbooks.com

Published in the United States by Beaufort Books
www.beaufortbooks.com

Distributed by Midpoint Trade Books
www.midpointtrade.com

Interior design by Elyse Strongin, Neuwirth & Associates, Inc.
Interior Illustrations by James Pharr
Cover Design by Amy King
Cover Photograph by Maureen Robinson at Dog Works Digital Photography

10 9 8 7 6

Printed in the United States of America

CONTENTS

Preface by David Horton, Ph.D.   VII

Introduction by Warren Doyle, Ph.D.   IX

1. LOVE   I
Abol Campground, ME, to the top of Mount Katahdin, ME—3.87 miles

2. TRUTH   7
The Appalachian Trail Institute, Banner Elk, NC

3. INEPTITUDE   13
Unicoi Gap, GA, to Springer Mountain, GA—50.9 miles

4. ADVENTURE   31
Unicoi Gap, GA, to the Nantahala Outdoor Center, NC—84 miles

5. ADVERSITY   43
*Nantahala Outdoor Center, NC, to Waterville School Road, NC—
103.4 miles*

6. HOME   55
Waterville School Road, NC, to Hot Springs, NC—33.4 miles

7. FRIENDS   65
Hot Springs, NC, to Cherry Gap Shelter, TN—84.5 miles

8. CONFIDENCE   85
Cherry Gap Shelter, TN, to Damascus, VA—104.9 miles

9. OPPRESSION   103
Damascus, VA, to a little past Pearisburg, VA—165 miles

10. DISCOMFORT   125
    Outside Pearisburg, VA, to Troutville, VA—92 miles

11. INSPIRATION   139
    Troutville, VA, to Rockfish Gap, VA—132.3 miles

12. GENEROSITY   155
    Rockfish Gap, VA, to US 522 (Front Royal), VA—107 miles

13. DIVERSITY   165
    *US 522 (Front Royal), VA, to Pen Mar Park, MD/PA—
    95 miles*

14. ABNORMALITY   177
    Pen Mar Park, MD/PA, to Delaware Water Gap, NJ—260 miles

15. MORTALITY   201
    *Delaware Water Gap, PA, to Bear Mountain State Park, NY—
    107.9 miles*

16. PERSEVERANCE   219
    *Bear Mountain State Park, NY, to Mount Greylock, MA—
    183.9 miles*

17. OPTIMISM   233
    Mount Greylock, MA, to Hanover, NH—160 miles

18. REGROUPING   241
    Hanover, NH, to Pinkham Notch, NH—123 miles

19. TRIBULATION   261
    Pinkham Notch, NH, to Monson, ME—199 miles

20. TRIUMPH   279
    Monson, ME, to Mount Katahdin, ME—118 miles

21. HOMECOMING   295
    Summer 2005 to Summer 2008—3 years

2008 Itinerary   301

Acknowledgments   303

Dedicated to...
The Glory of God,
My Love, my Husband, Brew Davis,
My Friend, my Father, Yorke Pharr.

PREFACE

Jennifer Pharr Davis is a modern day adventurer. Most folks in today's society do not seek out things that will test them. Most seek out things that will entertain them. As you read Jennifer's story, you can feel her pain and vicariously enjoy and relate to all that she goes through on her trip that shapes her into the special person she has become.

Even though I knew most of the events that happened during her trip, I could not put this book down. You will feel the same. I could not wait to see what challenge the Appalachian Trail presented to her next, and how she would deal with it. I believe that this is a book that everyone can relate to—not just hikers and runners, but anyone who has ever dreamed about doing something adventurous.

There has never been anyone so young who has accomplished what Jennifer has. She is one of the toughest, nicest, and friendliest people that I have ever known. She motivates me to seek new challenges. Reading this book will motivate you to seek challenges in your life.

I feel honored to call Jennifer a friend, and look forward to seeing what she will do in the future. You will feel like she is your friend after you read this book. The story you are about to read is just the start for this young lady.

David Horton, Ph.D.
Endurance Runner, Former Appalachian Trail Speed Record Holder
Professor of Kinesiology, Liberty University

INTRODUCTION

The Appalachian Trail is a simple, slender thread of individual freedom flowing between Springer Mountain in northern Georgia and Katahdin in central Maine. That such a footpath even exists in our modern cyber world is a testament to the visionary who conceived it in the early twentieth century and the thousands of volunteer trail builders working tirelessly over the last eight decades, along with the dedicated trail maintainers of today.

It is our nation's premier long-distance hiking trail, emulated and modeled worldwide. It is as significant to our nation's health as our interstate, national park, and Social Security systems, and at very little cost to the taxpayer. It provides the peaceful and beautiful green to offset the sometimes chaotic, dehumanizing gray of our daily existence. Those who tread this path for a morning, afternoon, dusk, dawn, weeks, or several months are more likely to feel better about themselves, and each other, after they have taken their respective trail sojourns.

The pilgrimage is an important part of many cultures. We need to get away from the familiar and explore not only what is around the next bend but also discover the strength and beauty that we have within us. A walkabout helps us to realize that we were just conditioned and trained in school, and with this realization we can take our first steps toward freedom and self-actualization. We develop our critical thinking abilities, rediscover being curious, and find ourselves asking questions again. We begin to more closely define what is real and what is trivial to us. We become more awake to beauty and truth, right and wrong. We rediscover a childlike sense of wonder at the essence of the natural environment.

The trail is a teacher like no other. It has no required reading, assignments, projects, or grades. It has no expectations. It has no prejudice or discrimination. It doesn't care about your socioeconomic class, age, gender, religious affiliation, race, ethnicity, education level, occupation, family name, the clothes you wear, or the car you drive. What a fantastic place for an individual to find out who she really is!

Over the past thirty-seven years, I have traversed the entire Appalachian Trail sixteen times. I have observed hundreds of people before and after their thru-hikes. In most cases, the trail has caused positive changes for these pilgrims. They are physically, mentally, and spiritually stronger and more confident about their abilities and capacities. They are more content, flexible, tolerant, patient, and adventurous.

However, it is troubling that not all those who set out on a thru-hike complete their journey. Estimates of the potential thru-hikers who drop out range from seventy-five to eighty percent. Why? Based on the eight groups of people I have led up the entire AT, with phenomenal completion rates, I offer these thirteen snippets of accumulated wisdom:

- Walking the entire Appalachian Trail is not recreation. It is an education and a job.
- Walking the entire Appalachian Trail is not "going on a hike." It is a challenging task—a journey with deeper ramifications. Are you willing to accept them and learn from them?
- Don't fight the Trail. You have to flow with it. Be cooperative with the Trail, neither competitive nor combative.
- Don't expect the Trail to respect or to be sensitive to your comfort level and desire to control your environment. In your avoidance of discomfort, you may become more uncomfortable. Fear is weight.
- Time, distance, terrain, weather, and the Trail itself cannot be changed. You have to change. Don't waste any of your energy complaining about things you have no control over. Instead, look at yourself and adapt you mind, heart, body, and soul to the Trail. Remember, you will be a guest in someone else's house the entire journey.

- The Trail knows neither prejudice nor discrimination. Don't expect any favors from the Trail. The Trail is inherently hard—there is no easy. Everything has to be earned. The Trail is a trial.
- Leave your cultural "level of comfort" at home. Reduce your material wants while concentrating on your physical and spiritual needs.
- Basic needs—food, clothing, shelter? Keep it light, simple, and frugal.
- It is far better, and less painful, to learn to be a smart hiker rather than a strong hiker.
- Leave your emotional fat at home as well. Feel free to laugh, to cry, to feel lonely, to feel afraid, to feel socially irresponsible, to feel foolish, and (most importantly) to feel free. Relive your childhood and play the GAME of the Trail. Roll with the punches and learn to laugh in the shadow of adversity. Be always optimistic—things could always be worse; don't become mired in the swamp of sorrow.
- If your goal is to walk the entire Appalachian Trail, then do it. People who take shortcuts do so because they are usually shorter, quicker, or easier. So where is the challenge and honor in that? We have enough of this in the real world.
- Expect the worst. If after one week on the Trail you can honestly say that it is easier than you expected, then you will probably finish your journey.
- We all have our own temperaments, levels of comfort, and thresholds of pain. If these are congruent with what the Trail requires, you should succeed on your pilgrimage.

What follows is an informative and inspiring narrative of a young woman's successful traverse of the entire Appalachian Trail after she finished her undergraduate education. She took many of these snippets of long-distance hiking wisdom to heart, and she was granted great rewards of insight, beauty, and truth that will last her all her life and impact the people who have the good fortune to meet her. I'm proud to be one of those.

Becoming Odyssa is a frank and fun story of a young female pilgrim becoming more than she ever was before through hard physical effort, perseverance, and her ability to adapt and be flexible. She learns to appreciate the simple pleasure of flowing by foot, gazelle-like, through the magnificent Appalachians from Georgia to Maine. It is a journey to be appreciated and honored. Knowing what she has done since her maiden voyage of 2005, I'm confident this will only be the first book of her accomplishments in the long-distance hiking realm.

It is both an honor and a privilege to introduce you to Jennifer Pharr Davis's story of becoming Odyssa.

Warren Doyle, Ph.D.
Director, Appalachian Trail Folk School
Founder, Appalachian Long Distance Hikers Association (ALDHA)

1

LOVE

JUNE 20TH, 2008

ABOL CAMPGROUND, ME, TO THE TOP OF
MOUNT KATAHDIN, ME—3.87 MILES

Mount Katahdin is one of the toughest climbs on the Appalachian Trail, but you don't feel it—at least, not like you would expect. Northbound thru-hikers who journey up the mountain are too consumed by the accomplishment, and Southbound hikers are too overwhelmed with anticipation to focus on the difficulty of the path. Hikers remember their emotions on the mountain more than its unique geographical features. It is a peak that has launched dreams and fulfilled goals. It is a summit that will change your life.

My wristwatch alarm went off at 3:30 AM. Finally. Despite my warm sleeping bag and soft foam pad, I had hardly slept at all that night, waiting to hear the rhythmic beeping that now filled the tent.

Sleepless nights were not unusual in this season of my life. I thought back to a week and a half ago when I didn't sleep in anticipation of my wedding ceremony the next morning. Twelve days ago it was pure excitement and an unrelenting smile that kept me from sleep, but this morning, anxiety and adrenaline filled the darkness. In both cases my elevated heart rate and insomnia were the result of starting a new journey—a journey down a road that I believed I had been uniquely designed and created to explore.

Brew, my new husband, began to stir beside me. Apparently the significance of the morning had not kept him from a deep sleep, which he now struggled to depart. Luckily, in a small tent, all my jostling prevented him from falling back asleep, and in accordance with our plan we were both dressed, with headlamps on our heads, packs on our backs, and half-consumed Clif Bars in our hands, by 3:45 AM.

It took us a little over an hour to navigate the dark forest and rocky terrain at the base of Katahdin, but at 5:00 AM we emerged from the woods and arrived at an endless uphill boulder field. The terrain ahead resembled a rock quarry, with stones scattered across the mountainside, masking the trail in front of us. But with the atmosphere now dimly glowing, we tucked away our headlamps and began winding our way up the rocky slope, scanning rocks and boulders for the painted blazes that would guide our path.

On June 20th in central Maine, the sun starts to break through the clouds too early for most to appreciate. The first rays hit our backs at 5:30, and I was thankful for the warmth and light that they provided. There were several moments during the ascent when I stopped to look out over the softening sky. I was inspired by the sea of clouds beneath us and the three distant mountain peaks that sat like islands amid the dense white depths. I struggled to keep my focus on the rocky path, and instead watched the vast shadow of Katahdin serve as a sundial, rotating over the ocean of clouds below us.

I was so taken by the beauty and stillness of the morning that the reality of the task ahead didn't sink in until we neared the top of the mountain. Walking across the rock-strewn field that led to the northern terminus of the Appalachian Trail, I was suddenly struck by the significance of each forward footstep that I planted in the soft, damp earth.

I had been on this same trail, in this same place, three years earlier. But my first climb up Katahdin wasn't as lighthearted or light-footed as my current traverse. I had arrived at the mountain after the four hardest months of my life, and had viewed my climb to the rocky apex as merely the means to an end—the end of physical hardship, the end of emotional distress, the end of unsavory encounters, and the end of spiritual unrest. I swore to myself that I would never come back to this mountain, and that I would never again entertain the idea of thru-hiking.

God must have been laughing down on me as I made those short-sighted vows. What I didn't realize at that time was that my climb up Katahdin had not marked the end of a journey, but the beginning of a new life. I had no idea that the challenges I faced as a twenty-one-year-old woman hiking the Appalachian Trail would so deeply impact who I am, what I believe, and how I want to live. And I certainly would never have guessed that my epic misadventures on the AT would lead to an enduring love of long-distance hiking.

The path was uneven, but Brew and I walked hand in hand to the worn wooden sign that marked the top of the mountain. It was 6:20 AM, and I was ready to set out on a new adventure, to begin a new chapter of my life, with the man I love by my side. Before I started, we took a few mountaintop photos, then I grabbed hold of my warm, sweet-smelling husband as he prayed over the next 2,175 miles. Together we asked God for safety and good health, we asked that He would strengthen our relationship, and that He would allow us to help others along the way.

After we said "Amen," I set off down the mountain. As I went forward, I reflected on the trials and trails that had led me back to this place. A large smile spread across my face as I considered the past five thousand miles and three and a half years, and remembered the preparation for my first thru-hike of the Appalachian Trail. As I transitioned from the upper plain of Katahdin to its rocky spine, I laughed as I thought about how far I had come from the insecure twenty-one-year-old who had started the trail in 2005. I was now able to look ahead and see where I wanted to go, but I was still close enough to look back and see where I had come from.

2

TRUTH
DECEMBER 2004

THE APPALACHIAN TRAIL INSTITUTE,
BANNER ELK, NC

It is impossible to fully prepare for a 2,175-mile hike. The only way to learn how to hike all day, every day, is to go into the woods and do just that. Since most people cannot or do not train for thru-hiking by thru-hiking, they have to get ready for the trail by reading guidebooks, scanning internet chat rooms, going on day hikes, and spending time at the local gym. To prepare for my first thru-hike, I decided to attend an intense three-day Appalachian Trail workshop led by Dr. Warren Doyle.

I t was a cold winter morning in December 2004. I woke up at 4:00 AM and drove two hours from my home in Hendersonville, North Carolina, to reach Lees-McRae College in nearby Banner Elk.

Lees-McRae was where Professor Warren Doyle taught undergrad courses in elementary education. But beyond being an educator, Warren was an Appalachian Trail legend. He had hiked the trail thirteen times and counting, and when the Lees-McRae students left the campus for winter break, Warren used the facilities to host his Appalachian Trail Institute: a course designed to help prepare hikers who intended to hike the entire trail.

At 7:57 AM, I found an empty desk in the professor's classroom and took a seat. There were nine other participants, and they all looked nervous. I fidgeted with my pen and rustled with my notepad until eight sharp, when Warren entered the room.

He was in his mid-fifties, he had a peppered gray beard and a larger belly than I would expect on such an accomplished hiker. He stood at his chair in front of the class and surveyed the Institute's participants, then he took a seat, clasped his hands together in front of his body, and in a resounding voice, he asked, "Why do you want to hike the Appalachian Trail?"

I was pretty sure he was staring right at me, but he might have had the power to make everyone in a room feel that way.

"Let's go around the room and have everyone tell the class who they are and why they want to hike the Appalachian Trail," he said, grinning like the Cheshire Cat.

There I was, sitting in the classroom of the legendary Warren Doyle, who had hiked the Appalachian Trail more than anyone else, and I didn't know how to answer the first question of his three-day workshop.

I had only spent three nights in the woods in my entire life, and I knew very little about thru-hiking. As we began to go around the room with introductions, I felt panicked and unsure of myself, like I was naked and everyone knew it.

The attractive young couple at the opposite end of the table were the first to respond: "My name is Doug, and this is my wife Sarah."

My mind began to shift back and forth as I tried to listen to what the other participants were saying while reflecting on why I wanted to hike the trail.

"We want to do it as a couple," said Sarah. "This has always been Doug's dream, but now we're married, so I want it to be *our* dream."

"I've wanted to hike the trail ever since I was a Boy Scout," added Doug. "But now that we're married, I couldn't imagine going off and leaving Sarah for six months. That's why she's coming with me. The only problem is that she's *really* prissy, and I don't know how she'll cope without her makeup and curling iron."

Everyone laughed, including Sarah, as she gave her husband a playful shove.

"It's true," she said. "I'm a priss, but I'm a stubborn priss."

I smiled and thought about the advantages of having a hiking partner, someone to share your gear, your day, and your memories. When I decided three years ago that I was going to hike the Appalachian Trail, I thought that my best friend or my father might come with me. As time passed, it became clear that none of my friends or family would be able to go on this journey with me. Most of them thought I would abandon my plans well before now, but I was still determined to do the trail. I had adjusted to the idea of hiking on my own, and I was excited about it, though my mother was not.

"Wesley, why do you want to hike the trail?" asked Warren

We were already almost halfway around the table. I was thankful to be positioned at the end of the nine-person panel, but I was still worried about what I would say.

"Well . . . " Wesley began. "I grew up on a farm in Alabama. I was outside every day doing work, hard work. After I graduated high school, I left the farm and started working in the city. I spent thirty years behind a desk, and the whole time I was there, I missed being outside and I missed manual labor. We sold the farm when my father died, but now that I'm retired I want to hike the Appalachian Trail. I want to work hard during the day and go to bed with the sun. That's what I think we were made to do."

"Do you think your body will remember what it's like to perform manual labor?" asked Warren.

Part of what made me nervous was that Warren responded to each answer with more questions. He was the king of *what ifs:* What if your hiking partner doesn't like it? What if you get injured? What if you don't finish in time to get back to work? What if your spouse wants you to come home?

Warren was especially hard on Jeff, the middle-aged man seated to my right.

"Whoa, whoa, whoa!" Warren interrupted Jeff's response, waving his hands and shaking his head. "You said you want to hike the trail for *fun?* Do you think hiking in the rain and snow is fun? Do you think walking twenty miles a day with blisters on your feet is fun? What are you going to do when you wake up one morning and decide that the trail isn't fun anymore?"

At least now I knew not to include the word "fun" in my answer.

Jeff tried to backtrack for several minutes, unsuccessfully, then Warren finally called on me.

"And last, young lady, we come to you. Tell us a little about yourself and why you want to hike the Appalachian Trail."

"My name is Jen," I began nervously, "and I'm twenty-one years old. I decided during my freshman year of college that I was going to hike the Appalachian Trail, and I arranged my classes so I could graduate a semester early—this past December. I'm planning to start the trail in March from Springer Mountain, Georgia, and I'll stay out there as long as it takes to reach Mount Katahdin in Maine."

"Okay, but *why* do you want to hike the trail?"

Ugh, I was hoping he would forget that part.

I took a deep breath. I had given people different answers to that same question for the past three years. I said that I wanted to hike the trail to be in nature, to push my limits, to meet new people, to put off getting a job, or to give my mother gray hair. I had given various answers depending on what I thought the person asking the question wanted to hear. But I knew that Warren would see through a trite response. So for the first time, I tried to tell the truth.

"I feel like I'm meant to . . . I mean, I feel like I was made to . . . I guess what I'm trying to say is that I think I'm *supposed* to hike the AT."

"What does that mean?" asked Warren.

"Well, when I think about doing anything else it just feels wrong. The thought of not doing the trail fills me with regret to the point that it almost hurts inside. The idea of thru-hiking the Appalachian Trail came to me three years ago, and since it entered my mind, not a day goes by when I don't think about the trail. It's not like I chose to hike the trail, but more like it chose me."

"Ah, yes," said Warren, looking surprisingly pleased. "So the trail is a calling?"

"Yeah . . . a calling."

Admitting to everyone—including myself—the real reason that I wanted to hike the trail made me feel good. A little crazy, but good. I felt lighter and breathed easier knowing that I was able to be honest.

Meanwhile, Warren had stopped asking questions and started whimsically singing, *"The trail is calling, calling, calling, calling to you and to me."* Then, with a more serious look on his face, he sat up straight and looked around the room.

"Thank you all for your answers," he said. "They were very . . . insightful."

Then, before wrapping up our morning session, Warren once again managed to look at me and stare at everyone else at the same time.

"You need to know that the trail can and will change you," he said. "Once you finish the trail, your life might not look the same as it did when you started. If you don't want things to change, then you need to rethink thru-hiking."

Then Warren, with a knowing gleam in his eye, let out a mischievous laugh that shook his soft belly, and with his arm outstretched and his palm facing up, he ushered us out of the classroom for an afternoon hike on the Appalachian Trail.

3

INEPTITUDE
EARLY MARCH 2005

UNICOI GAP, GA, TO SPRINGER MOUNTAIN, GA— 50.9 MILES

For a northbound thru-hiker, the southernmost fifty miles of the Appalachian Trail is the beginning of a new relationship rife with hopes, fears, and stomach butterflies. The anxiety and anticipation about what will come next are expressed by friendly smiles, nervous chatter, and numerous photos. The miles build up slowly as people adjust to the trail and their gear, and the learning curve is visible each day as hikers figure out how to set up tents, pop blisters, and exist in a wilderness that is full of strangers. For many northbound thru-hikers, the foothills of Northern Georgia are both the happiest and the most challenging part of the journey.

After three days at the Appalachian Trail Institute, I felt far more prepared for my thru-hike than I had before I arrived. I felt more confident planning my food resupplies, limiting my gear, budgeting my money, and preparing myself mentally for the trail. I was still uncertain about the alternative hiking methods that we covered, such as not packing a stove and not filtering the water from mountain springs or streams, and the alternative gear options, like using a tarp instead of a tent, a trash bag instead of a raincoat, or a ski pole instead of a hiking stick. But, most importantly, I left the Institute knowing that it was not my gear that would get me to Katahdin, but my heart and my head.

The other benefit of the Appalachian Trail Institute was that I made several good friends. In particular, I had grown close to Sarah and Doug. My first reaction to the couple and their overwhelming affection for each other included a lot of mental eye-rolling. But as the workshop progressed, I felt myself reluctantly drawn to their friendly personalities and the warmth of their love for one another. By the end of our three-day course, the three of us left the workshop with a plan.

We decided to start the trail together for the sake of companionship—and the sake of my mother—and to begin our thru-hike as an unbalanced "flip-flop."

There are three ways to thru-hike the Appalachian Trail:

1) You can start at Springer Mountain, Georgia, and hike to Mount Katahdin, Maine, as a northbound hiker.
2) You can start from Katahdin and hike to Springer as a southbound hiker.
3) Or you can start somewhere in the middle and hike to either Springer Mountain or Mount Katahdin, then return to your starting place and hike in the opposite direction to complete the trail as a flip-flop.

Most hikers who flip-flop start in the middle of the trail, near Harpers Ferry, West Virginia. We started our flip-flop in Georgia, fifty miles north of Springer Mountain. The idea was to meet in early March and hike the first fifty miles of the trail backwards.

Theoretically, there is no right or wrong direction on the Appalachian Trail, but in the month of March, in the state of Georgia, everyone hikes north—everyone except for us. We wanted to hike south to meet as many northbound thru-hikers as possible and learn from their mistakes. The more lessons we could learn vicariously, the better.

I met Sarah and Doug on March tenth in a gravel parking lot a mile north of Springer Mountain, and after gathering my gear and locking my car, I climbed into their SUV, and together we drove back down the mountain.

Unicoi Gap is only fifty trail miles from Springer Mountain, but on the road it took us winding two and a half hours to reach the trailhead.

The day so far had been sunny and cool, but at Unicoi Gap, the long afternoon shadows and increased elevation meant freezing temperatures and bitter winds. Before we left the car, I pulled all my extra clothing out of my pack and layered it on my body for additional warmth.

As I zipped up my raincoat and adjusted my pack, I heard Sarah call to me from the edge of the woods.

"Hey Jen, come look at this."

She had found our first white blaze. One of the things I loved about the AT is that it seemed idiot-proof. There are two-by-six white rectangles marking the trail every hundred yards. I didn't need a map or a compass; all I had to do to make it to Maine was follow the white blazes.

I walked over and stared with wonder at the simple stripe of white. I curiously grazed my fingertips along the bumpy rectangle of tree bark, and then, noticing that my friends were already twenty yards up the trail, I stepped past the blaze and began my thru-hike on the Appalachian Trail.

It was 4:30 when we started. In early March, deep in the Blue Ridge Mountains, that meant we had an hour and a half of daylight left.

Our first day's distance and ascent wouldn't be difficult for a seasoned hiker, but I wasn't used to hiking with a heavy, awkward backpack. It felt like I was giving a hefty six-year-old a piggyback ride up the mountain.

I tried to take my mind off the climb. Glancing around, I looked for the natural beauty that is synonymous with the AT, but all I saw were naked trees shuddering in the wind. Looking up into the blustery wind made my eyes water, so I dropped my head and stared at the trail. For the rest of our uphill journey, I concentrated on the rocks and roots on the trail, and the big white puffs of air that appeared every time I exhaled.

It took us just over an hour to hike the 2.2 miles from Unicoi Gap to Blue Mountain Shelter. The three-sided wooden shelters are an important part of the trail and trail culture. With a shelter approximately every ten miles, hikers will gather at the lean-tos during the day to socialize, and at night the structures provide cover for those who don't want to pitch their tents.

Peering into my first official shelter, I was not impressed. The floorboards looked dirty and the sides of the building had gaping holes. Sarah walked up behind me, put her hand on my shoulder, and said, "I guess we should try to stay here since there's not enough daylight to set up our tents. I just hope there aren't any mice."

Mice? I hadn't thought about rodents living in the shelters. Thankfully, Blue Mountain Shelter was too full of large, two-legged creatures for me to notice the small, four-legged kind. Amid the sleeping bags and backpacks, I met four college-aged girls who called themselves the Georgia Peaches. They were here on a spring break hiking trip. Even with just their noses poking out of their sleeping bags, it was clear that they were attractive, personable, and had already made quite an impression on the other hikers, especially Eskimo.

Eskimo was a retiree from Alaska who had situated himself directly beside the Georgia Peaches. He spent the evening bragging about his handmade gear and sharing his preferred hiking techniques with the cute coeds.

Two young men also occupied the campsite. One was tucked into a blue sleeping bag in the corner of the shelter. He wore a green ski mask that covered his entire face, and as Doug set up his bag nearby, I overheard the guy mumbling something about insulin and what Doug should do if he didn't wake up the next morning.

The other guy was wearing a navy blue down jacket and walking away from the campsite with his water bottle in hand. I grabbed my own empty water bottle and quickly followed.

The hiker stopped two hundred yards downhill from the shelter and crouched over the water source: a small puddle formed by an underground spring. With pump in hand, he meticulously filtered every ounce of water flowing into his bottle.

I watched him in awe: I didn't have a pump. I also didn't have iodine, chlorine dioxide, a SteriPEN, or any other acceptable form of water treatment. I had decided, based on Warren Doyle's advice at the Appalachian Trail Institute, that it would be fine to drink from the majority of water sources on the Appalachian Trail without treating the water. But staring down into the shallow puddle, I began to second-guess my au naturel approach.

Not wanting to look foolish without a form of water treatment, I stood back and waited for the young man to finish before I attempted to draw my water directly from the source. As he stood up to leave, I caught a glimpse of his face. Curly black locks escaped from the red bandana on his head. The lower half of his face was lined with a week's worth of coarse stubble ending right below his full cheeks. He glanced up and met my stare with hazel eyes, then smiled.

"Hi, I'm Matthew."

"I'm Jen."

"First night on the trail?" he asked.

"Yeah, my friends and I are thru-hikers, but we're hiking this section south, regrouping, then heading north."

"Cool. In that case, maybe we'll meet again farther up the trail."

When Matthew left, I quickly gathered my water and then turned on my headlamp to hike back to the shelter. My brief exchange with Matthew flipped a switch within me. Matthew was the first person I had met on the Appalachian Trail, and that made the hike feel real. It was reassuring to meet a complete stranger and immediately feel connected by a common goal. Plus, I had called myself a thru-hiker—in the present tense. I liked the way that sounded.

Back at the shelter, I set up my stove and eagerly placed my pot of murky water and Velveeta Shells and Cheese on top of the burner. The outside temperature was well below freezing, and my dinner took longer than I expected to cook. As I stared at the still water, waiting for it to boil, my fingers grew painfully numb. After fifteen minutes, the water was steaming but still not bubbling, and I impatiently decided that the noodles had soaked long enough. With shaking hands, I picked up the pot, drained off the brown water, added the orange goo, and awkwardly stirred the sauce around the glob of noodles.

I filled my spork and brought it to my mouth. Crunching down on the first bite, the concoction tasted like Easy Cheese and eggshells. I could only stomach a few bites before my decreasing dexterity and sensitive gag reflex caused me to surrender. Still hungry and not knowing what to do with the leftovers, I shamefully returned to the water hole and slung them into a nearby bush. I submerged the pot in the puddle to try and remove the orange crust cemented inside the pot. I was sure that this was not the proper way to clean camp dishes, but I was too embarrassed and too cold to find another solution.

Ready for bed, I threw my food bag and dirty cooking equipment into my pack and placed it against the shelter wall, then I squeezed my foam pad and sleeping bag between Sarah and Matthew.

"Night, Jen," said Sarah.

"Good night," I answered. Then, looking at the empty sleeping bag beside her, I asked, "Where's Doug?"

"He's putting our food bag up on the bear cables. He should be back any minute."

"Oh, all right. See you two in the morning."

I had seen the metal bear cables hanging from a tree near the shelter, but I had no clue that I was supposed to use them to suspend my food.

I thought about my pack full of food and dirty dishes leaning up against the side of the shelter. It was completely accessible to shelter mice, or, even worse, bears. I really wanted to see a bear on the trail, but not my first night, and not because I had done something wrong!

I was frustrated with myself for not knowing how to cook, how to clean my pots, or where to hang my food. The simplest everyday tasks were complicated on the trail. Even drinking water, finding a place to change clothes, and spitting out my toothpaste had become obstacles. I felt unprepared for my first night and overwhelmed by the thought of spending months on the trail.

I tried to fall asleep, but I couldn't stop shivering, and the wooden floorboards beneath me were too hard for me to find a comfortable position. I laid on my left side until my hip hurt, then on my back until it ached, then on my right side until my arm went numb, then on my stomach until the pain from the stiff wooden boards made me roll back onto my side. I felt like a rotisserie chicken stuck in a freezer.

The warmth and soft glow that greeted me the next day was a welcome relief. I had spent the majority of the night staring into the darkness and waiting for the sun to rise. And when the morning's first rays peeked into our lean-to, everyone in the shelter began to stir. Some fired up their stoves for a warm breakfast, and others fetched their food from the nearby storage cables and crawled back into their sleeping bags to enjoy Pop-Tarts in bed.

I didn't want to cook, I didn't want to reveal that my food bag was in my pack beside the shelter, and, unlike the four Georgia Peaches, I didn't know how to change clothes inside my sleeping bag. The last one didn't matter so much since I was already wearing all my clothes.

I decided that my best option was to roll up my sleeping bag, shove it in my pack, and start hiking.

I turned to Sarah, who now had Pop-Tart crumbs on her top lip.

"Hey, I think I'm going to get started."

"Okay, we won't be too far behind you. But if we don't catch up, remember, you can't leave Springer without us."

I laughed. "I'm sure I'll see you before then."

Then I hopped out of the shelter, collected my pack, and headed into the woods.

My second day on the trail featured a challenging ascent, scattered snow flurries, and excruciating pain. Although it was still early in the trek, I was already developing a routine. I would hike for thirty or forty-five minutes until my shoulders screamed and my hands went numb. At that point I would take a short break, remove my pack, and rest my arms and shoulders until I regained blood flow to my fingers. Then I would continue on my way.

My pack wasn't abnormally heavy; I estimated that with my gear, food, and water it probably weighed thirty pounds, but unlike most hikers, I never weighed it. Pack weight was a controversial topic among thru-hikers. Those with really heavy packs, over fifty pounds, will carry them with pride. They have increased joint pain and hike slower, but they feel tough and prepared for anything. On the other hand, light-weight backpackers struggle daily to reduce their fifteen-pound loads by a fraction of an ounce. They hike faster and get fewer injuries, but they sacrifice comfort at their campsites.

I was somewhere in the middle, and my head told me that my pack was manageable, but my shoulders gave me a different message. The pain throbbing in my narrow, boney shoulders was somewhat my fault: I was never fitted for a pack before I left to hike. Instead, I had gone to a downstairs closet in my parents' house and rummaged through thirty-year-old sleeping bags and campfire cookware to find an old external-frame backpack that my brother had once used at summer camp. Its faded gray color and worn hip belt weren't glamorous, but it was free.

My first full day on the trail, I passed twenty-five or thirty hikers headed north. I greeted all of them, and while some stopped to talk, others simply nodded their heads and kept going. It was strange to think that ten percent of the people I passed would quit before reaching the North Carolina border, and another sixty percent would quit before the half-way point. It was hard to believe that only one in four of the wide-eyed hikers I encountered would complete the trail.

I think most people would assess potential thru-hikers based on their physique, experience, and pack weight, but I predicted their odds of success based on facial expressions. If a person could smile in the blustery snow flurries and bare forests of North Georgia while carrying a cumbersome pack on his back, I decided he would make it to Katah-din. On the other hand, if a person offered a gruff greeting, didn't look up, or simply grunted as I passed by, I figured the odds were stacked against him.

As the sun reached the horizon, I encountered fewer and fewer peo-ple. The darkening sky meant that most hikers would be looking for refuge at a shelter or in their tents, but I was still alone. I reasoned that Sarah and Doug were not far behind me, so I decided to take a break and wait for them. We agreed that we might not spend every night together on our journey to Springer, but I didn't quite feel ready to spend the night on my own yet.

I stopped on a fallen tree to eat dinner. I didn't want to cook, so I substituted an energy bar and trail mix for a hot meal. It was better than a half-cooked pot of food, but the cold temperatures left me licking my frozen energy bar like a popsicle.

I finished my rock-hard dinner and there was still no sign of Doug and Sarah. I wasn't near a shelter and, with or without my friends, I would soon need to find a place to pitch my tent. As I began to look for a flat spot, I heard footsteps behind me. I turned to see Sarah and Doug making their way up the trail, and a wave of relief crashed over me as I realized that I wouldn't have to tent alone.

Together we hiked a hundred yards farther and came upon a makeshift campsite. There was one navy blue tent in the back corner of the flat clearing, but no sign of life. The three of us, tired and ready to stop, found two flat spots near the trail and began to set up our tents. I was more than happy to sleep on the ground after tossing tirelessly on the floorboards of the shelter the night before.

It was demoralizing how long it took me to pitch my tent. I had practiced putting up my one-man shelter several times before I left home, but tonight the frigid temperature made it impossible to push my tent stakes into the frozen earth. My fingers were so numb I could barely pull the zippers and tie the necessary knots. Finally, after thirty minutes, the structure was crooked and the wall fabric was sagging, but I had finished erecting my tent.

I walked over to wish Sarah and Doug a good night's rest. As we talked about the day and discussed our plan for the following morning, we heard a rustling noise from the one-person tent in the corner of our campsite. We watched as the blue rain flap slowly opened, and a red woolen cap emerged. A young woman with dark hair and a pale complexion looked up at us with red eyes and tear-stained cheeks. "I just wanted to see who was here," she said. And then, as quickly as she had appeared, the red hat disappeared and the rain flap was zipped shut.

It wasn't until I slipped into my own sleeping bag and the night's darkness overtook the dusk that I heard her muffled whimpers and tearful breathing carried by the wind.

Why was she crying? Was she scared or lonely? Maybe she was cold? (I wanted to cry because of the bitter temperatures, but I was convinced that my tear ducts were frozen solid.) I wondered if she would be one of ten who would quit within the first week. Then I realized that based on the statistics, only one of the four of us at the campsite would finish the trail. The odds were daunting.

I lay awake wishing there was something I could do for my unknown neighbor. I wanted to say something to her or do something for her, but I didn't know what. Didn't Sarah and Doug hear her muffled whimpers? Why weren't they doing anything?

In society, we tend to let people grieve on their own, especially people we don't know. But on this barren mountainside, it seemed cruel to allow someone to cry alone when I was so physically close to her. But I could not overcome my inhibition, and as her sniffles grew quieter, I said a soft, silent prayer for her inside the seclusion of my tent. I decided that as I continued down the trail I would try to help people who were struggling, regardless of whether or not I knew them.

Mountain Crossings Outfitter and Hostel at Neels Gap was the first sign of civilization I encountered on the Appalachian Trail. Located twenty miles into my hike and thirty miles north of the trail's southern origin, the outfitter capitalized on hikers with heavy packs and sore feet. Meanwhile, the hostel catered to hikers who were eager for a bed and a shower after several days on the trail. Surprisingly, at this point, neither the store nor the hostel appealed to me. But I decided to make the most of the public picnic tables and running water.

I was now on day three of cooking, and I hated it. I was appalled at the thought of having to deal with cooking, cleaning, and forcing down lukewarm mush all the way to Maine.

Nonetheless, I once again placed some pasta in water and waited for it to expand. Within minutes, Sarah and Doug arrived and began cooking as well. Talking about our first night in tents, we all agreed that they were more comfortable than shelters, as they offered added warmth, less snoring, and protection from mice.

When I was sure that my shells were tender, I added the cheese, and for the first time in over forty-eight hours I enjoyed a warm, fully cooked meal. I ravenously consumed the entire pot of food and then immediately felt full and bloated. As I stood up to leave, I struggled to connect the ends of my hip belt around my waist.

Since Sarah and Doug were not yet finished with lunch, I decided to continue on without them. I loved the confidence of knowing that friends were nearby, but after we reached Springer Mountain, I planned to restart the trail on my own. The thought of being part of the same group day after day felt restrictive.

The trail was becoming the adventure I had envisioned. I loved meeting new people, I loved learning new skills—despite my mistakes—and I loved the feeling of being self-sufficient. After three days on the trail, I felt more independent than at any other time in my life. I was completely responsible for my decisions and my own well-being. I felt scared and empowered at the same time.

Leaving Neels Gap, the path veered straight up Blood Mountain. It was the longest and hardest climb of the first fifty miles, and the heightened stimulation combined with a full pot of Velveeta in my stomach proved to be a terrible combination. My ascent was interrupted when I urgently raced into the woods and out of sight from the trail.

I squatted in pain and discomfort for several minutes, holding a fresh wad of toilet paper in my hand. Frozen in that primitive stance, I realized that this would be my reality for the next several months—a far cry from my padded seat cushion at home. But despite the unfamiliar routine, I emerged from the woods feeling lighter and more confident. I had overcome another reality of the trail.

Unfortunately, Mother Nature decided to reinforce my new skills half a mile later, then again a few hundred yards from the summit of Blood Mountain. My frequent side trips into the woods left me feeling weak and uncomfortable, but I did get a great photo at my final rest stop. I laughed thinking about how I was probably the only thru-hiker who would ever take a picture from this spot on the trail. Then, as I thought more about it, I decided that I liked using the restroom in a place that no one else would ever visit. It definitely cut down on the germs.

Our last full day of hiking before reaching Springer Mountain was the longest. By mid-afternoon I had covered fifteen miles, and I hadn't seen Sarah and Doug since I left the campsite early that morning.

Most of the thru-hikers who walked less than ten miles a day wore very heavy packs and hiking boots. Warren Doyle had recommended wearing a light pack and hiking in running shoes, and I'm glad I took his advice. Blisters were common for everyone on the trail, but those wearing boots seemed to have worse ones than the hikers who wore sneakers. Even the people who had taken great care to break in their boots before they started were still suffering from sore Achilles tendons and hot spots.

Doug and Sarah hiked in boots. I knew their feet had been hurting and I hoped that they were okay—and that I wouldn't have to spend the night without them. I wasn't scared of the dark or being alone at night, but the combination of the two was intimidating. I'd never even slept alone in a house before, let alone in the woods.

One of the spookiest attributes of the forest was that it felt timeless. I surveyed my surroundings and envisioned someone standing here two thousand years ago and enjoying an almost identical view. The only indications that I hadn't experienced a time warp were the dirt path and white blazes cutting a thin line through the woods.

As the shadows of the hardwood trees lengthened on the trail, my heart began to race. I decided to stop well before nightfall so my friends could catch up.

I arrived at a trail intersection and looked for a place to set up my tent. Searching for a flat spot off the trail, I heard something behind me and turned, hoping to see Sarah and Doug. Instead, an elderly couple wearing day-packs came walking down the trail holding hands.

"Hello there!" said the man. "I'm Daddy Lee and this is my wife Big Mo. Are you a thru-hiker?"

"I'm trying to be," I replied.

"Are you hiking by yourself?" Big Mo asked with a hint of concern.

I remembered Warren saying at the workshop that even if we were hiking alone we shouldn't share that fact with complete strangers.

"Nah, I have some friends right behind me. I'm waiting for them to catch up."

"Well, then you should come with us," said Big Mo. "We're hiking down this side trail to Long Creek Falls. It'll only take a few minutes and you'll get to see a waterfall and some Native American carvings. You can leave your pack here so your friends will be sure not to pass you."

I hesitated. I typically didn't accept invitations from strangers, especially if it meant following them deeper into the woods, but this couple was in their late sixties and they were holding hands, and I was desperate for company, so I accepted their offer.

My trust was rewarded when, after a quarter of a mile, we reached a cascading waterfall bordered on either side by large rhododendrons. Beside the falls, Big Mo led me to a large granite rock with faint figures carved into the side.

"Legend has it," she said, "that over three hundred years ago at this very spot the Native Americans sacrificed six European explorers who were part of one of De Soto's expeditions."

I traced the thin carvings with my fingers. Discovering this piece of history so close to the trail made me feel insignificant. I realized I was a small traveling vessel in the depths of an ancient mountain chain that was rich in stories.

Daddy Lee was well versed in Appalachian Trail news and culture, and on our hike back to the trail junction he warned me about hikers who were known for stalking and stealing from people along the trail.

"Watch out for a hiker named Tarzan; he'll steal your pack and gear. And look out for Fire Starter, he likes to hike with women and always ends up making them feel uncomfortable."

When we arrived back at the trail junction, I was relieved to discover that my pack hadn't been stolen, but disheartened that Sarah and Doug still hadn't arrived.

"Well, we'd better get going so we can make it to our car before sunset," said Big Mo.

"Have a great hike," said Daddy Lee. "Just stay with your friends and I'm sure you'll be fine."

Despite the couple's kindness, Daddy Lee's parting words proved unnerving, especially since I found myself alone once again.

I pitched my tent and waited to hear the sound of Sarah's and Doug's heavy boots approaching. I ate a cold dinner of trail mix and peanut butter, then I brought out my headlamp and read an evening devotion outside my tent. Still my friends did not appear.

My hope faded with the daylight, and after searching in the darkness with my headlamp one final time, I entered my tent to prepare for bed.

I would have been less intimidated about my first solo campout if I hadn't just heard a harrowing story of Indian sacrifice and been warned against criminals who lived along the trail. My mind was racing and my body was too tense for rest. I was tossing and turning when a soft rain started to drum a gentle rhythm on my tent. The steady shower turned into a harder rain, followed by thunder and lightning, followed by sleet. I decided that this would be a very unpopular night for looting and marauding along the trail. Eventually, feeling warm, dry, and relatively safe inside my tent, I fell asleep.

"Jen, are you in there?"

"Wake up, sleepyhead!"

The rain had lulled me into a deep sleep, and it took me several seconds to realize that it was morning and Sarah and Doug were calling to me from outside my tent. I slowly unzipped my rain fly and squinted into the fresh morning air. Looking up, I saw my friends standing a few feet away, dressed in colorful rain gear and obscured by a heavy white mist.

"I'm glad you slept right by the trail," Sarah said. "I was worried we wouldn't be able to see your tent through all this fog."

"Yeah, we had to stop yesterday afternoon because of our blisters, but we woke up early to catch up so we could all climb up Springer together."

Springer Mountain was just four miles away, and the thought of climbing the legendary summit and seeing my car, which would take us down the mountain to showers and food, gave me a sudden burst of energy.

"You guys go ahead, I'll be right behind you," I promised.

Sarah and Doug hiked away, and I began to pack up my things. I was happy with how well my tent had held up under the precipitation the night before. There was some condensation on the inside walls, but by contorting my body and changing clothes at a 150-degree angle without touching the tent fabric, I managed to stay relatively dry. But taking down the wet tent with numb hands and trying to shove the saturated fabric into a small dry sack proved impossible, so I finally decided to just shove the soaking tent inside my pack and let everything dry out at home. Hiking away from my campsite, my pack weighed down with water, I began to rethink the practicality of trail shelters.

Initially I thought that the morning's heavy mist was temporary or isolated to a certain valley, but it never lifted. The trail remained shrouded in white and I struggled to define objects ten feet in front of me. The white blazes blended in with the atmosphere, and it became difficult to follow the trail amid the haze. After two hours of hiking, I was relieved and excited when I walked out of the woods and into the Springer Mountain parking lot where Sarah and Doug were waiting beside my car. The fog could not hide their smiles, and I responded with a proud grin of my own.

From the parking area, we still had one mile to travel to reach the summit. Hiking to the crest, we rose above the fog cover and could see distant sapphire peaks jutting up through a white blanket of clouds. I stumbled along the trail and stubbed my toes on large rocks that littered the path, unable to take my eyes off the breathtaking vista.

We were so focused on the scenery that it was almost a surprise when we reached the plaque at the mountain summit. Looking at the rock monument that marked the southern end of the Appalachian Trail, I was hesitant to approach it. I didn't think that arriving at Springer Mountain would feel so overwhelming, but being at the southern terminus of the Appalachian Trail—the spot where thousands of dreams are launched every year—I felt so many different emotions. I was proud to have finished our first fifty miles and excited about the journey ahead, but also anxious about what the trail had in store for me, and scared that I wouldn't be able to make it all the way to Maine.

"Hey Jen, can you take our picture?" Sarah called.

I dropped my pack and turned to photograph my friends on top of the mountain, then I had them snap a few pictures of me. We were proud to document our arrival at Springer Mountain, and after finishing our photo shoot we searched for the Springer register so that we could sign our names in it.

Trail registers are a tradition along the path and are located in almost every shelter from Georgia to Maine. Some hikers sign almost every booklet, while others sign very few. I had not signed one yet but was looking forward to leaving my signature in the trail's southernmost journal. We found it in a metal box carved into the side of a rock. As I sat down and prepared to sign the journal, I realized there was a small problem: I didn't have a trail name.

Trail names, an Appalachian Trail tradition, are titles or nicknames hikers use in lieu of their normal identities. Some people come to Springer with trail names already in mind, while others travel hundreds of miles before they settle on one. I hadn't come to the trail with a trail name, but over the past four days I had been bombarded with suggestions. Other hikers recommended Stretch, Amazon, and Sasquatch, which all alluded to my six-foot frame and long gait. For me, these physical descriptions had worn out their welcome in middle school.

So when Sarah handed me the journal, I paused. There was so much I wanted to say. I was uncertain about how to express my expectations for this adventure and, more significantly, I was unsure who I would become over the course of this journey.

Finally, I pressed the pen to the paper and wrote:

I've always heard New England is nice; look forward to being there this summer.

—Odyssa

I was a Classics major in college, and over the past four days, I had compared the Appalachian Trail to Homer's *Odyssey* several times. One hiker suggested that my trail name should be Odysseus. But I didn't want to be a guy; there were too many guys out on the trail already. So I decided to re-gender the name and call myself Odyssa.

I thought about what the name meant. Maybe I was a wanderer on a long journey back to my home. But then what was I walking away from? And did I really even have a home? After all, I no longer lived with my parents, and I was out of school but without a job. I didn't even know what the word "home" meant anymore. Maybe that was why I was out here. Maybe I was searching for a home.

I shook my head to clear my thoughts. I wasn't a three-thousand-year-old Homeric character, I was just a girl who wanted to hike the Appalachian Trail. I closed the book, looked at my friends, and together we walked back down the trail to the parking lot.

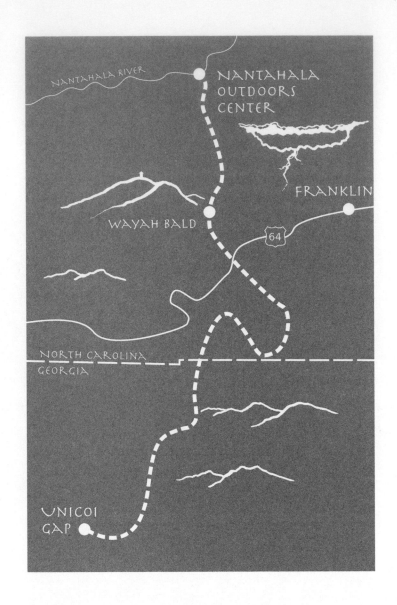

4

ADVENTURE

UNICOI GAP, GA, TO THE NANTAHALA
OUTDOOR CENTER, NC—84 MILES

Just when you start to gain confidence on the moderate hills of northeast Georgia, you enter North Carolina and find your first real mountains. Several of the summits are home to fire towers, which, on clear days, provide stunning views of the dark blue peaks reaching out to the north. Much of the trail is lined with rhododendron thickets, and clear creeks cross the path every few miles. A long descent to the winding waters of the Nantahala River and the welcome amenities at the Nantahala Outdoor Center mark the end of the section.

The lessons of the first fifty miles were abundant. After reaching Springer Mountain, I decided to spend a week at home to regroup and repack, and then return to Unicoi Gap to start hiking north toward Katahdin.

I made a lot of changes after spending several days on the trail: I replaced my heavy Nalgene water bottle with an empty Gatorade bottle to save weight, I left a wool sweater at home but added a lightweight fleece jacket and an extra pair of socks, and I put more food in all of my mail drops. But more than anything, I repacked my thoughts. After the first fifty miles, I'd realized that hiking the trail wasn't going to be recreation; it was going to be hard work.

By hiking the section from Unicoi Gap to Springer Mountain, I had completed just two percent of the entire trail, and it had been substantially more difficult than I had expected. In spite of that, I was surprised how much I missed the trail when I got home. I was only at my parents' house for six days, but they seemed to drag on endlessly. When I wasn't repacking, I was sharing stories from my first fifty miles with my friends and family. And at night I would lie in bed trying to imagine the adventures that awaited me.

The night before I returned to the trail, I struggled to sleep, and when the morning came I got up eagerly and gathered my belongings. I went upstairs to find my father sitting on the edge of a chair with a steaming mug of coffee in his hand. Together we loaded up his white pickup and started our three-hour drive to Unicoi Gap.

Most parents would not be thrilled if their twenty-one-year-old daughter decided to hike the Appalachian Trail alone—and my mother was one of them. But my father was different.

"I know that you're gonna make it all the way to Maine," he told me. "If there's anyone who can do it, it's you. And when you get up there, I'll come pick you up."

"Mom doesn't think that I'll make it," I said.

"You know your mother, she's just worried. But the main thing you have to worry about on the Appalachian Trail is people, and people are a threat everywhere. So if this is what you want to do, then you should do it. Just trust your instincts and you'll be fine."

Even though my dad was supportive, that didn't make leaving his youngest child and only daughter on the side of the road any easier. When we arrived at the trail, he gave me a big hug and tears welled up in his eyes as he helped me hoist my pack out of his truck bed and onto my back. As I turned to start my northbound journey, my dad held his camera to his eye and captured every step as I disappeared into the forest.

The excitement of being back on the trail helped me climb out of Unicoi Gap quickly, but when I looked behind me and no longer saw the road or my dad, my stomach began to twist into knots. As I continued hiking, I began to panic. Part of me wanted to sprint back down the trail and jump into my father's arms. But I slowly kept placing one foot in front of the other, distancing myself from my dad and hiking farther away from where I started. I told myself that this is what my dad would want me to do. And this is what *I* wanted to do.

After several miles, the path leveled out on a ridge, and because the trees were barren, I could see the neighboring mountains in every direction. I finally stopped thinking about the life I had left behind and began to focus on the adventure ahead. My body was energized, and my optimism quickly carried me down the trail. I longed for the challenges that awaited me, and I raced down the path to find them.

The following afternoon, all that racing left me sidelined on a fallen tree. I had spent the last few hours trying to hike through the discomfort inside my sneakers. At first my feet just felt hot, and then increasingly sore, but now with each step the roots on the trail felt like daggers and the rocks like broken glass.

I sat down on a rotting log and buried my face in my hands. If I was going to continue hiking, I had to do something. I carefully unlaced my shoes and gently removed my socks to examine the soles of my feet. I had been blister-free for the first fifty miles and had acted rather self-righteous about not wearing boots, so looking down upon the dime-sized, pus-filled sacs that dotted my feet, I wondered what had happened.

I started sifting through my pack, looking for something sharp to pierce the tough outer layer of skin. At the very bottom of the bag, beneath my sleeping bag, I found my pocket-knife. It wasn't a sterile needle, but it was the only sharp item I had so it would have to do. I carefully unfolded the blade, then I pressed the sharp tip to a swollen white sac near the ball of my foot and slowly began to skewer the thick skin. Once I penetrated the outer layer, I gently squeezed out the clear liquid as if deflating a balloon. I repeated this procedure again and again, and after half an hour, my feet no longer resembled a relief map.

I covered the smooth but tender skin with antibiotic ointment and then, knowing that a Band-Aid wouldn't stick, I wrapped the soles of my feet with duct tape. Every trail book, blog, and briefing I'd read suggested bringing duct tape, and already I was discovering one of its many practical uses. I put my socks and shoes back on and packed up my gear to test my new feet on the trail.

I knew that my makeshift surgery wasn't the most hygienic operation, but as I pushed myself off the log and slowly transferred my weight to my feet, I was pleased to discover that much of the pressure and some of the pain had disappeared.

Hiking nimbly through the bright afternoon sun, my feet continued to feel better, but my legs started to burn and a dull ache filled my head. For the next three miles, the trail never really seemed to gain or lose substantial elevation, but it constantly went up and down. With each short, steep incline on the trail, I became increasingly drained of energy and motivation.

It came as a much-needed morale boost when I passed a small sign on a tree marking the North Carolina border. It gave me confidence to know that I had been able to start at a random point in Georgia and walk to a neighboring state. And not just any state—my state.

My sense of accomplishment didn't last long. The first two mountains in North Carolina were the most challenging yet. Their extended demands left me physically exhausted and emotionally fatigued. Hiking down the second descent, I looked down to see my legs visibly quivering beneath me. I put my hands on my thighs to stop the shaking, but as soon as I let go they began twitching again. With each quaking footstep, I became persuaded to end my day earlier than I had planned. Stumbling my way downhill and into Deep Gap, I was relieved to find a flat plot of land near a stream where I could set up camp.

After pitching my tent, I pulled my food bag and stove out of my pack. Most hikers look forward to a warm meal at the end of the day, but for me, cooking had already become a chore with little reward. I hated the bland pasta and rice meals in my food bag, and I didn't like feeling forced to devour an entire pot of food, either.

After receiving several dirty looks from other hikers, I'd learned that throwing unwanted food into the woods and cleaning out my pot in the streams were not acceptable ways to dispose of dinner scraps. If you didn't eat your food, you were supposed to pack it out with you and throw it away at the next town. But I didn't want to eat my food *or* pack it out.

With great annoyance, I gathered water and lit my camp stove in order to heat the pasta shells. When the noodles were tender, I drained the water and added the pungent, neon orange Velveeta goo to the mix. I then set aside the pot and began to disassemble the stove, but as I unscrewed the burner from the fuel canister, my numb fingers fumbled the stovetop directly into the pot of gluey pasta.

I grabbed the stovetop, but not quickly enough. The small gas holes that the flames passed through were now filled with the cheese-like substance, which had thickened and expanded into its pores. For half an hour, I tried to wash and burn the fake cheddar out of the stove, but my efforts were futile and my stove remained clogged and broken.

I was discouraged and upset with myself for being so clumsy, but as I ate my dinner, I decided that hot food was overrated. From now on, I would just skip the cooking and substitute cold food for hot meals. After all, I didn't like cooking when I was at home, so I don't know why I thought it would be different on the trail. If anything, cooking was worse on the trail.

I vowed to send my pot and stove home at the next post office and skip the warm meals until I could enjoy them at a restaurant in town where I wouldn't have to cook or clean.

After dinner, I was desperately ready for sleep. I cradled my sore, tired body in the warm folds of my sleeping bag and shut my eyes. Before slipping into complete unconsciousness, I heard two sets of boots pass nearby. I was startled awake when I heard a deep male voice call out, "Hey, anyone in there?"

I looked out of my tent and squinted into the setting sun to see two older men with wide-brimmed hats and moustaches staring down at me.

"Yes?" I mumbled.

"We just wanted to make sure you saw the sign about the bear," said the first.

"Yeah, it says he's been aggressive in the past," the second man added.

"Bear? Aggressive?" I replied, trying to shake myself out of a stupor.

The taller of the two sensed my confusion. "Yes, it says right here on the sign. You saw the sign, right? It says that the bear will approach hikers who camp here. Don't you think you should hike to the next shelter?"

An hour ago, I didn't have the energy to go another step, but fear is a powerful motivator. I thanked the two men and assured them that I would not be far behind them.

When they left, I crawled out of my tent and hiked a few yards down the trail to look for the sign about the bear. I must have been blind with fatigue a few hours beforehand, because it was almost impossible to miss the bold warning nailed to a tree. This new information gave me a second wind and, without a thought of sore feet or aching muscles, I quickly packed my gear and raced up the hill to make it to the next shelter before nightfall.

I arrived at Standing Indian Shelter at dusk and was disheartened to discover that it was already packed past capacity with hikers. I walked behind the building and was forced to set up my tent again, on uneven ground. The chore would not have been as difficult if it had still been light outside, but the encroaching darkness meant I had to use my headlamp to see what I was doing. I was not yet comfortable setting up my tent in full daylight, let alone at night.

Ten minutes passed and the tent was leaning heavily to one side, but after such a strenuous day, I decided that the caving side walls would have to do.

Tonight, of all nights, I expected to sleep soundly. But within a few minutes, the chainsaw snoring of a hiker in the shelter thirty yards away filled the night air. Strangely, it was the only noise that filled the air—as if even the birds and insects had been scared away by the sound.

The snorted breathing was so loud that it kept me awake and made me reconsider my odds with the bear. I can't imagine how dreadful it would have been trying to sleep inside the wooden lean-to.

I spent the majority of the night longing for the morning, when I could hike away from the deafening sound. And even before the sun had crested the horizon, I was on the trail and hiking away from the shelter and the unpleasant memories of the night.

I hiked with motivation and without distraction for most of the day. My limbs were still sore and my left knee felt tender, but I was determined to out-hike whoever had made the unbearable noise at the previous shelter. I hiked purposefully until late afternoon, when I encountered an unexpected blockade on the trail.

Actually, I smelled it before I saw it.

With my nose pointed toward the sky, I became convinced that the ever-stronger aroma of a fire-cooked dinner was either the work of a gourmet Scout troop or a cruel conspiracy between my mind and my stomach.

The smell continued to grow, and when I finally felt as if I were swimming in the scent, I rounded a corner to find a dirt road with a small RV parked beside the trail. Near the RV was a fire with several pots suspended above the flames. A circle of empty lawn chairs stood beside the fire, with a cooler in the middle.

I approached the fire and discovered black pots filled with beans, rice, and corn cooking above the flames. My attention was drawn to the nearby table boasting cheese, lettuce, salsa, sour cream, and flour tortilla shells. This couldn't be real. What if it was a ploy? This full-on fajita buffet could be a Hansel-and-Gretel–like trick designed to trap thru-hikers.

My mind said go, but my stomach said stay.

Crrreeeaaaaaak! The door to the RV opened and I jumped back in surprise. A middle-aged woman stepped out with a smile on her face and an apron around her waist.

"Hungry?" she asked. And before I could respond, she handed me an empty plate and began to guide me around the buffet.

"Take whatever you want," she continued. "And make sure to come back for second and third helpings. We don't want any thru-hikers leaving here hungry. My name's North Star, just let me know if you need anything."

"Are you a thru-hiker?" I asked.

"No, darling, but my husband and I love the Appalachian Trail. We live near the path in Maine, and this winter we decided to sell some property so that we could escape the snow and come help thru-hikers as they started their journey north from Georgia. My husband is out getting more wood for the fire right now. We try to have hot food available to hikers around the clock. There are also sodas in the cooler and condiments inside the RV. When you have everything you want, just pull up a lawn chair by the fire and enjoy."

As I sat down with a plate weighted down by burritos, the two older men with moustaches who had warned me about the bear turned the corner. They seemed as startled as I had been to find such a pleasant obstruction on the path, and after meeting North Star, they followed her direction to fill their plates and sit by the fire.

"Hey guys, thanks again for warning me about the bear yesterday. By the way, did you sleep okay last night?" I wanted to feel them out to see if maybe one of them had been responsible for the snoring.

"Are you kidding me?" asked the man with orange-tinted facial hair. "I didn't sleep a wink, thanks to that hiker Big Foot."

"We've been hiking fast all day to make sure we don't have to spend another night anywhere near that guy," said his friend with the gray moustache.

"Me too," I replied, relieved that I wouldn't have to drop my plate and start running.

Together, we sat there laughing and talking between large bites of food. It was amazing how relaxed and accepted I felt sitting around the fire.

I had heard about the concept of "trail magic" before I started hiking. As I understood it, trail magic was a term used to describe gifts, particularly food, that were given to thru-hikers simply because they were thru-hikers, without anything expected in return. North Star's RV was my first encounter with trail magic, but she had given us more than just food. She had given us community.

I enjoyed a long visit and two full plates of food with my new friends before I felt the need to hike away from the oasis and increase my distance from Big Foot. I thanked North Star with a big hug and then bid farewell to the moustache men.

With a light heart and a full stomach, I climbed up and over Albert Mountain and down to Rock Gap Shelter. It was nearly dusk, but I didn't want to take any chances setting up in the shelter, so I pitched my tent a few hundred yards down the trail. I smiled as I remembered not wanting to sleep alone my first few nights on the trail. Now, only a week later, I was seeking out solitude.

When I awoke, it was Easter Sunday. It didn't feel very warm outside and there was a steady rain beating against my tent. I struggled to change clothes without rubbing against the wet sagging tent walls. My awkward movements resembled some form of alternative yoga, and I received a substantial core workout from suspending my body for long periods of time without using my arms.

I tried to take my time getting ready inside my tent, but finally, when I couldn't procrastinate any longer, I repeated the mantra: "No rain, no Maine. No rain, no Maine." Then I stepped out into the cold, wet forest.

The conditions were dreary, and my mood didn't improve when I crossed Highway 64.

For most hikers, this road would signify a spot to hitch a ride into nearby Franklin, North Carolina. But for me, it meant one thing: home.

I knew that if I traveled east on this road for two hours, I would end up within a stone's throw of my childhood home. I wondered what was taking place there right now. I wondered if my parents were at home, and whether or not they were thinking of me. I wondered if my brothers were coming over for lunch and if I would be the only family member missing—and for what? To be alone, outside, cold, and wet, on Easter?

I stood on the pavement in a daze until a car sped out of the fog and chased me to the other side of the road. And with one last glance at the hazy yellow lines, I turned and hiked away from Highway 64.

Easter was much the same from start to finish—the cold rain and dense fog never lifted. I only encountered one hiker all day, an older man with a disgruntled expression who responded to my, "Hello there!" with a silent nod.

My breakthrough of the day came when I discovered that I could eat and hike at the same time. Stopping to eat made me cold, so I stuck several semi-frozen energy bars in my pockets and sucked on them throughout the afternoon. This discovery would affect the way I hiked for the rest of the trip. It wasn't that I didn't want to stop and take breaks, it was just that sometimes the trail was more bearable if I kept moving.

Not stopping to rest finally took a toll on me. My last mile-and-a-half climb to the evening's shelter started very slowly. It wasn't until the rain strengthened and the thunder and lightning rolled in that my pace quickened. The storm gave me the incentive I needed to shake off my exhaustion and run the last mile uphill and into the already crowded Cold Spring Shelter.

I was relieved that, although the place was packed past capacity, the eight male occupants in the shelter were willing to make room for a rather wet and pathetic-looking young woman. Thankful to have a space inside the lean-to, I quickly unbuckled my metal-frame pack and laid it down next to my hiking stick. It felt good to move away from the gear that I feared might electrocute me.

Next, I located the trash bag in my pack filled with my dry sleeping clothes, and I went behind the shelter to change. By hugging up as close to the wooden beams as possible, I remained relatively dry and protected, thanks to the roof's two feet of metal overhang.

I began to peel the wet synthetic top off my torso and over my head . . . and then it hit me. Literally. A bolt of lightning struck the roof of the shelter and continued to the earth through my body.

The jolt stiffened my spine and sent a sharp momentary ache through every inch of me. But the pain had vanished by the time I realized what had happened. I began to assess my physical well-being. I wiggled my toes, poked my stomach, flapped my arms, and counted my fingers. My ears felt hot and I could hear a faint buzzing, but besides that I couldn't see or feel any ill effects.

I was filled with relief and adrenaline; I quickly finished dressing and ran back around to the front of the shelter.

"Hey, guys, guess what. I think some lightning just struck the roof and then went through my body!"

A bright headlamp near the back wall of the shelter pointed my way. "I *thought* I felt a buzz," said the person behind the light.

Then another voice, in the opposite corner of the shelter, confirmed it, "Yeah, I just got shocked by touching a nail inside the shelter. Something definitely hit us."

"It's called splash lightning," said a rosy face sticking out of a red sleeping bag. "The bolt must have hit the roof and then taken several different paths to reach the ground."

Right in front of me, a hiker looked up from his stove and said, "You're lucky it didn't hit you directly."

"Even if it did hit you straight on, you'd probably be okay," another man objected. "I read that only about fifteen percent of people who get struck by lightning die. There's a ranger in the Shenandoah National Park who's been struck by lightning seven times, and he's just fine."

"Well, once was enough for me," I said.

After a few minutes, my heart stopped racing and I rolled out my sleeping bag to prepare for bed. As I lay down, I wondered if perhaps the electricity that shot through my veins would somehow leave me altered in the morning. I was no longer worried about any negative side effects; I figured they probably would have run their course by now. But I wouldn't have been opposed to waking up the next morning with different-colored eyes, a white steak in my hair, or maybe the gift of telepathy.

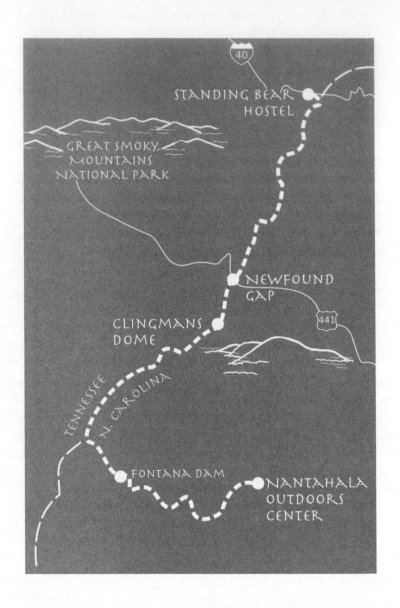

5

ADVERSITY

NANTAHALA OUTDOOR CENTER, NC, TO WATER-
VILLE SCHOOL ROAD, NC—103.4 MILES

*On a clear day in the Great Smoky Mountains National Park,
the nearby mountains appear navy blue and then fade into
softer hues before interlocking with a cyan sky. The evergreen
trees that line the side of the trail give the feeling of a green
labyrinth. Snow and ice remain on the trail into May, and fog
hugs so close to the ground that you will struggle to see your
shoes on the trail. The Smokies offer untamed wilderness that
make you feel subject to the environment, not in control of it.*

By week two, my once-burning flame of wanderlust began to die down to a flicker. And when adventure begins to lose its appeal, it starts to feel more like adversity. I had gained knowledge and strength on the trail. My miles were increasing and my ineptitude around the campsite was decreasing, but I still felt intimidated as I approached Great Smoky Mountains National Park. The seventy-mile section of Appalachian Trail that straddles the high ridges of the Smoky Mountains was supposed to be the most difficult terrain south of New Hampshire, and I wasn't sure if I had the skill, ability, or provisions to traverse the looming peaks.

I arrived at Fontana Dam, the park's southern threshold, with low self-confidence and an empty food sack. When I reached the doors of the Fontana Dam Visitor Center, I found a sign that read CLOSED UNTIL MAY. Ignoring the sign, I tried knocking on the door. I knocked and knocked and knocked, but to no avail. I walked around to the left and right of the building searching for a sign of life, but there was no one in sight. I had planned on taking the daily shuttle from the Visitor Center into a nearby town to resupply. Feeling helpless, I plopped down against the cold stone wall that surrounded the building.

I was exasperated at the thought of having neither food nor transportation, but worst of all, I was stuck. Before the hike, I had sworn to my mother that I would not hitchhike by myself. She accepted that hikers depended on serendipitous rides to and from town to restock their provisions, but she made me promise that I would not attempt to "thumb it" alone. So there I sat, stranded at the base of the Smokies, weighing Maslow's hierarchy of needs against my own moral integrity.

When a car pulled up beside the Visitor Center, I didn't think much of it. In fact, it was almost satisfying to watch the disappointment of the two young men inside the vehicle when they discovered the sign taped to the door. When the driver noticed me, he drove over and rolled down the window.

"Excuse me, do you know if there's somewhere we can find hiking information?" asked the driver, who wore an Auburn baseball cap.

"What do you want to know?" I asked.

His buddy wiped the shaggy brown frat-boy hair out of his eyes and leaned over to respond. "We're on spring break and wanted to go back-packing for a few days, but neither one of us has a map."

"Here, this might help." I pulled out my Appalachian Trail Data Book to let them look it over, and then helped them piece together a manageable route from the obscure numbers and abbreviations.

In the midst of our conversation, it struck me: I had told my mom that I would not try to hitchhike by myself, but hitchhiking connoted standing on the side of the road and sticking out your thumb. These two guys had trusted me for trail information, and now we had formed a relationship—we were practically friends. There wasn't a rule about riding with friends!

I explained my circumstances to the young men and, easily per-suaded, they agreed to shuttle me to the closest resupply point.

Too bad the closest resupply point turned out to be a gas station with three shelves of hiker food that hadn't been restocked since last year.

I still wasn't sure how much food I required to satisfy my no-cook diet, especially with variables such as my increasing appetite and more difficult terrain. After digging through the meager selection, I bought a small pile of crackers, Pop-Tarts, candy bars, fruit chews, and a jar of peanut butter. I was aware of the lack of nutritional value, but with few other options, I just hoped that my resupply would provide enough calories to get me through the Smokies.

When we left the store, we drove back to Fontana Dam, where I said good-bye to the two young men from Alabama and watched as they hiked away from the parking lot in blue jeans and cotton t-shirts, with packs that were twice as big as mine.

I was eager to set out as well, but I wasn't willing to enter the park until I exploited an earlier discovery. Poking around the Visitor Center that morning, I had found an open restroom. In the corner, much to my delight, there was a working shower stall.

More than food, warmth, or shelter, what I longed for the most was a hot shower. When I stepped into the steaming cascade, the warm water melted my frozen skin and rinsed away the dirt that was caked on the skin of my inner ankles and lower calves. I had never appreciated a shower this much before, and I stayed under the hot spray for over half an hour.

I didn't have a towel, so when I was finished I pulled out ten feet of brown paper towels from the dispenser and blotted my body with the harsh, nonabsorbent material. Oh, how I missed my soft plush towels, and amenities like shampoo and conditioner! The only soap I carried on the trail was all-natural liquid soap which was so oily and pungent that it could easily have been mistaken for pure peppermint extract. After using just a few drops, I smelled like a candy cane.

Showered and scented, I headed back into the woods. Entering the park, my afternoon was spent climbing a never-ending series of switchbacks, zigzagging my way higher and deeper into the park. When the sun finally descended to meet the still-ascending trail, I turned off the path and hiked to nearby Russell Field Shelter.

Drawing close to the wooden structure, I was shocked by how many hikers I saw. I had heard that the Smokies were a popular spring break destination, but I hadn't seen anyone since this morning, so it was a surprise to see nearly thirty people at the campsite. I identified families, college friends, and several high school kids with their chaperones, but I didn't see any other thru-hikers. I was the only one at the campsite who wasn't part of a group.

The shelter itself had a chain-link fence and small gate to enclose the open side of the building. It seems that in order to keep the bears away from the hikers, the park employed a "zoo in reverse" model, and arranged the people in caged shelters while allowing the animals to roam free and observe.

Since I couldn't sleep inside the exhibit space due to species overpopulation, I was forced to tent on a nearby hillside. While setting up camp and retrieving my water, I struck up a conversation with members of a youth group from Michigan. They invited me to share devotionals with them that evening, and I accepted. Part of me longed for the fellowship, and another part hoped for excess dinner scraps.

I watched hungrily as they all devoured every bite of their dinners, but I appreciated the nourishing discussion that followed. The group talked about their time in the Smokies as a mountaintop experience that could only last momentarily before they returned to the valley. They frequently referred to their backpacking trip as a "getaway" or "retreat." I thought back to all the things I wanted to get away from in high school, like tests, social pressures, and college applications. I empathized with the teenagers in the circle. I'd rather be anywhere than back in high school.

As I listened to the group, it became clear to me that, while going into the woods for a few days was socially acceptable, living on the trail for weeks at a time was viewed as controversial. And the questions I received around their campsite reinforced my perception: "How can you afford to hike the trail?" "What do your friends and family think?" "Why would you want to live in the woods for that long?"

I could afford to hike the Appalachian Trail because in college I babysat, worked in a church nursery, and held a summer job for three years in a row to save up money for the trip. In fact, my summer boss had offered me a full-time job after I graduated. When I declined, he looked at me sternly and said, "You need to think very seriously about what you are trying to run away from."

Run away? I had just experienced the best three and a half years of my life. I wasn't trying to escape anything, and if I had been, I'm sure there would be an easier way to do it. At the end of college I was independent for the first time in my life. I was free to live where I wanted to live and do what I wanted to do. The trail was not a retreat for me. For the next few months, it was my job and my home. It was where I wanted to be.

Halfway through the night, I was woken by gusts of wind thrashing at my tent. I could hear the currents approaching and crashing like waves into the thin shelter walls.

My eyes were heavy, but the violent wind kept me awake. To make matters worse, as the night progressed, I started to hear small ice pellets bounce off the sides of my tent, and even in my stupor I became concerned.

I grew up relatively close to the Great Smoky Mountains National Park, and I recalled annual spring newspaper reports of hikers trapped or killed in the park due to late-season snowstorms. I worried that, instead of hiking north tomorrow, I might have to retrace my steps out of the park in a snowstorm. It was an answer to my prayer when I peered out of my tent the next morning to find that the icy weather had subsided into a cold rain.

I knew that my second day in the Smokies would take me to the top of Clingmans Dome, the highest peak on the Appalachian Trail, but the white clouds that infiltrated the forest made it difficult to tell how far I had hiked and where the trail was leading.

I decided I must be getting close to the summit when the hardwood forest gave way to small brushy evergreens that smelled like a fresh-cut Christmas tree. I hadn't seen a view all day, but the mist wrapped around the saturated alpine limbs of the spruce trees formed an image more tangible and mysterious than any mountain panorama.

When the trail stopped angling upward, it also split in two. I stopped to look around. This couldn't be the top of the mountain, could it? I didn't feel like I had worked hard enough to reach the tallest point on the trail.

Then I saw the sign a few feet ahead: CLINGMANS DOME 6,643 FT. The bleak isolation of the fog had masked the distance and effort it took to reach the mountaintop, and now I had it all to myself.

I followed the signs to the observation tower and, laying my gear on the wet ground, I slowly climbed the spiral ramp to the top. I don't know why I walked to the top. I couldn't see ten feet in front of me, let alone the distant peaks, but there was something about coming so far and still not being at the highest point that made me want to go farther.

Descending from Clingmans Dome, I found patches of ice and snow still covering the trail. The winter sun doesn't shine on the north slope of the mountain and as a result, snow remains on the ground until late spring.

Instead of risking a dangerous fall, I chose to sit and carefully slide down the ice on my bottom. During one particularly long and steep slide, I lost control and skidded off the trail. When I stopped I found myself five feet downhill from the trail tangled in a web of evergreen branches. I wasn't hurt, but I had little desire to stand up and continue hiking. I propped myself up amid the tree limbs and dug through my pack for a snack.

I sat still for nearly an hour, nestled against the trees, watching the mist particles dance and swirl in the breeze. Finally, the darkening sky prompted me to rise and walk—or rather skate and slide—to the lonely Mount Collins Shelter. I don't know where the thirty hikers from last night's shelter had disappeared to, but I now felt like I was the only one left in the park; me and whatever animals roamed in the darkness outside the chain-link fence.

Generally, I'm a positive person, so the next morning I awoke hoping for a warm, clear, sunny day. However, when I looked out on the same cold, wet fog, it shattered my optimism. I was starting to feel like a cartoon character who was followed everywhere she went by a storm cloud overhead.

Besides affecting my attitude, the cold, damp weather had greatly increased my appetite. I still had a day and a half left in the park, but I was down to a few remaining Pop-Tarts, some crackers, and the dregs of my peanut butter. I would need to start conserving food to make sure I would have enough to get me through the park.

It was disheartening to struggle through another day of cold rain. My clothes were wet, my core was chilled, and I couldn't see anything except the trail at my feet. I needed something to do, something to take my mind off the discomfort, so I sang. Not well (I never sing well), not loudly (that would come with time), just a quiet off-key tune to help me down the trail. My playlist included popular rap songs and well-known musical numbers like "My Favorite Things" from *The Sound of Music* and "Tomorrow" from *Annie*. The rap songs were fun and didn't require much of a melody. And as for the musical selections, I decided that if refugees and orphans could have a good attitude, then so could I.

When people asked me before my hike what I was most afraid of, I responded that being cold and wet was my worst fear. Yet there I was in the freezing rain, and I was singing.

I entered Tricorner Knob Shelter at twilight and introduced myself to bundled faces wrapped in sleeping-bag cocoons. After my first day in the Smokies, I had only encountered a handful of thru-hikers. I felt a fond admiration for the fellow hikers bundled up on the wooden boards. They had all been outside today, doing the same thing that I had been doing, in the same conditions. We hadn't hiked together, but we had shared a really hard day.

The four male hikers in the shelter related stories from the day's adventures and their previous miles. However, one hiker had more stories than the rest. Dude was an older man who spent his time off-trail as a bartender, and his laid-back attitude and surfer jargon were the root of his trail name. He had a cinnamon-colored beard down to his chest that put the blossoming facial hair of the other male hikers to shame. His skin was tanned and dirty, and his voice was even more overpowering than the strong hiker-stench that surrounded him.

The stories, the smell, the weathered brow and beard—they all stemmed from the fact that Dude had not started his thru-hike from Georgia; he had started in Maine. Dude began his southbound expedition last fall. He had traveled nearly two thousand miles and only had two hundred left before he would reach Springer Mountain. I respected and envied Dude. He had accomplished something amazing: He had hiked here from Maine.

When I woke up, I knew that I was still in the South, but it felt like Maine outside. I had spent the night submerged in my sleeping bag, which was rated for twenty-degree temperatures, holding my fists between my knees in the fetal position and shivering to keep warm. The shelter was at 5,920 feet, and the weather and elevation combined to make it my coldest morning on the trail. At least the sound of rain no longer resonated from the roof above. Finally, the two straight days of precipitation had come to an end. Then I glanced outside . . .

SNOW.

It was 5:30 in the morning, and already several inches of white powder gleamed in the remaining moonlight.

Seized with adrenaline, I threw on my top layers, packed up my sleeping bag, and slipped on my shoes, which were covered with a thick layer of ice.

I ran outside and over to the bear cables to retrieve my food sack. I was still having trouble working the cables in good weather, and now that the metal lines and clasps were frozen it was almost impossible. I finally took hold of the sack and wrestled it off the wire. Under the snow that surrounded the food bag was a stiff layer of ice. I had to put it on the ground and step on the sack several times before it was malleable enough to fit in my pack. Forcing it into the compartment with cold fingers, I closed up my icy zippers, picked up my pack, and sped down the trail.

My mantra for the day was "hostel or bust." According to the data book, I still had eighteen more miles inside the park and then I would reach a lower road with a hostel nearby. I didn't know what to do in a snowstorm, I was almost entirely out of food, and I was wearing every item of clothing that I had. If I didn't make it out of the snow and out of the Smokies today, I would be in big trouble.

The snow in the air was blinding, and it continued to build up on the ground, and since it's impossible to run effectively with a pack through the snow, I did a sort of speed-shuffle. While I was striding along, watching my shins cut through the white powder, I smacked my forehead hard on a tree that had been suspended five and a half feet in the air by neighboring trees. At a normal hiking speed, it wouldn't have hurt too much, but due to the speed-shuffle, the impact raised a small goose egg on my forehead.

Great—no food, no dry clothes, *and* a possible concussion . . . Hostel, here I come.

Fortunately, almost all the hiking was downhill. In parts, the decline was so steep that, by using my hiking stick as a side-to-side stabilizer, I could almost ski down the mountain.

For most of the morning, I was sheltered from the worst of the wind and snow by hiking under the cover of the forest. But every now and then, the trees would open up to an exposed ridgeline that left me completely vulnerable to the elements.

On one long stretch of exposed ridgeline I ducked my head and closed my left eye, trying to shield my face from the snow and freezing rain. The wintry mix battered my face and left my exposed skin feeling as though it had been nicked countless times with a razor blade.

When I finally reached tree cover again, I lifted my head and tried to open my eye, but it wouldn't open. My eye was frozen shut!

A blizzard was disorienting enough; now I was going to have to navigate blustery conditions, try to stay on a snow-covered path, and locate erratic white blazes with only one eye?

Pawing at my face with my gloves, I managed to wipe the frozen crust away from my eye. Several long seconds passed before my eyelid opened and I regained my sight.

I didn't want to stop until I was completely out of the snow, so I kept hiking as hard and as fast as I could. My body was now running completely on fumes. I hadn't stopped to rest or eat all morning, and there was an acute pain in my left shin that felt like some sort of muscle pull or tear. But after five very trying hours, I reached a lower elevation and higher temperature, which turned the snow into rain and let me walk on a slushy but visible trail.

I had made it out of the blizzard. I was safe, but I was still cold, still weak, still hungry, and I still had nearly two thousand miles to go.

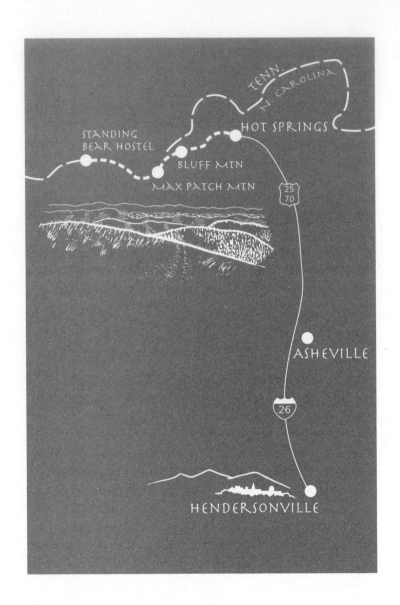

STANDING
BEAR HOSTEL

TENN.
N. CAROLINA

HOT SPRINGS

BLUFF MTN

MAX PATCH MTN

25
70

ASHEVILLE

26

HENDERSONVILLE

6

HOME

WATERVILLE SCHOOL ROAD, NC, TO
HOT SPRINGS, NC—33.4 MILES

The trail starts to feel a little easier after descending out of the Smokies. The climb to the top of Max Patch is gradual, and the summit offers a breathtaking panorama. From this viewpoint, in the heart of the southern Appalachians, the mountains start to appear less like the opposition and more like friends. Thick rhododendron tunnels lead hikers off of Max Patch and then triumphantly into the small town of Hot Springs, North Carolina.

After hiking down the last set of rock stairs and crossing the final river to exit the Great Smoky Mountains National Park, I was desperately looking forward to the comfort of a hot shower and a night indoors. When I spotted a sign for Standing Bear Hostel, I turned off the trail and journeyed up a remote dirt road in search of food and warmth.

Throughout the frightening weather and difficult hiking that day, I had envisioned the hostel as beacon of hope and civilization. I was disappointed and a little dismayed when the road dead-ended at a collection of shoddy log cabins. The ramshackle hostel was eerily quiet. I became apprehensive about my decision to stop for the day. Under other circumstances, I probably would have hiked away from the deserted hostel, but after completing eighteen snow-covered miles in six hours, I didn't have the energy to leave.

I walked up to the largest of the shacks and noticed a sign welcoming hikers. I pushed open the heavy door, and in the darkness I could barely make out several bunks and a small woodstove. I heard something rustle in the back corner of the room. One of the bunks moved and a man emerged whose clothing, deep-set wrinkles, and expressive eyes made me feel as if I had stepped back in time to rural nineteenth-century Appalachia. His mouth opened to display very few teeth, and in a gruff voice he said, "Welcome to Standin' Bar. I'm Snapper. I'll get Mr. Curts." Then he headed out the back door of the bunkhouse.

The door slammed. Snapper was gone, and I was alone.

Feeling very uncertain, I removed the heavy, wet pack from my back and edged toward the woodstove in the center of the room.

I had almost regained feeling in my fingers when the back door creaked open. Snapper reappeared with a taller, slightly less sinister man in tow.

"Hey there," he said. "Welcome to Standing Bear, I'm Curtis."

"Cur-*tis*?" I asked.

"Yeah, Curtis. Here, let me show you around the place."

I was still cold and wet, and I didn't want to leave the warmth of the woodstove, but I reluctantly followed.

Curtis showed me the surrounding log shacks which housed the main sleeping quarters, a shower stall, laundry hut, and snack shed. During our tour, Curtis reassured me that Snapper helped him run the hostel, and although he could come across as a bit backwoods, he had a heart of gold. After our tour, Curtis walked me back to the bunkhouse. I now felt far more comfortable than when I had arrived.

Before leaving me by the woodstove where he'd found me, Curtis asked me where my home was.

"I'm from Hendersonville, North Carolina," I answered.

"Hendersonville?" he said with surprise, then bluntly asked, "Well, then what the hell are you doing here?"

I was confused by his response, but then Curtis explained with a smile that Hendersonville was only an hour's drive from the hostel. He suggested that, if I wanted to, I should call my parents and spend the night at home.

Home? I hadn't intended to go home for five months, until after I reached the end of the trail, and at this point I had only been gone for two weeks. Going home felt like cheating. But the thought of my parents, my room, my clothes, and my bathtub led me to at least consider the option.

Curtis pointed me in the direction of the phone. I hesitantly dialed the number, and as soon as I heard my dad's voice on the opposite end, I suddenly felt okay not spending the night at the hostel. Before I had even suggested the idea, my father asked me where I was and then turned his truck toward the Smokies.

My dad's comforting voice was incentive enough to return home, but the mention of watching the University of North Carolina men's basketball team play in the NCAA Final Four sealed the deal. Tar Heel basketball was a family tradition. In my mother's opinion, the only thing more grievous than the fact that I would be in constant peril and out of touch for several months was that I was missing March Madness.

While I waited for my dad at the hostel, I decided to make the most of the surrounding shacks. I started with a load of laundry and then took one of the coldest showers of my entire life. I stood under the breath-stealing stream in the outdoor stall, with the temperature of the surrounding air somewhere just above thirty-two degrees. I thought

that the water would have to warm up at some point, but I finally gave
up mid-shampoo, my fingers blue and my body covered in goose bumps.

With soap suds still in my hair, I returned to the bunkhouse, where
Snapper sat near the stove. Too cold for inhibition, I sat down directly
beside him, as close to the fire as possible.

As my teeth slowed their violent clacking and my cold stiffness and
social tensions began to ease, we began to talk.

"I'm glad you git to go home," he said. "But it's too bad it's tonight."

"Why is that?" I asked.

"It's Friday, so Mr. Curts take us to the Mexican restaurant. They's
got a real good bluegrass band on Fridays."

A bluegrass band at a Mexican restaurant? That would be something to see!

"I'm sad that I'll miss it," I said. "Especially the food, I'm starving."

In response, Snapper got up and left the room. Five minutes later he
returned with some leftovers from the nearby Mexican restaurant.

"These's from last night. Go 'head, e't it," he insisted.

Snapper watched proudly as I enjoyed his leftover tamales. And after
I finally reached a point where I was warm, happy, and no longer ravenous, my dad appeared. I was elated to see him, and I ran over and threw
my arms around him. We were both ready to head home, but before we
left, my dad went to settle up with Curtis. Curtis greeted my dad but
refused to take any money from him. I had spent most of the afternoon
at the hostel, and taken full advantage of their shower and laundry, yet
Curtis refused payment.

"Just take your daughter home and take good care of her," he said.
"That'll be payment enough."

Curtis picked up my pack and helped me carry it to my dad's truck,
then he stood in the driveway and waved good-bye as we disappeared
down the dirt road.

As we drove home, I gushed to my dad about my first few weeks on
the trail. The only break in our conversation came when he stopped at
a McDonald's drive-thru to order a Big Mac value meal. I typically
didn't eat much fast food, but the past few weeks made two beef

patties smothered in sauce on a sesame-seed bun rank high on my list of delicacies.

My dad and I didn't go straight to our house, but rather to the home of some friends of the family, where I ate my second dinner, took my second shower, and soaked my feet as we watched the first half of the basketball game.

As a six-foot-tall North Carolina native, basketball had been an intrinsic part of my life growing up. I don't remember consciously choosing to play basketball, but due to my height, I'd been recruited by every YMCA and AAU coach in the area. Eventually my ball-handling skills and shooting improved, and I learned to love the sport. But despite years of playing the game, my fondest basketball memories are of gathering in the living room with my family and friends to cheer on the Tar Heels.

My dad and I drove home for the second half, and although it was a close game, I found myself strangely distracted. I laid on the floor with our golden retriever and began flipping through my Appalachian Trail Data Book, calculating mileages and planning my next few days on the trail. When I did glance up at the TV screen, I was more interested in the spectators than in the basketball players. It was odd how much energy was expended by the stadium full of screaming, yelling, cheering fans, urging both teams to victory. It was strange to think how much vocal support and enthusiasm surrounded these athletes when, back on the trail, I knew that I would have to push my physical limits and athletic aptitude in solitude and silence.

That night, after the Tar Heels won, I went to bed at 1:00 AM. On the trail I had been falling asleep around 8:30 every night, but at home the electricity, cable, and running water kept me awake much later than I had planned. The late night, combined with daylight saving time and a 6:00 AM wake-up call, translated to just under four hours of sleep.

One might imagine that after spending so many nights on the cold hard ground, I would have been inclined to spend a little more time in my own bed. However, my dad promised that if I could hike the thirty-three miles from the hostel at the base of the Smokies to nearby Hot Springs in a day and a half, then he would bring me home to watch Carolina play in the National Championship.

After an hour-long car ride back to the Smokies' eastern boundary, I hugged my dad, said good-bye, and started to hike uphill away from the road. I had a little over thirty miles to cover in just over thirty hours. And as I hiked up and out of the gap, I discovered the trail was still covered in snow.

At first, just a few inches covered the ground, and I had fun shuffling my feet through the undisturbed white blanket. It felt special being the first one to pass through the winter landscape. As the trail continued to climb, however, the snow on the ground grew deeper, and by the end of the morning, I found myself trudging through three-foot snowdrifts. At that point, I didn't feel as special, and the snow didn't seem as fun.

I had to stop often and take off my shoes to dump out the excess snowmelt and wring the cold water out of my socks. I was thankful that the sky was clear and not threatening further precipitation, but the morning breeze had developed into a strong headwind that chilled my body and sapped my strength.

The powerful gusts of wind nearly knocked me on my knees as I left the tree-line to pass over the bald at Max Patch. Southern balds are one of the highlights of the Appalachian Trail. They are mountaintops or tall ridges that are devoid of trees, providing 360-degree views. They're not a natural feature in the Southeast, so the forest service has to maintain them with controlled burns and grazing livestock.

Because there are no trees on top of a bald, there's no protection from storms or strong winds. As I stumbled my way to the summit, I was beaten down by the fierce currents. The only way I could make progress without toppling over was to struggle forward with my head down and body leaning at a sixty-degree angle into the oncoming wind.

In the rare moments when I was able to glance up and take in the view, I was captivated and left in tears. (Maybe the tears were caused by the piercing wind, but the view was truly one of the most stunning displays of natural beauty that I had even seen.) The taller mauve mountains with white peaks that encircled the bald made me feel like the centerpiece of a divine coliseum. It was as if I were a gladiator struggling against the forces of nature. The deafening wind evoked the roar of the crowd. I thought about the noisy, attentive fans at the basketball game the night before. Out here, the mountains were the spectators.

Escaping the coliseum with a rush of adrenaline, I returned to the inner chambers of the forest to face a new challenge. As the snow stopped gleaming and the sun started to hide behind the trees, I grew worried. I had not seen any other thru-hikers all day, and the miles in the Data Book no longer seemed to be corresponding to my trail miles. I was concerned that I had somehow diverted myself onto an adjoining trail and I wouldn't be able to find my intended shelter for the evening. Suddenly I didn't trust myself, the Data Book, or the white blazes leading me forward.

I finally arrived at a dark three-sided structure and let out a huge sigh of relief. My legs had never been off-track, just my mind.

With no one else at Walnut Mountain Shelter, I silently arranged my sleeping area and began preparing for bed. I was frightened to be the only one in the shelter. I no longer feared solo-camping in my tent, but in a shelter I never knew who might show up and join me. I wasn't specifically worried about other hikers, but I think most women have a fear of waking up next to a strange man and not knowing how he got there.

Waking the next morning to an alarm on my wristwatch, I looked around in the dark shelter and discovered that I was still alone. I packed up my belongings and started on a very dark morning hike. I needed my headlamp for the first few miles up Bluff Mountain. The alarm on my watch hadn't been set any differently, but daylight saving time meant that my usual start time was now an hour before sunrise. Ordinarily, I wouldn't have been so keen about hiking in the dark and snow, but my promise to meet my dad in Hot Springs propelled me forward.

When the sun rose over the mountaintops, it was such a bright hue of electric orange that the snow beneath me glowed like the embers of a thriving fire. The brilliance was blinding, which made it hard to look up or down. The vividness of the color was breathtaking and left a memorable impression even as it softened to a calm yellow.

The early morning splendor rejuvenated my spirits and reinvigorated my aching body. The trail descended for the majority of the morning, and lower elevations meant less snow and better footing. It also helped that I had eaten most of my food, so my pack felt extra light.

When I arrived in Hot Springs, I was proud to have overcome thirty miles of snowy trail and excited to return home and watch the Tar Heels. Since my cell phone didn't work, I found a pay phone and called my dad to arrange a pickup time. Once our rendezvous was established, I began to explore.

Hot Springs was the first town that the trail traveled directly through. It was a scenic town surrounded by mountains and nestled in a narrow valley beside the French Broad River, but I was shocked at how small it was. There was a half-mile-long Main Street with a few small businesses that backed up against the river and a few dozen houses that led up the hillside away from the water, but that was all— that was Hot Springs.

As a thru-hiker, I appreciated the manageable size because that meant I could find everything I needed without having to do too much extra walking.

Waiting for my dad to arrive, I went to the post office, where I picked up a mail drop filled with food, fresh socks, a razor, and a bar of soap. It was strange to be receiving a package that I had assembled, addressed, and mailed to myself just a few weeks earlier.

After I left the post office, I crossed the street to visit Bluff Mountain Outfitters. I was amazed that a town of this size could support an outdoor store, but I suppose it benefited from the ill-equipped hikers on the Appalachian Trail; the cold, wet rafters who paddled the French Broad River; and the tourists who came to the town's hot springs and then wandered down Main Street in search of a souvenir.

I didn't need anything from the outdoor store, but that didn't stop me from perusing the aisles and examining the brightly colored camping gear, which seemed much better than the archaic and monochromatic gear on my back. As I made my way to the back of the store, I noticed a map on the wall. It showed the entire Appalachian Trail from Georgia to Maine, and there, near the very bottom, was a small sticker marking Hot Springs.

I thought back on how hard the first section of the trail had been for me and how much I had overcome; it seemed unfathomable that I could still be so close to the beginning. I was suddenly overwhelmed by the sheer magnitude and distance of the trail. When I saw how little I had covered, making it to Maine seemed impossible. Momentarily frozen, I had to literally give my body a quick shake to free it from self-doubt.

I left the outfitter and went in search of the most important component of a trail town—food. I found a quaint convenience store and sandwich shop near the edge of town, where I ordered a large sub and waited for my dad to arrive. When he pulled up in his white truck, I eagerly jumped inside and was once again whisked away to the world of hot showers and basketball.

My second trip home wasn't as enjoyable as my first. Entering my room, I found a "to do" list that needed to be accomplished before that evening's game. I started to check off each chore one by one. Several of them included packing up the personal items in my room and separating out old clothes and books to be given away. I was struck by the fact that this room, and this building, was no longer my home but my parents' house. I would never again stay here for an extended period of time, and the fact that my mother was trying to convert my childhood memories into a guest bedroom only intensified that notion.

At first I was angry. I felt abandoned and forgotten. But soon the self-pity melted away, and I began to understand that it wasn't my parents who were changing, it was me. I was the one leaving. I was the one who had outgrown childish things, school projects, and collages on my walls. I had to keep reminding myself that for the next five months my home was on the trail. And it made it a lot easier to stay out there, knowing that I didn't have a room full of pictures or a closet full of clothes waiting for me.

That night we sat around the TV as a family and watched the Tar Heels win the National Basketball Championship. Some families look forward to Christmas so they can spend quality time together; I look forward to basketball season for the same reason, and this had been a particularly good season. I no longer had a bedroom to come back to after the trail, but sitting and yelling at the TV in the living room, I knew I would always have my family.

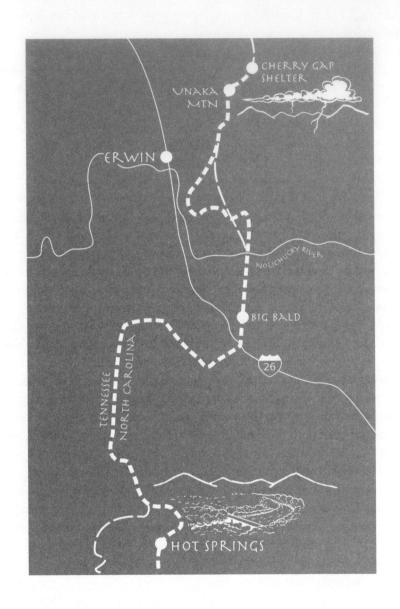

7

FRIENDS

HOT SPRINGS, NC, TO
CHERRY GAP SHELTER, TN—84.5 MILES

After climbing out of Hot Springs, the trail travels along the mountain ridges and crosses into Tennessee. Near Erwin, Tennessee, the trail descends to cross the Nolichucky River. It briefly contours the serpintine Nolichucky before beginning a steady climb up Unaka Mountain. On a clear day, the strenuous ascent is rewarded with scenic views at Beauty Spot, but on a cloudy day, you will not be able to recognize Beauty Spot and might become lost in the pine tree maze that covers the mountain summit.

The first several hundred miles of the Appalachian Trail are awkward for a solo hiker. Since leaving Sarah and Doug, I had wanted to hike by myself, but many hikers use the Southern states to search out compatible partners and form hiking groups that will last until Katahdin. I worried that when I talked to other hikers for an extended period of time, they would think I was putting out signals that I was looking for something more long-term.

It was like going stag to a dance. You want to dance, that's why you're there, so you eagerly accept any offer to get up and get moving. But then when you start dancing you become paranoid and try not to send the wrong signals to your partner, for fear he'll think it's more than just a dance. The plan is to boogey all night with as many partners as possible. But if a song ends and someone asks you to join him for a second dance or a breath of fresh air—that's when you know you're in trouble.

That's why I appreciated trail encounters that felt friendly without feeling permanent. And when I returned to the trail in Hot Springs, I was fortunate enough to dance down the trail with one partner after another.

The first on my dance card was Steam. I didn't have to introduce myself to Steam because we already knew one another. That is, my mother reported that we had once played together as three-year-olds. I hadn't seen him for eighteen years, but when our parents discovered that we both planned to hike the Appalachian Trail this spring, we had a dinner reunion to discuss it. I hadn't seen or heard from him since then, but returning to the trail, I found Steam packing up his tent a mile outside of Hot Springs. I waited briefly for him to finish breaking down his camp, then we hiked together for the rest of the morning.

Steam bounced down the trail ahead of me carrying a lightweight pack with a trimmed-down foam sleeping pad strapped to the side. Instead of watching the trail, I stared at his defined calf muscles and the black elastic bands circling just below his knees.

"What are those black bands on your legs?" I asked.

"They're braces that help hold my kneecaps in place. I had a lot of trouble with my knees playing soccer as a kid, and I wanted to take some preventative measures to make sure they last two thousand miles on the trail."

"Like what?"

"Well, besides wearing the braces, the biggest help is using my two Leki hiking sticks to alleviate some of the stress of hiking downhill. Plus I'm trying really hard to keep my pack under twenty pounds, even with food and water. I did a lot of research on lightweight gear before getting on the trail. I have some great homemade gear, and the rest I bought at a discount through the outdoor store where I worked this winter."

We stopped on the side of the trail so that Steam could collect some water from a nearby spring. After he filled up his water bottle, he took out a clear two-ounce plastic bottle with an eyedropper.

"What's that?" I asked, as I watch him release two drops of the liquid into his bottle.

"It's bleach."

"You mean, like Clorox bleach?" I was both shocked and a little concerned.

"Yeah, it's just household bleach—granted, I try to steer clear of the lemon-scented kind—but two drops per liter, when dissolved, will kill bacteria without harming humans. The military uses this method, and I've also seen it presented as an option at some state parks, plus most U.S. cities add chlorine to the water supply at their treatment facilities. On the trail it's the lightest, least expensive, and most readily available option."

It had never even crossed my mind that bleach could be used to purify water, partly because there was a poison control warning on the bottle. I still wasn't treating my water, and I knew that maybe that meant I was taking in some things that weren't too good for me, but bleach or iodine or other chemical treatments didn't seem healthy either.

Steam then told me how challenging it was for him to be a vegetarian on the trail. He said he was struggling to take in enough calories and protein in his diet.

"I've heard of a few vegetarians on the trail who drink bottles of olive oil or eat sticks of butter to maintain their body weight," he said.

"Are you going to do that?"

"I think if I'm tempted to drink olive oil then I'll just go ahead and add some meat to my diet."

Above his gear and water purification, the aspect that interested me most about Steam was that he was hiking the trail as a Christian missionary. He had partnered with a group called Appalachian Trail Servants and he raised support to hike the trail and share his faith. I knew that I would share my beliefs if the subject came up in conversation on the trail, but purposely trying to start that conversation terrified me.

It's not that there weren't Christians on the trail—there were. But Christians on the Appalachian Trail are like bears: you might run across a handful on your way to Maine. On the other hand, left-wing anti-fundamentalists are the squirrels of the trail, and you're guaranteed to encounter several every day. As a bear, I was scared of squirrels because they were scared of me. They kept their distance and feared I would eat them, when really I just wanted to dine on berries and live peaceably in the woods. I admired Steam because he was proud to be a bear, whereas I was a bear trying to look like a groundhog. Groundhogs are a lot less threatening than bears. Plus, they're cute. You'd be crazy not to like a groundhog.

"How is it sharing your faith on the trail?" I asked.

"It's been great so far," he said.

There was a long pause, and I could tell he was reflecting.

"I never bring it up right away, and just try to look for ways to help people. You know, give them water, or a little extra food, or just listen to what they have to say—things that I would want people to do for me. In conversation there are a lot of natural ways for me to bring up my faith, so I can do it organically and without judgment."

As we started a long, gradual uphill section, Steam continued to tell me how blessed and comfortable he felt as a Christian on the trail, and how meaningful interactions and moments of peace constantly reassured him. I was happy to listen to Steam and his stories because they seemed to strike a chord of truth. They also meant that I didn't have to talk while hiking uphill, which always made me grateful. By the time we reached the top of the mountain, I started thinking that maybe I should just be happy to be a bear and not worry about what the other woodland creatures thought.

Steam and I continued to hike and talk until the early afternoon when we arrived at Spring Mountain Shelter. There was a young male thru-hiker in the lean-to named Second Gear, who briefly introduced himself and then continued hiking. I also had the urge to continue hiking, but Steam decided that he was done for the day and would spend the rest of the afternoon at the shelter.

I said good-bye, wished him well, and continued down the trail. It struck me that Steam was out here to love and encourage me as much as anyone else. He was out here for the bears as much as he was for the squirrels.

For much of the afternoon, I walked within view of Second Gear. We didn't hike together and we didn't talk to one another. That didn't bother me. What did bother me was that he was listening to his iPod.

IPods didn't bother me because they were antisocial or because they were a way to disassociate from the trail; they bothered me because when you listen to an iPod, you can't hear external noises, and that seemed dangerous. Bopping down the trail to his music, Second Gear couldn't hear me behind him, he couldn't hear animals in the woods, and if he needed water, he wouldn't be able to hear a stream and locate water if it was out of sight. I had seen numerous hikers wearing earphones on the trail, and if I had to guess I would say more than half of thru-hikers used them on their journeys, but they didn't seem safe to me. The more I thought about it, the more validated I felt in singing out loud when I needed music.

Late that afternoon, I noticed Second Gear stop walking and remove his earphones. He stood frozen at a road crossing, and I soon saw the cause for hesitation. He was staring at a handmade sign that read TRAIL MAGIC above a large red arrow pointing to the right.

Hearing my footsteps behind him, Second Gear turned.

"The sign says trail magic," he said.

"Let's do it," I replied.

There had been lots of trail magic in the Southeast. About every other day there would be a box of snacks or a stash of drinks left by the roadside for hikers. I now almost *expected* trail magic, which made me very disappointed when it more or less disappeared as I hiked farther north.

Second Gear and I walked down a road looking for a car or cooler or another sign of trail magic, but it took us by surprise when the next red arrow pointed up a gravel driveway to an attractive log cabin. Except for the Burrito RV, trail magic had always come in the form of provisions left beside the trail, but this sign was pointing toward someone's home. We approached the steps cautiously, uncertain whether we were in the right place. When we were a few feet from the porch, the front door flung open and a kind-looking man with salt-and-pepper hair invited us inside the house. I had never been invited into a stranger's home before.

"Come in, come in," he said. "My name is Zeus and that's my wife, Spring, in the kitchen."

We stepped inside, took off our muddy shoes, and waved to Spring, who was standing over a pot that filled the cabin with a smell of rich, salty broth.

"Thanks for inviting us in," said Second Gear. "This is a really cool place you've got here."

"Thanks," said Zeus. "We moved here two years ago after we thru-hiked the AT. We wanted to be close to the trail so we could hike all year round, and so we could encourage other hikers on their journeys. Here, let me show you around the place."

As we walked around the bottom floor of the cabin, Zeus took particular pride in pointing out and explaining the numerous Appalachian Trail photos and maps that lined the walls. The home had enough trail paraphernalia to pass as an AT museum or gift store.

After Zeus finished showing us around the house, Spring invited us to the kitchen table, where our places were set with bowls of home-made vegetable soup. While we sipped the warm broth, Spring recounted stories from the thru-hike she and Zeus had shared.

"We didn't think we were going to make it," she said. "At least, not in six months. We were plagued by injury and illness. I had to take a week and a half off the trail to heal a twisted ankle in Virginia, and Zeus experienced flu-like symptoms for much of New England. For a while we thought that he had contracted Lyme disease. But on October eleventh, four days before they closed Katahdin for the winter, we reached Baxter State Park and finished our hike."

"It was the best day of our lives," said Zeus.

"Well, that and our wedding day," laughed Spring. "But it's true, after thirty years, the trail did make us feel like newlyweds again."

Spring diverted her attention from refilling our bowls and turned to look lovingly at her husband. She stared at Zeus with raw emotion, and then, without averting her gaze, she said to us, "You think you're just out there hiking, you think the Appalachian Trail is just a footpath. But it's more . . . so much more."

Zeus returned his wife's loving gaze and then looked at us. "You must enjoy every day," he said. "There are no guarantees on the trail. I don't care how healthy you are or how good a hiker you become, there are always going to be loose rocks, slick roots, water parasites, and disease-carrying ticks. There are factors that you can't control and you can't prevent, so you just need to enjoy every day, because it is a rare few who are strong enough and lucky enough to make it to Katahdin."

Zeus and Spring's hospitality was uplifting, and the wisdom they imparted would serve as a reserve of strength for the rest of the trail. The fact that Second Gear and I had been crossing the nearby road on one of the days that Zeus and Spring opened their home to thru-hikers felt predestined. I guess with the trail name Odyssa, it's no coincidence that I spent an afternoon with Zeus and his wife.

When we were warm and full, Second Gear and I thanked our hosts and started back to the trail. There were five miles until the next shelter, and I walked with Second Gear the whole way.

I had found out a little about him while sitting around the table with Spring and Zeus, and now that we were back on the trail I wanted to know more. On our walk to the shelter, I learned that he had grown up two hours away from my hometown, on the other side of the Appalachian Mountains in Johnson City, Tennessee, and that, like me, he had just graduated from college.

It was becoming clear that an overwhelming number of thru-hikers were recent college grads. The obvious reason was that college graduates were able to devote four to six months to the trail without leaving a career and family behind. That also explains why recent retirees are so prevalent on the AT. But more than that, I think college grads are called to the trail because we have a lot of figuring out to do. We've spent our entire lives under the influence of family, school, and religion, and we need to test our doctrines. The trail provides a place to sort through the fact and fiction of our childhoods.

That was one reason it was so important to me to meet as many different people as possible and not become part of a group: I wanted to retell my story and explain who I was until it made sense. And, just as importantly, I wanted to listen to other hikers and learn from them.

When we arrived at Little Laurel Shelter, I could hardly remember what the previous stretch of trail looked like, but I knew all about Second Gear's family, his high school experience, his ex-girlfriend, and his post-trail ambitions.

Instead of sleeping in the shelter that evening, I decided to tent a few yards away. I was glad about that decision when, just as I drove my last stake into the ground, a tall middle-aged man hiked up the trail.

I could hear him swearing to himself from fifty yards away, and not an "Ouch, I stubbed my toe on a rock" type of cursing, but rather a constant stream of four-letter words occasionally interrupted with coherent English. His angry, aggressive rant made me imagine him grabbing the tree in front of him and violently shaking the roots up from the ground, then lifting the trunk over his head and hurling it into the bushes.

When the towering brute looked my way, I quickly shifted my eyes back to the ground. In an effort to look preoccupied with my camp chores, I re-staked the last tent peg into the ground, calmly unzipped my tent fly, carefully removed my shoes, and then dove as quickly as possible into the sanctuary of the synthetic walls. Once I was safely inside my tent, I listened to the ruckus near the shelter for another twenty minutes, until the profanity sputtered to a stop.

With my mind still racing and my heart pounding inside my chest, I decided to write in my journal until I was calm enough to fall asleep.

April 5th

Out on the trail, I don't know whether to trust people or to run from them. This afternoon I went from trusting complete strangers and spending time in their home to wishing that I was back at my parents' house, away from the crazy guy at the shelter who is cursing at the top of his lungs. It's not the profanity that bothers me, it's his anger and unpredictability. I want to pack up and find another spot to camp, but that would be too obvious. I'll try to wake up extra early tomorrow and hike extra fast so I can get away from him—I just hope nothing happens before then.

The night proved uneventful, and the next morning I held to my plan. I pushed out of camp as dawn broke and didn't stop for a rest until the sun reached the middle of the sky. But just after I finished making my peanut butter and Pop-Tart sandwich, my spine stiffened as I heard the rustling of someone coming down the trail. I stood frozen and breathless until Second Gear rounded the turn and I could relax.

Second Gear had also decided to tent last night. Well, actually, he didn't really tent because Second Gear used a hammock, but regardless, he stayed outside the shelter and avoided any interaction with our unsavory neighbor. And, like me, he decided to rise early and hike hard this morning to distance himself from any more obscenities.

By now, I had seen several hikers use hammocks instead of tents. By suspending a lightweight cocoon between two opposing trees and then hanging a tarp above the hammock, they were protected from the elements, but they didn't have to sleep on the ground. It seemed like a cool concept, as long as there were trees around.

As he sat down to join me for lunch, Second Gear commented on my sandwich.

"Peanut butter on Pop-Tarts?"

I admit that my trail nutrition was not what it should have been, and I was still experimenting with my no-cook diet, but I was quite confident in one culinary truth. "Peanut butter tastes good on everything," I said.

"Everything?" inquired Second Gear.

"Yes, everything."

Then, looking at the contents of my food bag, Second Gear proposed that I test my theory using Slim-Jims.

Unwrapping the processed stick of beef jerky, I dipped it in my peanut butter jar, stuck it in my mouth, and confirmed: "Yep, everything." Two weeks ago I had never eaten a Slim Jim; now I was eating them with peanut butter and enjoying it.

After lunch, Second Gear and I spent the remainder of the day hiking together. It's amazing how much you can learn about someone in a few hours when there are no distractions. Except for short stops to admire the view, or to analyze a tuft of wild boar hair in a berry thicket, we spent the afternoon engrossed in conversation.

As I talked with Second Gear, it struck me how honest we were with one another. I wasn't trying to be exceptionally open or sincere, but there was something about walking through the untamed forest with a relative stranger that allowed me to share more of myself than I ordinarily would have.

The thru-hiking community was the first group I had been part of that didn't have a hierarchy. Being a thru-hiker was not like working at a job where you answered to a boss, or like being part of a family that was subject to its elders. On the trail, I wasn't expected to be mild-mannered, but I also didn't need to be authoritative. Everyone was on an equal playing field. I think that helped hikers to express themselves openly. That and the confidentiality.

Most people you encounter on the trail you will know for less than a day, and even those you see more than that will most likely not be part of your life once you return home, so the chances of a leaked confession are slim to none. Counseling and Catholicism finally made sense to me: there was something cathartic about sharing my thoughts, desires, sins, and successes without worrying about rumors and public perception.

At the end of a six-hour stretch with Second Gear, I felt absolved. I had shared so much with him in such a short time, and after just over twenty-four hours together, I felt that I knew more about him than friends I had known for four years in college. Then it struck me: I knew his background, his preferences, and his ideology, but I didn't know his real name—and the nice thing was, I didn't need to.

The intimacy of the afternoon was disrupted that evening when we found Hogback Ridge Shelter full of weekenders. Until now, I had viewed weekenders as backpackers who couldn't take six months away from work and family, so instead they would spend twenty-four to forty-eight hours in the woods at a time. Tonight my opinion changed.

Tonight they felt like overindulgent, inconsiderate houseguests. They came to the trail with full stomachs, and they continued to eat throughout the weekend, filling the campground with tempting aromas and stuffing their faces in front of starving thru-hikers. They hiked less than ten miles a day and usually settled into camp before 4:00 PM. And worst of all, on nights like tonight—nights when the clouds hung low and threatened rain—they filled an entire shelter with their stogies, whiskey, and laughter without leaving any room for tired thru-hikers.

As I set up my tent near Second Gear and three other unfortunate thru-hikers, my frustration festered. It just didn't seem fair that I had to sleep outside in the rain tonight and pack up a wet tent tomorrow morning, carry it all day, and unpack a wet tent again tomorrow night, when the weekenders only had to hike two and a half miles to their cars at Sam's Gap and drive home to their warm, soft, dry beds. There might not have been a hierarchy among thru-hikers, but I definitely felt like we should be able to pull rank over weekenders.

As I had predicted, when I awoke the next morning, I heard a heavy rain falling. After much delay, I began the Tai Chi of getting dressed inside my sagging shelter before grudgingly stepping out into the dreary downpour. I packed up my soaking tent with cold fingers and stuffed it inside my drenched pack. Then, leaving behind the giggling, dry weekenders and their breakfasts that smelled of bacon, I started hiking uphill, in a layer of rain gear, with just my nose sticking out.

The trail began that morning with an unrelenting climb up a muddy slope. My rain gear kept out most of the external moisture, but my base layer became soaked with sweat from the lack of airflow inside my "breathable" rain clothes. As the elevation gain brought me into increasingly colder air, the damp sweat chilled my core and left my teeth chattering and my body shivering.

When I reached the ridgeline, I found myself on a long stretch of exposed trail that wandered over the supposedly scenic Big Bald. The only view I had was of the faint dirt path beneath my feet. The bald was smothered with a fast-moving fog that was pushed across the grassy landscape by a strong, blustery wind. I could not lift my foot off the ground without the wind forcing it several inches off the trail. The way my legs crossed and my feet flew up in the air, I felt more like a country-western line dancer than a hiker.

I thought back to Max Patch and the challenge of crossing over its exposed summit. These balds were supposed to be the most rewarding sections of the Appalachian Trail in the Southeast, yet I found myself wanting to hike over them as quickly as possible.

I was absorbed with the task of walking forward when a strong gust of wind swept over the mountain and blew my pack lid open like a sail. The added resistance caused me to stumble off the trail and land with my hands and feet planted on the frost-covered straw that lined the path.

I quickly jumped to my feet and tried to secure my pack, but the wind made it almost impossible, and before I could fasten the buckles, my fleece mittens flew from the top of my pack into the dense white mist. I desperately tied a quick knot in my pack strap to keep the rest of my belongings contained, then threw it over my shoulder, and started into the abyss to find my mittens.

Thankfully, they were caught in a frost-covered hedge a few feet away. I immediately put them on, and then looked around to try to locate the trail. All I could see was a fast-moving sheet of white and the ground directly below my feet. I zigzagged for several minutes looking for the small strand of dirt. Then, when I found it, I guessed which direction to follow it in.

Praying that I was in fact on the Appalachian Trail and headed north, I soon caught the outline of someone hiking in front of me. As I drew near, I could make out a petite woman who was struggling even more than I was to press through the toppling wind and thick fog. Sensing my presence a few feet behind her, she momentarily glanced back and caught my gaze with her youthful brown eyes. I felt an immediate connection, and I knew that my success in escaping this bald was now tied to making sure this woman made her way to safety, too.

As I watched her struggle in front of me, I wished there was something I could do for her, but the wind carried my words off before they reached her ears, and I was so preoccupied with my own footing that all I could do was walk slowly behind her and make sure that, finally, we both reached tree cover.

Tall, guardian-like pines finally appeared through the mist. Passing underneath their protective limbs, I fell beneath their branches in exhaustion. The hiker ahead of me collapsed nearby, and again we caught one another's eye, this time with a softer look and a sigh.

"That was horrible," she said. And then, out of nowhere, she started to laugh. I wasn't sure if she was laughing with shock or relief, but it was contagious.

"I know, right?" I said through my laughter. "That was insane!"

"This trail is the worst idea I have ever had. By the way, my name's Iris."

"Is that your real name or trail name?" I asked.

"It's my trail name. Iris is the Greek goddess of the rainbow, and I saw a rainbow on Springer Mountain. Plus I was a Classics major in college."

"Really?" I was dumbfounded. "My name . . . I mean, my trail name is Odyssa, and I was a Classics major too."

Iris laughed even harder. "That makes sense. It figures that two people who both chose to study dead languages would also lack the practicality to stay off an exposed mountaintop in this horrendous weather."

"So where did you go to school?" I asked.

"I graduated five years ago from UNC Chapel Hill."

"I love the Tar Heels," I stammered. "In fact, I was the only person in my family to not go to Carolina."

Then I looked closely at her. On second glance, something about her did look familiar.

At twenty-seven, Iris was six years my senior, and the youngest female hiker I had met on the trail. And since I had no clue what I was going to do with my Classics major, I eagerly listened to her recount the past five years of her life.

Iris sat at the base of the tree, resting, snacking, and telling me about the year she lived in Greece working at archeological digs and the two years she had just spent in West Africa with the Peace Corps. She explained that she had left her boyfriend in West Africa, as he still had six more months in the Corps, and the trail was a way to occupy her time until he returned.

"When I started the trail, I cried myself to sleep every night because I missed him so much. Well, because I missed him so much and because it was miserably cold outside. It is a little hard to adjust to winter after spending two years in Africa."

Wait a minute . . . she cried herself to sleep? The pieces began to come together. I knew that I had felt a strong sense of familiarity toward Iris, but it wasn't just an inner connection—I had already met her.

When I thought back to my second night on the trail, I was certain that Iris was the young woman who had been crying in her tent near where I had camped. I looked at her face and could now envision her poking her red wool cap out of the tent and briefly looking around the campsite before darting back inside.

She confirmed my story, and then laughed as she confessed, "I still take my cell phone out on top of every mountain, searching for a signal strong enough to call Africa. It's really hard being half a world away from the man you love."

"What will you two do in the fall?" I asked.

"Oh, my boyfriend will move to New Haven with me and look for a job when I start back to school."

"For what?"

"Law."

Yale Law School—I was in awe. I wanted a poster of Iris to hang on my wall after the trail. Moreover, I wanted my mother to meet Iris, so she could maintain hope that I would eventually do something productive with my life.

"Okay, so one more question," I said. "What's harder, the Appalachian Trail or the Peace Corps?"

"The Appalachian Trail," she said. "*Definitely!*"

Putting my food bag back into my pack, I was shocked to look at my watch and see that two hours had elapsed since I had started talking to Iris. I was exhausted, and I still had several more miles to go before I reached No Business Knob Shelter.

"Hey Iris, I'm gonna keep hiking. I'll see you at the next shelter, okay?"

"Sounds good—if I make it. If I don't, then it was nice meeting you, Odyssa."

When I arrived at the shelter, I was hoping to see Second Gear, but he was nowhere in sight and had probably pushed on down the mountain to the nearby town of Erwin, Tennessee. Instead, the shelter was full—not with a group of weekenders, but with a couple from Washington State. They had commandeered the entire eight-person shelter by spreading out all of their wet rain gear.

"May I move a bit of your stuff to make room for my sleeping bag?" I asked.

Scowling with displeasure, the woman responded, "There are tent sites in the area if you want to tent."

"Actually, I slept in the pouring rain last night and walked through it all day today, so all my stuff is wet. I *want* to sleep in the shelter."

"Fine, do whatever makes you happy," she snapped.

I was now on day three of a bad luck streak when it came to sharing the trail shelters: first Mr. Obscenity, then the weekenders, and now an unfriendly couple from the West Coast.

After sharing the shelter in silence for an hour, I was elated to see Iris approaching. Without asking the couple's permission, I cleared a space for her next to my sleeping bag.

That night, as we went to bed, I was very satisfied to be dry, still, and lying on the dusty wooden floorboards next to another new friend. I had almost forgotten about the disgruntled Washingtonian couple several feet away, until I began to hear their loud rustling and heavy breathing. I had no clue what they were doing—well, okay, I did have a clue, but they couldn't be . . . Oh, yes, they were!

I wasn't going to pull my headlamp out and shine it on them, and I was too grossed out and mortified to say anything, but after hearing one final deep gasp followed by a heavy sigh, I was quite sure what had just happened eight feet away from where Iris and I were sleeping. No wonder they'd wanted me to tent outside! I was scared, annoyed, and ready for the sun to come up so I could leave.

The next morning, I was on the trail before daybreak. It seemed that trying to put distance between myself and undesirable company was becoming the motivating factor that would get me to Maine.

Once again, the day began with a cold, steady rainfall. It was four miles downhill into the Nolichucky River Basin and the outskirts of Erwin, Tennessee. I longed to stop. I knew that Second Gear was in Erwin and that Iris would be arriving there shortly. There were hostels and hotels in Erwin, grocery stores and restaurants, and the register at No Business Knob Shelter mentioned a hot tub and an all-you-can-eat pizza buffet. But I needed to continue hiking. I had arranged to meet friends in Banner Elk, North Carolina, on Sunday, and that meant I needed to cover fifty miles in forty-eight hours.

It took every ounce of willpower to overlook the wooden hostel to my left and the paved road that led into town, and instead begin the four-thousand-foot climb up Unaka Mountain. I only stopped to have a snack after I had walked far enough that I wouldn't be tempted to turn around and go back into Erwin.

During my first few weeks on the trail, my appetite had actually seemed to diminish, but since leaving the Smokies, I began to notice an exponential rise in my hunger. This morning, as I stared into my food bag, I knew that even though I needed to stretch the contents out for another two days, I was hungry enough to eat all of my remaining food. Balancing self-restraint with desire, I ate more than I should have, but not everything.

The climb up Unaka was hard—really hard. There were no views and my disrupted sleep the night before, combined with a calorie deficit, left me utterly drained, and the entire section was uphill.

For the first time since I started the trail, I thought, "This is not fun." Not that being struck by lightning, caught in a blizzard, or getting lost in the fog on top of Big Bald had been fun, but it had all been new, and I had been filled with adrenaline. Hiking uphill in the rain was not new anymore.

I was tired, I was hungry, and the whole experience of walking day after day had started to feel, well . . . repetitive. I began to think about how far away Maine was, and about all the other cold, wet climbs that awaited me along the way. I started to doubt that I could physically make it to the end of the trail. And as my despair grew, so did the mountain.

I tried to occupy my mind with thoughts other than hiking, but the ache in my shoulders, the hunger pains in my stomach, and the burning in my calves made it impossible to think about anything else. In the midst of my struggle, I held onto the simplest, most concise piece of hope that I could think of: *Every step I take is a step closer to Maine*, I thought. *Every step I take is a step closer to Maine.*

At first I repeated it in my head, but then I began to say the words aloud, and with every new step I would utter my mantra.

"Every step I take is a step closer to Maine. Every step I take is a step closer to Maine!"

I knew that Maine was still a long way off—over eighteen hundred miles—but I needed to think about it. I needed to know that, although I was currently in a state of pain and discomfort, I was also constantly moving toward an end-goal. This sense of progress propelled me up the mountain, and when I finally reached the summit, I was depleted, but I was there—a little farther than where I had started, and a little closer to Maine.

To celebrate my summit, dark clouds gathered overhead and clapped in applause. Soon their thunderous approval was accompanied by a stunning light display and a downpour of rain. The electrical storm gave me what I had lacked all morning—adrenaline. I slalomed through the confusing pine forest on top of Unaka, desperately searching for white blazes.

The entire mountaintop was covered in pine trees, and the ground was blanketed with pine straw. I couldn't see a definitive dirt path anywhere, and the lightning had me panicked. Everything looked the same, and I felt like I was stuck in a maze or an amusement park funhouse.

I kept having flashbacks to being struck by lightning. Every time a brilliant white flash lit up the forest, my spine stiffened and my body froze in fear. My mind now associated each bolt of lightning with the intense pain that had traveled through my body weeks before. I remembered the story about the ranger in Shenandoah National Park who had been struck by lightning seven times, and I tried even harder to find my way off of the mountain.

Once I was through the evergreens, the path again took form, and I quickly descended the backside of the ridge. Trying to rush, I stepped on a slick rock and slid several feet down a muddy slope to the switchback below. My fall served as a shortcut, but it also left me sore, scraped, and covered in mud. I continued to hobble along at a decent pace, trying to use rainwater to rinse the brown sludge off my body, but when the downpour let up and the lightning ceased, I lost all motivation.

I knew I was within a mile or two of the shelter where I planned to spend the night, but I still couldn't do anything more than plod clumsily down the trail. I felt as if I were inebriated: there was little connection between my mind and body, and I had a hard time focusing on the forest or my feet. The only thing that kept me moving forward was three weeks of muscle memory.

After trudging along for what seemed like an eternity, I arrived at the Cherry Gap Shelter—only to look around in dismay at the many people who already occupied the small building. I didn't have the energy to set up my wet tent tonight.

With my head down, I muttered halfheartedly, "Is there any more room in the shelter?"

I wasn't even sure if anyone had heard me, but then a mature Southern accent quickly called back, "Of course there's room, darlin'! I'll move my bag over and you can sleep here."

The voice triggered a sense of recognition. I lifted my head and peered into the corner of the shelter.

"Wesley?" Paralyzed with joy, I stood there staring at my friend, who sat grinning and waiting for me to acknowledge him. Wesley had attended the Appalachian Trail Institute with me, and aside from Sarah and Doug, he had been my closest friend at the workshop.

He was a tall, thin man with tanned skin and deep laugh lines contouring his face. He was a retiree from Montgomery, Alabama, and he embodied a true Southerner—loud, opinionated, and kind.

With a crooked smile on his face, he rose from the floorboards and engulfed me with open arms. I held on to Wesley as if he had returned from the dead. I never thought I would see him again, and meeting him here, now—there couldn't have been a sweeter reunion.

Wesley helped me situate all my belongings, sweetly prodded me to get my cold, damp body into a warm sleeping bag, and shared some of his dinner with me, which he unconvincingly claimed that he couldn't finish. All I could do was lie there and smile as he tended to me with care and conversation.

When he was satisfied that I had eaten enough, Wesley began to regale me with stories from his first month on the trail. At the workshop, he had told Warren that he wanted to hike the Appalachian Trail so he could work hard and be outside, and he had gotten just what he wanted. His stories from the first few weeks on the trail were epic, but it seemed that each adventure ended with either sickness or injury. He rattled off a litany of ailments, including a broken rib, pneumonia, and a stress fracture in his foot. Then he followed that up with an even more impressive inventory of prescription drugs he was taking for his infirmities.

After Wesley was finished recounting his many mishaps, he looked to his left and introduced me to Deputy, who reminded me of Wesley, except that his accent was stronger, his beard was longer, and his skin was a deeper shade of caramel. Deputy and Wesley had been hiking together for several weeks. Eager to match his companion's list of set-backs, Deputy immediately dove into how this was his fourth attempt to thru-hike the AT. In fact, I got the impression that Deputy enjoyed relaying the annals of hardship that had kept him from Katahdin. One year it was a broken leg, another it was family tragedy, and once it came down to budgeting and finances. Once, Deputy made it all the way up to Connecticut before having to stop. But despite his setbacks, he would start over at Springer Mountain each spring in an attempt to hike the entire trail.

I admired Deputy's persistence, but after a day like today, I was convinced that I was only going to try this once. This was my one chance, and if I wanted to finish, then I needed to give it my all, because I wasn't coming back.

That night I fell asleep as Wesley and Deputy tried to convince the five New Englanders in the shelter that the South had not tech-nically lost The War—God bless those two if they ever make it past Maryland.

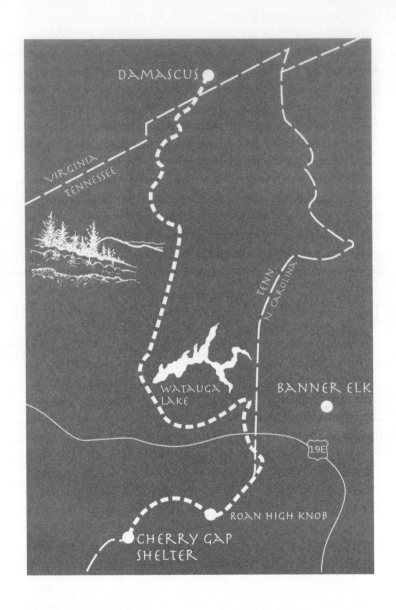

DAMASCUS

VIRGINIA
TENNESSEE

TENN.
N. CAROLINA

WATAUGA
LAKE

BANNER ELK

19E

ROAN HIGH KNOB

CHERRY GAP
SHELTER

8

CONFIDENCE

CHERRY GAP SHELTER, TN, TO
DAMASCUS, VA—104.9 MILES

The rolling fourteen-mile descent off Roan Mountain to High-way 19E reveals some of the best scenery on the Appalachian Trail. The views from Big Hump and Little Hump stretch beyond the open fields of waving grass and provide glimpses of neighboring mountains in North Carolina, Tennessee, and Virginia. As the trail nears the Virginia border, it transitions from high peaks into level ridges and more gradual elevation changes. And the triumphal entry into Damascus, Virginia, marks a new state and the completion of four hundred and fifty miles.

I t baffles me how I could feel weak and sore beyond repair and then, after nine hours of sleep, wake up feeling healthy and strong. When I opened my eyes and saw Wesley snoring beside me, I felt refreshed. Even though I had almost sworn off hiking the day before, it was a new day, and I felt drawn to the trail and eager to hike.

For the first time in two days, it wasn't raining. After rustling Wesley to a waking stupor and wishing him good-bye, I left the shelter and continued walking north.

The trail was peaceful, the wind was calm, and a quiet serenity pervaded the woods. The only noise came from my shoes gently snapping a twig or lightly crunching the leaves on the trail. I entertained myself with thoughts of the new friends that I had made, thoughts of an upcoming visit in Banner Elk, thoughts of my proud father at home telling every person he knew what I was doing, and my mom standing beside him and rolling her eyes.

Suddenly, a noisy footstep interrupted my thoughts. Steps in the woods make a distinct sound, and what I had heard was clearly a footstep, but it wasn't mine, and it hadn't come from the trail. I looked to the right of the path and there, peering out from behind a tree ten feet away, was a large man in head-to-toe camouflage holding a shotgun.

"Ya seen any turkeys?" asked the man.

"Turkeys?" I repeated, wide-eyed and still in shock.

"Yeah, *tur*-keys." This time he enunciated very clearly, in an attempt to make me feel like a moron.

There was a pause. I wasn't opposed to hunting, but I didn't like being surprised. In particular, I didn't like being surprised by men dressed in tan-and-green unitards holding big guns, especially if they were targeting wildlife that I hoped to see alive. But what scared me the most was that I hadn't seen this hunter until I was within a few yards of him. He had stayed completely still and well disguised, silently watching me approach, then appeared unexpectedly and without warning. Weren't these guys supposed to wear bright orange caps or something?

I wanted to tell him that I had been out here for several weeks and had not seen a single wild turkey, and that he should just give up and go home.

But instead I scowled and replied, "Nope, no *tur*-keys."

Realizing the negative impression he had made, the hunter tried halfheartedly to redeem himself. It sounded forced, but as he turned to leave, he said, "Well, have a good hike and watch out for hunters, 'cuz it's the first day of the season."

The season—turkey season. Great. I didn't have to worry about thunderstorms today, but I did have to worry about men in camo running around the woods with loaded guns. For the rest of the day I was paranoid, especially when I had to pee and couldn't be sure that men weren't hiding behind trees and watching.

Thankfully, most hunters aren't motivated enough to climb a six-thousand-foot mountain to look for turkeys, so I made it to the top of Roan Mountain without any further encounters. Roan, like Unaka, offered a beastly climb to the summit. Its rocky slope and steep grade is said to rival the peaks in New Hampshire and Maine, but unlike Unaka, I completed the long ascent with relative ease.

Roan's summit is covered in a spruce forest and doesn't offer any panoramic views from the top. However, after navigating a mile and a half off the peak, the trail reaches an exposed ridge, which is covered in tall golden stalks of grass that roll like waves in the breeze.

Within the swaying expanse of amber hues, there are several dark green islands of rhododendron. Up until now, I had mostly seen rhododendron bushes with their leaves tightly curled like cigars and pointing to the ground, but when the temperatures warm up, a rhododendron bush will unclench its fists and open them to the sky. That afternoon, the plants on Roan Mountain unfurled their leaves and lifted them heavenward.

Imitating the rhododendron, I lifted my hands to the clear blue sky. It felt so good that I stopped walking, looked to the sky, and began to spin in circles. I felt safe and free like an uninhibited child. Then I felt dizzy, really dizzy. I stopped twirling and took several drunken steps up the trail until I could once again walk in a straight line.

When the path reentered the forest, I was filled with awe by the surrounding vegetation. The forest had soaked up two straight days of rain and now looked greener and smelled more alive than I had ever experienced. Each step I took was filled with wonder, and the path itself seemed eager to please as it continued to slope gently downhill.

I hadn't passed anyone that day except the hunter. When I reached Little Hump, I could once again see the trail stretch into the distance before me, and there wasn't another person in sight. It felt as if I had the entire mountain all to myself.

Little Hump offered uninterrupted views of the Blue Ridge Mountains, which, true to their name, were now transforming from a barren brown to a kaleidoscope of blues. I followed the ridgeline to the top of neighboring Big Hump to watch the sunset. The sky was lit up with hues of orange, pink, and yellow that could never be duplicated in manufactured colors. And when the sun set, the mountains shed their shades of blue to reveal a majestic coat of purple.

I was overcome with awe. Spontaneously and without thought, I shouted, "Praise God!" into the wind.

Then I felt like a dork.

I had become comfortable singing out loud on the trail. But shouting into the wind—to a God that most folks on the trail rejected—felt weird. I mean, what if someone had heard me? What if a hunter had been hiding in the grass and now thought that I was some crazy person screaming to God on top of a mountain?

I hadn't meant to think so much about God on the trail. I wasn't really counting on Him to challenge me or change me. I thought that we would just maintain the status quo until I finished in Maine and started going back to church. But this evening, with the sunset, the scent of the mountains, and the noise of the crickets, I knew that God had planned it out for me. I remembered a verse in the Bible that said that even if humans failed to praise God, the rocks would sing out his glories. And that's what they were doing—the mountains were singing the praises of God beautifully and without shame. I wished I could be more like a mountain.

The next morning I had a short jaunt to 19E where I planned to meet Heather. I woke up early, eager to reach a familiar face and a shower. I packed up my belongings and started hiking while the sky was still gray. As the sun rose over the horizon, I began to notice how faint the white blazes had become. It was almost if someone had tried to remove them from the trees and rocks that lined the path.

Eventually the trail left the woods and joined a gravel road through a rural neighborhood. The mobile homes that dotted the road were rundown: some were slanted, one had a crooked roof, and several had missing siding or broken windows. But *all* the modular units had at least one guard dog that came charging at me with teeth bared and slobber streaming down its jowls.

Big, small, it didn't matter—I was terrified of every terrier, bloodhound, and indistinguishable mutt that ran in my direction. To make matters worse, I saw one woman stand at her window and smile as her two pit bulls growled, barked, and prepared to pounce.

When I arrived at the highway without being mauled, I breathed a sigh of relief. I had made it to the road, and soon Heather would be here to take me to her house. But then I remembered that Heather had said there would be a parking area here, and a sign . . . but there was nothing of the sort.

This wasn't our meeting spot!

How could this have happened? I'd followed the white blazes here, but I must have taken the wrong trail—or the old trail.

I knew that the Appalachian Trail was slightly rerouted from year to year. Sometimes it was altered because of natural forces such as floods or rockslides, other times because of property rights and land easements, and occasionally trail maintainers decide to relocate the path for better views or easier climbs. I could see why the rerouting was necessary, but I didn't know that the old blazes still existed and could lead hikers astray!

Without any clue where I was or which direction I should walk, I pulled out my cell phone to call Heather. It was dead.

I started to walk along the roadside, hoping she would drive by or that I would come across the official Appalachian Trail. But after five minutes, I hadn't seen a single car, let alone Heather's, and I feared that I was heading in the wrong direction.

Standing there dumbfounded, I saw a white pickup truck approaching. I took several steps away from the road and stood aside as it passed. But as it roared by, the loud vehicle began to slow down, and a few dozen yards in front of me, it stopped completely. I wasn't sure if it had stopped for me or not, and if it had, I wasn't sure if that was good or bad.

A sturdy man with blond hair stuck his head out the driver's side window and yelled out, "You need a ride?"

I wasn't crazy about the idea of climbing into a truck with a man I didn't know, but I thought maybe he could point me in the right direction.

"Um . . . I'm trying to get to the Appalachian Trail on 19E to meet some friends."

"Well, that's a good ways from here, and you're walking in the wrong direction. But I can take you just up the road to where you can call your friends."

I knew that I had said no hitchhiking—or rather, my mom had said no hitchhiking—but someone offering me a ride was different than me soliciting one. Right?

Hesitantly, I nodded. "Okay . . . th-that would be great." I placed my pack in the truck bed and started to climb in the back.

"It's illegal to ride in the back," he said. "I won't bite, I promise."

I approached the side of the truck and cautiously climbed inside the cab.

Butch, the driver, seemed friendly. He smiled and asked me about the trail, which helped to ease my nerves. However, when he insisted on taking me back to "his place," I began to second-guess my decision.

"It's just up the road," he said. "You can use the phone there for free."

"Oh, no, really you can just drop me off at a gas station or restaurant or something."

"Nah, don't worry about it," he said. "My place is closer than the nearest gas station, and it should be pretty quiet this morning."

Quiet? I nervously checked to make sure the passenger door was still unlocked.

Butch continued, "You see, on a Friday or Saturday night there can be a lot of commotion there, a lot of drunk locals with nothing better to do. But today it will just be you and me."

I slowly moved my hand toward the door handle in case I needed to jump out at a moment's notice.

When we pulled up to Butch's Beer Wash, everything made sense. It would have helped put me at ease if Butch had told me from the beginning that he owned a bar.

At Butch's Beer Wash I called Heather, and in the thirty minutes it took her to arrive, Butch fed me breakfast and told me stories from the summer that he had hitchhiked from Tennessee to Alaska.

"So many people were good to me that summer and went out of their way to help me out. Now it's my turn to help others. I know you have friends near here, but if you need any more help or a ride back to the trail, here's my number. Just call me and I'll be happy to help you."

I felt embarrassed for having been so apprehensive during the car ride. Sure, Butch looked worn and tough, like he was from the remote mountains of Tennessee. But that was who he was: a third-generation Appalachian mountaineer, hardworking, decent, and kind.

The Smiths were lifelong family friends who lived a few miles from the trail in neighboring Banner Elk. Heather was my mom's friend, and I was better acquainted with her grown children, but I had known the family my whole life and had been looking forward to this visit since I started the trail. And while I had felt a little bit guilty getting off the trail and going home after the Smokies, I had no qualms about spending time with the Smiths in Banner Elk.

Before I started the Appalachian Trail, I had decided that this trip was about more than just hiking. Granted, a lot of it was about hiking, but I also wanted to invest in the people and places along the way. Experiencing the towns and cultures en route was just as important to me as my time spent on the trail.

The day I spent in Banner Elk was wonderfully ordinary. It was Sunday, so we went to church, where Heather's husband, Jeff, was the minister. We spent the afternoon watching their youngest daughter play soccer, and that evening, we enjoyed a family dinner together. But throughout the everyday events that filled our time, I never had an agenda other than to be present, share, and listen. I didn't have anywhere I needed to go or anybody else that I needed to see; I didn't have work or school to think about. I could focus entirely on our visit.

That night, I stayed up several hours past my trail bedtime, sitting in the kitchen and talking with Heather. At one point, she even ordered me to take off my shoes so she could massage my sore and swollen feet.

"So what do you think you'll do when your daughter graduates high school and you have an empty nest?" I asked.

"A lot," she laughed. "I never really got to put my master's in architecture to use after we had our first child. I think that maybe I'd like to get back to design. If I could combine that with my love of photography, it would make me happy."

"I never knew you had an architecture degree," I said with surprise.

"Ahh, yes," she smiled. "That's because by the time you came around, my kids had become my job. I've been driving carpools, going to after-school sports, and hosting sleepovers for so long that it's strange to think about it coming to an end."

I started to think about my own mother and the years she gave over to me and my brothers. I honestly had never thought that she might prefer to be doing something else.

"So, um . . . well, do you regret not working?" Part of me felt like the question was too personal and that I shouldn't have asked, but I really wanted to know the answer.

"No, no, not at all. Some women want to work or have to work, and I appreciate that, but I consider myself very fortunate to have been able to spend all those years with my children."

I give my mom a lot of grief, a lot of the time, but talking with Heather made me see my own mother in a new light. I loved my mom, I had always loved my mom, but now I was starting to appreciate her too.

Being on the trail had given me time to reflect on the people closest to me, and even though I was geographically separated from all of them, I had started to feel closer to them and more thankful for their presence in my life.

The trail had also taught me that everyone has a story. Before my visit in Banner Elk, I had viewed Heather simply as a loving mom, but now I also saw her as an avid photographer, a supportive wife, an architect, an outdoors enthusiast, and a terrific hostess.

After my visit with the Smiths, I returned to the trail—the current trail—feeling strong and rested. I had missed the woods and was happy to return. It was a beautiful spring day, with mild temperatures and a blue sky, the kind of day that draws everyone outdoors.

I wished that some of those people had stayed inside.

I could have done without the man in the white tank-top and cutoff jean shorts driving his ATV madly down the trail and running me off the path. ATV—I didn't even know what that stood for. I just knew that the loud, noisy four-wheelers tore up the path and were prohibited on the trail. Maybe the skinny man with the mullet was unaware of the restriction. Perhaps he thought that ATV stood for Appalachian Trail Vehicle, but my new interpretation was Asshole Traveling Violently!

A moment after he recklessly sped by, hollering and spraying mud on my legs, his two dogs—two familiar-looking pit bulls—cornered me at the base of a poplar tree. They barked, growled, frothed at the mouth, and fed off my fear until their owner called and they raced down the trail after him.

A few miles later, the trail came out of the woods at a rural cemetery and then crossed a paved road in front of a small brick church. Forty yards down the road, by the edge of a field, a pack of eighteen- and nineteen-year-old boys stood next to a pickup truck. Several were smoking cigarettes (I think they were cigarettes), and one was drinking from a flask.

Walk fast, I told myself.

But it was too late. They had seen me, and the catcalls ensued: "Hey, sweetheart, what's your name?" "Don't you want to come see us?" "C'mon, baby, what's the rush? You scared?" They all laughed, and a couple of them started moving in my direction.

My heart rate began to speed up as they started jogging toward me. I could handle the heckling, but this felt threatening. I was a few steps from the forest, so I pretended not to hear them and tried not to speed up until I passed behind the trees, then I started to sprint. I ran at least a quarter mile before I slowed down to a very, very fast walk.

"Harmless," I told myself. "Those boys were probably absolutely harmless; they were just teenagers with nothing to do." But despite my attempts to reassure myself, my stomach felt uneasy and I was filled with anxiety for the next few hours.

As the afternoon wore on, my distance from civilization grew and I slowed to a deliberate walk. Eventually I stopped replaying the day's earlier encounters in my head, and I became lost in thought, which I very much enjoyed.

In society, I never felt like I was able to follow a thought to completion. Instead, one thought would lead to another thought, which would lead to another thought, and then I would be distracted by a loud noise, a bright light, or a prior commitment and never finish my thinking. On the trail, however, I would have an idea, and that would lead to another, followed by a contrary opinion that would bring up a totally different concept, and at the end of exploring that concept there would be quiet and my brain would feel still. Not still as if it were empty or without intelligence, but just the opposite—still as if it were full and at peace.

Sometimes I would challenge myself to think and think and think, to see how long I could think and put off the peace, but no matter how long my thoughts lasted, the end was always the same. There was peace, the world was silent, and I was by myself.

I was at just such a place of peace when, out of the corner of my eye, I saw the black stick beside my foot move and then race to the side of the trail. I jumped to the opposite side of the path and squealed with fright.

A snake!

This was the first snake that I had seen on the Appalachian Trail. I hate snakes. I don't know why I hate snakes, but I do. That said, I knew that black snakes weren't poisonous, so I stood several feet away and watched to see what it would do next. For the most part, it just laid still, sunning itself on the trail, but when it did slightly adjust or wiggle its forked tongue in the air, I cringed in disgust.

I was amazed that the snake hadn't bitten me. My foot had landed within a few inches of its head, and it easily could have sunk its fangs into my exposed ankle, but instead it had just slithered in the opposite direction.

I was shaken up after coming so close to the legless reptile, and I promised myself I would be more careful and perhaps less "thoughtless" in the future.

Thirty minutes later I almost stepped on another snake. I hadn't seen a snake in four hundred miles and now I had come across two within an hour?

Once again, it was a long, thin, black snake that I had taken for a fallen branch. When I stepped within a foot of its body, it quickly moved away and actually started retreating up the bark of a nearby locust tree. As much as I despised snakes, it was neat to see this one climb up a tree. He used the grooved bark for support and wove his way up the trunk in an S-shaped pattern. He was already six feet off the ground when I decided to continue hiking.

Even though I still don't like snakes, looking back on the day, I decided that they had been my favorite unpleasant encounter.

I had forgotten how much I didn't miss the rain until I woke up the next morning to a cold drizzle. I had enjoyed two beautiful trail days since the last downpour, and I was not thrilled to once again take down a dripping tent and shove it into my soaking pack. I even preferred snow over a thirty-five-degree rain. At least with snow I could still stay relatively dry, unlike the piercing wind and pouring rain that chilled my core and numbed my extremities.

By now, I had also noticed a direct correlation between the weather and my appetite. At this point on the trail, I was experiencing ravenous hunger every few hours regardless of the weather, but when the temperatures dropped and the rain started to fall, my appetite became insatiable all day long. I now wished that I hadn't eaten three Snickers bars to end my lunch yesterday, and had saved one or two more for today.

My logic yesterday was that I had five Snickers, so I could eat three for dessert, which would make my pack noticeably lighter, and then I would enjoy one a day until I reached Damascus. At the time, I couldn't believe I was eating three candy bars at once, but they tasted so good and went down so easily that I probably could have eaten all five.

I was amazed at how much I could eat now. At the past three food resupplies, I thought I had bought enough rations that I could feast on the trail and still have leftovers when I reached the next town. Instead, my food continued to disappear far more quickly than I expected, and by the end of each section I would stumble into town starving and with an empty food bag. At lunch today, I realized that, once again, I would have to measure my food intake carefully until my next resupply.

The one upside to the cold rain is that I became highly efficient. When I could see my breath but not feel my fingers, all I wanted to do was put in my miles for the day and then curl up in my sleeping bag. Aside from a brief stop for lunch, I hiked continuously for twenty miles and was able to reach Vandeventer Shelter at 4:00 PM.

I was the only person there, and the first thing I did inside the empty building was strip naked. I peeled off my wet clothes as quickly as possible and changed into my warm, dry ones before any-one else arrived. Next, I unpacked my warm sleeping bag and wrapped it around my shivering body. I was very hungry, but I was worried that if I started eating, I would eat the rest of the food in my pack and have nothing left for the next day and a half.

After warming up for a few minutes, I decided to look around the shelter for the register, and that's when I spotted the trash in the corner. At least, I thought it was trash, and apparently somebody else had thought so too, which is why it had been left here. But as I investigated, I found an open bag of tortellini.

This wasn't the type of pasta that is hard and comes in a box. This was the type you find in the refrigerator section of the grocery store that's already soft before you cook it. If I still had a camp stove, I would have boiled water and cooked the pasta, but instead I just stuck the cold cheese-filled shells in my mouth one by one. I had no idea how long this pasta had been here, who had been eating it, or whether mice had already gotten into it, but I was really hungry, and the pasta was helping. I felt both ashamed and thankful, and I finished the entire package.

Eventually other hikers, none of whom I had met before, began arriving at the shelter. I was joined by two men in their mid-twenties, then three boys just out of high school. I was amazed that three kids who weren't even in college yet were out here hiking the trail together. Their youth and enthusiasm were infectious. Their stories about their countless mishaps and poor decisions on the trail made me realize that they were even more naïve and reckless than I was.

Just before dark, one of the boys became a little too bold and outspoken for my liking.

"Did you guys know that someone was murdered at this shelter?" asked the grinning seventeen-year-old.

I thought he was kidding, and so did the men in their twenties, because one of them said, "Yeah, right."

"No, seriously," another kid confirmed. "One of the first AT murders happened here. This twenty-two-year-old girl hiking by herself got hatcheted with an axe. And I hear some people think this shelter has been haunted since then."

Then the third kid chimed in with a ghostly moan followed by a rendition of *The Twilight Zone* theme song.

I was mad that they were joking about a murder, and completely ticked off that they had mentioned it in the first place. I knew there had been homicides on the Appalachian Trail, but I didn't want to know anything about them—especially the ones that had happened to young women hiking alone.

I thought it would take another day and a half to reach Damascus, but after covering twenty miles before 2:00 PM, I was faced with a decision. Stopping yesterday at 4:00 PM had been hard. I didn't like waiting around for the sun to go down. And if I stopped now, I wouldn't have anything to do for the next six hours.

On the other hand, I had already hiked twenty miles, and it was ten more to Damascus. My farthest day of hiking so far had been twenty-seven miles, and that had been a struggle. Usually I was happy to hike twenty to twenty-five miles, but today the trail had been surprisingly flat, I still had energy left, and all of a sudden I was craving pizza. But thirty miles? That seemed too far.

As I tried to decide what to do, two thru-hikers in their twenties walked up behind me. They were brothers. I hadn't met them at the shelter the night before because they had decided to tent a little farther down the trail.

"We didn't want to stay where someone had been killed," the older brother explained.

Without a history of homicide at the current shelter, they both started to unload their packs.

"Are you going to stop?" asked the younger brother.

"I don't know. I usually don't stop this early, but I've never hiked thirty miles in one day, and I don't know if I can make it to Damascus before dark."

He replied, "Yeah, we're too tired to make it there today, but we can't wait until tomorrow. Damascus is awesome. There's a pizza joint, a burrito shop, and a Subway in town. Plus, it will be our first shower in two weeks."

Two weeks? I thought I smelled something. The longest I had gone without a shower on the trail was four days.

In the end the decision was simple: pizza, shower, and a hostel trumped PowerBars, floor planks, and putrescence. I was on my way to Damascus.

Damascus is the preeminent trail town. All the businesses are hiker-friendly, meaning they don't mind dirty, stinky vagabonds with packs on their backs hanging around. And each May the town hosts a thru-hiker festival called Trail Days, which serves as a celebration for current hikers who have made it to Virginia, and a reunion for thru-hikers from years past. The main event at Trail Days is a hiker parade, where current thru-hikers parade down Main Street carrying water balloons to combat the hoses and water guns that the crowd points at them.

The sun was setting when I arrived in Damascus, and although there weren't water balloons or a crowd, I paraded down the center of Main Street filled with happiness and pride. The quaint town was beautiful and, like Hot Springs, it was next to a river and bordered by mountains.

The fading sun lit up the Main Street windows in pink, and everywhere I looked there were signs greeting hikers or providing information about specific services, such as trail shuttles, hostels, or resupply options. In other towns along the trail, thru-hikers were a spectacle, but in Damascus I felt like the guest of honor.

I celebrated my arrival with an immediate trip to Sicily's Italian Restaurant. At first, I was solely focused on food, but after a few slices of tomato, feta, and banana pepper pizza, it struck me—I had hiked almost five hundred miles. I had completed one of the toughest sections of trail along the North Carolina–Tennessee border, and I had made it to Virginia.

I sat there with a sense of accomplishment and enjoyed rewarding myself with pizza. It occurred to me that this was the first time I had ever eaten at a restaurant by myself. I thought back to how nervous it used to make me to go to my college cafeteria alone, not knowing whether I would find a friend to sit next to. I was self-conscious that sitting alone would make people think I didn't have any friends. But tonight sitting alone didn't bother me. I was more comfortable with myself and with silence than I had ever been, and I was filled with confidence—the confidence of five hundred miles.

The Place is a simple two-story building that a local church transformed into lodging for hikers and bikers. For a suggested donation of three dollars, I was treated to four walls, a wooden bunk bed, and indoor plumbing.

After arriving at The Place and taking a long, hot shower, I walked to the back rooms in search of a quiet bunk. I found a room without any people or packs, shut the door, and rolled out my sleeping bag on a nearby wooden frame. Mileage-wise, it had been my longest day, and

I hadn't slept well the night before, so I was much more interested in sleep than socializing.

Just as I closed my eyes, I heard someone slam the front door of the building. My body grew tense as the heavy footsteps grew louder.

There was a momentary pause before the door to my room swung open and an extremely large, rugged middle-aged man entered. His clothes were dirty and damp, and he had a nappy beard that reached down to his protruding belly. He glanced over at me and said, "Arrr . . . greetings, me lady. Is there room in here for a pirate?"

A pirate?

Although taken aback, I did my best to engage in conversation. "Well, there are lots of bunks open . . . except this one. I guess you can have whichever one you want."

"Ahh, thanks, lassie. It feels good to rest me weary bones."

"What's your name?" I asked.

"My name's Captain Jack Daniels, but you can call me Captain."

I asked Captain where he had hiked from that morning. He responded that he had just come from the Smokies.

"But Captain, aren't they two hundred miles away?"

"Arrr, you're right, me lassie, but it was too cold there, so I hitched up to Virginia."

I asked him if he was a thru-hiker, and he informed me that he had been a thru-hiker for the past fifteen years.

"The past fifteen years?"

Captain went on to explain that he owned several small businesses along the trail, and he spent his time hiking or hitching from one town to another to check on them.

He began to list all of his entrepreneurial ventures: one which involved GPS, one that sold hot dogs, and another that rented bicycles. I couldn't fully understand any of them, but I was very tired. Captain even offered me a job at one of his establishments. I declined, but told him that I might find him after I finished the trail.

Captain's lifestyle of continual hiking even had a formal club. He and two of his friends were part of a "long-term, short-distance" hiking organization known as Hiker Trash. To my surprise, the club had its own marketing materials, such as embroidered hats and business cards.

Captain gave me his business card. Looking it over, I was surprised to find a Bible verse on one side, an open slot in the middle, and bold print on the back that read, "PEEING—DON'T TOUCH!" He told me the slot in the middle was so he could slip the card over his beer bottle and protect his beverage while he went to the restroom. Captain concluded his show-and-tell by turning his pack around and pointing to his hiking mascot: a stuffed pirate doll that looked exactly like him.

Finally, suggesting that I looked tired and should get some sleep, Captain placed his possessions on the bunk beside me, grabbed his Nalgene bottle—which curiously smelled of something other than water—and took off to see if he could find any of his friends in town.

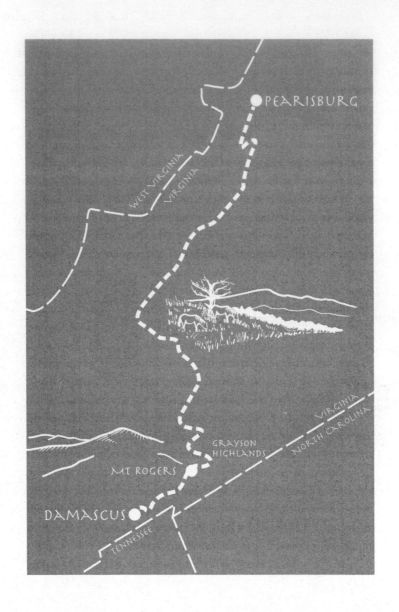

9

OPPRESSION

DAMASCUS, VA, TO A LITTLE PAST
PEARISBURG, VA—165 MILES

The pastoral setting of southwest Virginia is breathtaking. It is one of the most remote sections of the trail and begins with the open expanses of Grayson Highlands State Park, which is often compared to the rugged hills of Montana. While the scenery is stunning, for many, the highlight is the wild ponies that roam free inside the park's fence. Past Grayson Highlands, the trail travels through rolling farmland and beside grazing livestock. The scenic vistas of North Carolina and Tennessee make you feel like you're looking at a work of art, but crossing through the rural countryside of southwest Virginia and caressing the tall grass with your fingertips, you feel like you're part of the painting.

The next day, I awoke to the sound of Captain's rattling, rhythmic breathing. Unable to sleep through the vibrations, I gathered my belongings and headed to the laundromat.

I enjoyed my time in the fluff 'n' fold, especially after a local programmed the jukebox to play every Hank Williams song. But when my "quick-dry" hiking clothes were still wet after two cycles in the dryer, I gave up, threw them in my backpack, and headed back to the trail.

On my way out of town, I decided to make one last stop: Subway. I think it was the only chain restaurant in Damascus, and while I believe in supporting local businesses, I *really* like Subway. I like the fresh ingredients, I like the efficiency, but most of all, I love the fact that Subway offers me complete control. I love being able to dictate exactly what goes on my sandwich and watching it immediately take form. That morning, my six-inch sub on Italian parmesan bread was piled high with turkey, lettuce, tomatoes, onions, green peppers, banana peppers, jalapenos, oregano, a touch of mayonnaise, a lot of mustard, and a sprinkle of parmesan cheese. And as I selected chips and a drink to complete my meal, I noticed another hiker sitting toward the back of the store.

Hikers are fairly easy to pick out. They're typically male, typically hairy, usually smelly, and they often have a huge backpack and two hiking poles somewhere nearby. This hiker was a young man, medium height, extremely thin, with skin so pale I could see the blue veins at his temples. His white complexion contrasted sharply with his dark brown eyes and wiry black hair. When I first spotted him, he looked so deep in thought that I could almost see his brain working behind his translucent forehead.

When I introduced myself, his demeanor and even his coloring quickly changed. Shades of pink flooded his cheeks, and he seemed both pleased and surprised by my greeting. I asked if I could sit with him and he immediately made room for me.

I learned a lot about Moot during our lunch together. I learned that he had finished college last spring and had spent the past few months working at a boatyard on the Cape.

"What Cape?" I asked.

"*The* Cape," he said. "You know, Cape Cod, in Massachusetts."

I felt stupid for not knowing that, because the way he responded, it seemed like I should have known. There was a lot Moot knew that I didn't. I was amazed at how eager he was to bypass idle chatter and dive into thought-provoking topics like philosophy and obscure political issues. When he brought up theology, Moot described himself as an "existential atheistic Quaker." I didn't know exactly what that meant, but I was pretty sure I had never met one of those before.

Well aware that this conversation was going to take more time than a six-inch sub allowed, I finished my sandwich and suggested that we start back to the trail together. Moot eagerly agreed, and he continued his personal discourse as we rejoined the trail. It was clear that he had spent a lot of time formulating his beliefs, and he explained himself well, but there were still key concepts that I couldn't grasp.

One point of confusion was that Moot didn't believe in good or evil. He did, however, believe that humanity could be bettered through politics.

"Okay, so I definitely agree that politics are powerful and can positively or negatively affect people, but how can it better humanity without good or evil? What is it better than if there's no evil? And what is it striving toward if there's no good?"

"You don't understand," he said. He sounded annoyed and changed the subject.

Despite the many times we agreed to disagree, I appreciated Moot's honesty and enjoyed listening to his reasoning. It was refreshing to meet someone my age who was so contemplative and passionate, and Moot certainly didn't mind sharing his ideas or talking for long stretches without taking a break.

When he did finally stop to ask me a question, I knew what he was going to say, but that didn't mean I was ready for it.

"What about you, do you believe in a God?" he asked.

"Yes, I'm a Christian."

He turned and looked at me for a moment, then asked, "Why?"

It was times like these that I grew frustrated with God. I knew He had the power to create us with the capability to understand the divine, but He chose not to. So I was left trying to explain my relationship with an all-powerful, highly controversial Creator of the universe using the intangible evidence of miracles, the mystery of faith, and the concept of grace.

I loved these ethereal building blocks of faith, but they didn't make explaining it any easier, especially to someone like Moot. Moot was one of the most pragmatic people I had ever met, so he wanted a rational reason why I would base my life on faith in a man who came to earth two thousand years ago and upset people to the point of being executed.

Taking a deep breath, I began:

"I'm a Christian because if you know Jesus, then you have to decide whether He is God or whether He is a maniac. And I think He's God. I have thought that from a young age, and since then it feels like God has been revealing Himself to me in ways that make me know He is real.

"Christianity helps me to understand things both good and bad, and when I can't understand, I can rely on trust and faith, which is often better than an answer.

"And, well, most importantly, I have always felt loved—not loved like I feel around family or friends, but loved with a deep, strong, constant, overwhelming embrace that I know comes from God.

"I know I can't explain it very well, but if you could feel what I feel on the inside, you'd understand."

There was a pause when I finished. When Moot spoke, he changed the subject.

Thank God.

I had enjoyed hiking with Moot, but after spending the night with several other hikers at a shelter that evening, I was excited to wake up the next morning and continue hiking alone.

I enjoyed a pleasant morning on the trail. I climbed up the slopes of Mount Rogers, the highest mountain in Virginia, but it seemed like a hill compared to some of the climbs in North Carolina and Tennessee. The sun lavishly blanketed the ground and encouraged shoots of green to rise out of the earth.

After crossing a small stream, I decided to stop for lunch. Midway through my meal, I looked up to see Moot walking down the trail. I was glad to see him again, and the feeling seemed mutual, as he quickly threw down his pack to have lunch beside me.

"You didn't say good-bye this morning," he said.

"I didn't think you were awake," I responded

"Well, it took me a long time to catch you."

Catch me? The way Moot said that made me feel a little uneasy. It sounded like he had made it his objective for the day to find me.

When lunch was over, we hiked together toward Grayson Highlands State Park. At the park boundary there was a trail register, and I was slightly annoyed when Moot took the pen and wrote MOOT AND ODYSSA into the guest log. I hadn't signed a register since Springer Mountain in Georgia, and I didn't like that he'd signed it for me. But I was sure he was trying to be helpful, so I decided not to say anything.

Grayson Highlands State Park has two of my favorite things: beautiful views and wild ponies. The rolling hills inside the park feature undulating fields of grass and dramatic rock outcroppings. The exposed terrain makes it easier to spot the wild ponies that find sanctuary within the park's border. Even though the ponies were advertised as "wild," that didn't stop me from attempting a close encounter.

At first, my off-key neighs and whinnies weren't enough to convince them that I was a friend, but after I pulled some Twizzlers out of my food bag, they quickly warmed up to me. I grew excited as the ponies drew near and began to eat directly from my hand. And as their comfort level increased, one little guy even tried to steal a Twizzler from my mouth.

I freely admit that candy probably wasn't the best dietary choice for the small horses—or for myself, for that matter—but in the absence of apples or carrots, the red straws were the best I had to offer. I am glad that I hadn't come across the signs on the opposite end of the park that warned against feeding any of the animals, because then I would have felt a lot more guilty as I distributed the licorice.

When I had a good-sized herd around me, I heard someone behind me. Knowing that Moot was nearby, I assumed it was his shadow cast beside me, and I was surprised to look up and see a non-thru-hiker.

Or, at least, he looked like a non-hiker, but when he introduced himself as Red Wolf, I began to wonder.

"I was a thru-hiker last year," he quickly explained.

"Really? You did the whole trail?" I asked in awe.

His voice lowered and he sheepishly replied, "No, I should have. But I reached Virginia and missed my girlfriend so much that I got off the trail, went home, and proposed. We were engaged for a month before I found out that she had been cheating on me with my best friend while I was on the trail."

"Oh, I'm so sorry," I mumbled, not knowing what else to say.

He waved away my concern and continued, "I have two more semesters at Appalachian State University, and after that I'm going to start hiking the trail again—and next time, I'm not getting off."

Red Wolf then explained that he was at Grayson Highlands today for two reasons. One was to record the sound of the ponies for a school project. That was why he was drawn to my drove. Apparently, he had been trying all morning to lure them with carrots to no avail. I gave him some Twizzlers, and he had better luck.

The second purpose of his outing was to provide trail magic to thru-hikers. As Moot approached to see who I was talking to, Red Wolf told us he had stashed some food farther down the trail, and that he would be happy to hike with us and show us where he'd hidden the goodies.

When we arrived at Red Wolf's hidden cooler, I was impressed with the wide range of treats that he had dragged out to the trail. From the blue Coleman, he began to pull canned vegetables, fresh fruit, and donuts. We dug in, stuffing our faces with the treats until he interrupted us.

"I almost forgot," he said, extracting a half gallon of chocolate ice cream from the cooler. "I had it hidden at the bottom to keep it cold."

It took me less than five minutes to polish off half of the container, and I would have kept going if Red Wolf hadn't interjected.

"Hey, I could probably slackpack you guys tomorrow if you want."

Slackpacking meant carrying a light backpack or daypack with just the supplies needed for the day, and having someone drive the rest of your gear to a road crossing farther down the trail. I had never done it, but the thought was enticing.

I knew from an earlier conversation that Moot was opposed to slack-packing, as some hikers are. Those opposed believe that having some-one else carry their gear for a portion of the hike will discredit their thru-hike. I respected those folks and understood where they were coming from, but after hiking five hundred miles with my sadistic pack digging into my shoulders and making my fingers go numb, I had no qualms about handing over my gear.

"I would *love* to slackpack!" I said.

Moot quickly agreed: "Yeah, I'd be up for it, too."

What? Mr. High Ideals had told me just this morning that he didn't agree with slackpacking, and now, a few hours later, he jumped at the chance? I should have called him out on it, but I was so shocked that I couldn't say anything before Red Wolf asked us how far we wanted to go.

I took out my Data Book, looked at it for a minute, and then, star-ing directly at Moot, I said, "Forty miles."

I didn't like it when people contradicted themselves, and during our conversation about slackpacking, Moot had also said that he didn't like the idea of doing high-mileage days. I had no problem with high miles, but until two days ago, thirty miles had seemed above my limit. I don't know if it was my desire to test Moot that made me say forty miles, but I didn't really mean it.

"Oh my gosh, you guys can totally do forty miles!" Red Wolf shouted.

I looked at him, and he was grinning from ear to ear. I had been so focused on Moot that I had temporarily forgotten about Red Wolf. As soon as he heard me say forty miles, he became ecstatic.

"I did this section last year," he said. "It's not that bad. I mean, it has a few ups and downs, but I can meet you at the roads, and without packs you can definitely make it."

I looked back at Moot, convinced he would fold. But to my surprise and dismay, he anted up. "Yeah, I think we should do it."

What? Moot was a hypocrite, Red Wolf was living vicariously through us, and now I was supposed to hike forty miles tomorrow!

"You better get going," said Red Wolf. "There's a shelter close to the next road. You can spend the night there and I'll meet you with my car in the morning. This is gonna be awesome! You guys are awesome!"

As Moot and I hiked to the next shelter, I sure didn't feel awesome. I felt like an idiot. An idiot hiking with a hypocrite.

I wanted to go to bed soon after reaching Old Orchard Shelter. There was still daylight, but I wanted to get as much sleep as possible if I was going to hike a marathon and a half the next day. Moot stayed up a bit longer to read the shelter register, and probably sign both of our names in it.

I had already closed my eyes when Moot said, "Hey Odyssa, did you know that, according to this register, two hikers were murdered on the trail somewhere in southwest Virginia?"

Public registers should be censored, and so should Moot. I didn't comment, I just pretended to be asleep and then tried without success to forget what he had just told me.

The next morning I awoke at 5:30 and hiked with Moot to a dimly lit roadside where we met Red Wolf and his car.

Eager to get a start on the day, I grabbed a PowerBar and an extra layer of clothing, then dropped the rest of my belongings into Red Wolf's car.

"I'm ready," I said.

"I'll just be a minute," said Moot.

But a minute for Moot meant a half hour. First, he sifted through his food bag to find his granola. Then he poured the granola in a bowl, added a packet of powdered milk, measured some water in a cup and carefully poured it on the cereal, then stirred the concoction together for several minutes. Next, I watched him slowly spoon the dripping cereal into his mouth. He sat there for five minutes eating his breakfast with a satisfied grin on his face. Then, after he finished, he decided he needed to brush his teeth. Even if my dentist had been watching, I wouldn't have brushed my teeth with the attention to detail that Moot did.

After he packed his toothbrush, I turned to start hiking across the road, but Moot calmly called, "One more minute."

Then he brought a roll of toilet paper out of his pack and disappeared into the woods for ten minutes.

I would have moved on alone, but having Red Wolf slackpack us meant that Moot and I had to stay close together so we could rendezvous with our four-wheeled Sherpa. So I just stood there tapping my foot, annoyed, cold, and ready to start.

When Moot was finally ready, we started down the trail. I hiked quickly, trying to make up for lost time.

My brain was fast at work too. I spent a lot of time sorting through my frustration with Moot, and then I started to consider the enormity of a forty-mile day, and just when I had come to terms with that, I began to realize the frightening reality of a slackpack.

I had just given everything I owned and needed for the next few months to a complete stranger. I hadn't even removed my credit card or ID from my pack. And at this point, all I could do was hope that Red Wolf was honest and would show up as promised at the next road crossing. If he didn't, I was in trouble—big trouble. I mean, what was I going to tell the police? "Um, yeah, a guy named Red Wolf stole all my stuff. How? Oh, well, I kinda put it all in his car this morning."

After two and a half hours of hiking, I was excited and relieved to see Red Wolf. He was at the road, just like he said he would be, and he had even brought us some bananas.

It was no longer as cold as when we had first started, so I left some clothes in the car and discreetly retrieved the wallet from my pack before we continued our hike.

This time, Red Wolf hiked a stretch with us before turning around to shuttle the car once again.

I really enjoyed the time Red Wolf spent with us on the trail. When I hiked with Moot, everything felt heavy and serious, but when Red Wolf hiked with us, we sang eighties songs at the top of our lungs.

The next road we came to was Virginia Highway 16, directly past Partnership Shelter. On any other day, I would have forgone any predetermined plans and stayed there. It was the Cadillac of shelters: spacious, clean, with cold running water and a clean privy (a.k.a. outhouse). But Red Wolf had promised to meet us just ahead at Highway 16.

When we arrived at the road, Red Wolf stood there cheering and holding a brown rectangular box. He had stopped in a town and picked up a large supreme pizza for the three of us to split. Moot and I could not have been more thankful, or more ravenous. Together we devoured the pizza and celebrated the completion of twenty-six miles before 2:00 PM.

When we left Highway 16, Moot and I both knew we would be able to finish our forty-mile day. The nervous energy that had propelled us through the morning evolved into a relaxed confidence. And, since he was no longer preoccupied with the miles, Moot once again brought up theology.

"So, I don't really agree with you," he said.

"Agree with what?" I asked.

"I don't agree with your idea of God, and I think I know why you believe what you do."

"Okay."

This should make the next twelve miles interesting, I thought.

"You grew up going to church, so you were indoctrinated. My theory is that the church tells you about God so that you don't have to think for yourself or question reality. You said that you're okay with not understanding things because you trust God. I think that's a cop-out, an excuse for not digging deeper and looking for the truth. Because you believe in God, you're a nice person, you do nice things for people, and you help those less fortunate. I think *that* makes you feel loved, not God."

I suddenly realized that it became a lot easier to talk about my faith when I felt attacked. "Well, I don't think I'm a nice person, and God knows that I'm not a nice person."

"Yeah, that's what they tell you to guilt you into being nice and giving more money to the Church."

"Listen, Moot, you're right. I decided to believe in God at a young age, but it was my choice and not the Church trying to brainwash me. Just because I was young doesn't mean I couldn't understand love, and I know my life has felt different since then.

"It's kinda like . . . well, I guess it's kinda like slackpacking. When I agreed to slackpack, I wasn't exactly sure of everything it entailed, but it made sense, and I knew I wanted to do it. And as soon as I gave Red Wolf my pack, I knew I'd made the right decision. Right away, I felt lighter and more comfortable on the trail, and the hiking was easier.

"Being a Christian doesn't mean that you never have doubts about God. There were times this morning when I wondered whether Red Wolf would meet us or just run off with our stuff. In the end, it's not as much about you doing what you say you will as it is about God holding up His end of the deal. I know He will always be where He says He will be. I know that if I want Him to walk with me, He will, and I know that if I get lost, He will come looking for me.

"I don't need to know what roads He took to find me, and when He gives me pizza, I don't need to know where it came from. I just need to know that He will be there. And He is."

"I think I need to know where he got the pizza," Moot replied.

When we finished our twelve-mile stretch, we met Red Wolf at the last road of the day. He congratulated us, returned our packs, and wished us well.

Moot and I put our packs on and finished our forty-mile day by hiking two more miles to the Davis Path Shelter. I didn't feel like sleeping inside the shelter, but I was too tired to set up my tent, so I spread out my mat and unrolled my sleeping bag under the night sky. And, looking up at the beautiful complexity of the stars, I knew that He was watching over me.

The next morning, I awoke and slipped out of the campsite without saying a word to Moot. I was ready to hike alone.

That morning I enjoyed my independence and my miles. The Virginia countryside is beautiful. Instead of meandering inside the forest, the trail passes through open pastures and beside rolling meadows. The fields are home to cattle and donkeys, and are visited by deer and coyotes that easily circumnavigate the surrounding fences. But by late morning, the only creature I saw gliding across the countryside was Moot.

I could see him behind me, a white fleck with a dark top slashing through the tall grass. I increased my speed, but still the fleck grew and Moot gained ground. If it wouldn't have been completely obvious, I would have sprinted.

Within another twenty minutes, Moot was within talking distance. I didn't understand how he was able to hike so fast. I was walking as quickly as I could, which so far had been fast enough to outpace everyone else on the trail. But not Moot.

"Hey, are you sore from yesterday?" he asked.

"No, not really. Are you?"

"Not too sore, but I smell really bad." I didn't want to get close enough to find out. "I think we'll pass a large creek today and I might take a dip. Want to join me?"

"I don't do cold water," I said. It was the truth. I didn't care how bad I smelled; if it was cold outside and the water was cold, I wouldn't even splash it on my face.

"Well, then, you don't mind if I bathe naked, do you?"

Naked? Noooooo! The mental image of Moot's pasty white body and sinewy limbs frolicking in the icy current made me taste a little bit of bile in the back of my throat.

"Moot, if you decide to swim naked then I'll just keep hiking. I really like to hike by myself anyway." *Hint, hint.*

"Are you uncomfortable with nudity?" he asked.

Where was he coming up with this stuff? Just because I didn't want to watch Moot skinny-dip, all of a sudden I'm embarrassed by the human body?

"No, I'm fine with nudity," I said. "I think it's very important to be comfortable with your body. In college, my girlfriends and I used to sneak out on rainy nights and streak the practice football field. It was harmless fun, and no one ever saw us." Without thinking, I added, "In fact, I wouldn't mind hiking naked."

As soon as the words left my mouth, I regretted it. When I said, "I wouldn't mind hiking naked," I meant by myself, at night, under a full moon, in the summer, and for a very short stretch of time. But I immediately knew that was not how Moot envisioned it.

"Let's do it!" he exclaimed.

"No, no, Moot. Not in the cold and not with a guy."

"Have you ever seen a guy naked?" he asked.

"Yes." I couldn't pinpoint a specific time, but it seemed probable that at some point in my life I had seen a guy naked.

"When?"

"Uh, well, you know . . . I've seen naked babies . . . and R-rated movies . . . and stuff."

"Wait, does that mean that you've never had sex?"

"No, Moot, I've never had sex."

"Do you think that you're the only virgin on the trail?"

"I don't know, Moot. Maybe you should take a poll."

He was silent. I thought my sarcasm had finally deterred him from his questions. Then, after about fifteen minutes of silence . . .

"So . . . do you ever pleasure yourself?"

He was a disease, a fungus, a parasite. No matter how hard I tried, I couldn't get rid of him.

That night, before we went to bed, Moot asked me to call his name in the morning so that he would know I was awake, and then we could leave camp together.

But the next morning, I woke up and left without a word.

I hiked fast all morning. Still, although it had failed previously, my main tactic to escape Moot involved trying to outpace him during the day.

I had dropped hints too. Big hints. Hints like, "I'm so glad that I'm hiking this trail solo. I can't imagine having a hiking partner."

To which he would reply, "Yeah, me too."

I wanted to be brutally honest with him, but I didn't know how. My Southern upbringing had taught me to communicate through inference, not directly. The idea of telling Moot to his face that I didn't want to hike with him seemed impossibly cruel. Plus, I was worried about how he would react if I told him bluntly how I felt.

But even without saying anything directly, I felt like I was unmistakable in communicating my desire to part company. I left camp without waking him each morning, and hiked as fast as possible until he caught up, at which point my body language expressed displeasure, and my voice dripped with disappointment.

This particular morning, around the time I expected to start hearing Moot's rapid shuffle behind me, I came to a dirt road. At the road sat an old pickup truck. An old man stepped out of the truck in worn denim overalls and gave me a big grin with the few yellow teeth he had left.

"Hey, darlin', I'm doin' some trail magic with tha church. All tha ladies, they make a big breakfast for tha hikers. I'll take ya down the road to the church if ya's interested."

I felt like I was in the middle of nowhere, and it was hard to believe that there was a church or any other sign of civilization down that gravel road. But I was hungry and I thought the detour might be just what I needed to throw Moot off my scent, so I climbed into the truck bed with my pack and held on tight as we traveled swiftly down the bumpy road.

Within ten minutes, we arrived at a quaint, white chapel at the edge of an open field. The building was no more than a one-room sanctuary with a steeple, but this morning the cinder-block basement had been transformed into an all-you-can-eat buffet, complete with muffins, pancakes, cookies, casseroles, biscuits, sausage, bacon, juice, and cof-fee—all the delicious food you could imagine, and no Moot? Double sanctuary!

The breakfast spread sat on a small round table covered with a red-and-white checked tablecloth. A handful of thru-hikers sat around the table, and around the thru-hikers hovered every loving grandmother who lived within a ten-mile radius. About fifteen gray-haired women circled the table, ready to refill plates and top off glasses. In between their duties, they would engage the hikers in conversation.

"Oh, don't you look nice and fit! Here, try my marmalade."

"You're doin' so good on that trail! Have another one of my muffins."

"You are some of the first thru-hikers that've come through this year. Let me get you some more casserole."

Each woman insisted that you try *her* dish or have seconds on *her* recipe before you could consider yourself finished. Food is certainly one of the best ways to express love, especially to a thru-hiker, but I spent most of the meal feeling like an overwhelmed tasting judge at a rural county fair.

When it was time to leave, the women packed us to-go bags to take back to the trail. Then, with two other thru-hikers, I gathered my belongings and walked outside to wait for our blue jean-clad chauffeur to return from his next run.

When the truck arrived, Moot was sitting in the back. As we traded places in the truck bed, he started to object to my departure, but within seconds the swarm of grandmothers descended on him and surrounded him with an impenetrable wall of love and affection, and an artillery of baked goods. I knew that Moot would have to spend at least an hour eating before our hosts would let him return to the woods, and that gave me some breathing room.

When I arrived back at the trailhead, I followed Kid and Chilly up the next mountain. They were both thru-hikers, both tall, cute, and in their mid-twenties. However, while Chilly was easygoing and personable, Kid was one of the most cold and standoffish thru-hikers I'd met.

Kid hardly spoke, hardly smiled, and hardly did anything but look at the ground and hike. Both of them were strong hikers and I enjoyed trying to keep up with their pace. I loved it when Chilly prodded Kid into short bouts of conversation. I could tell that Chilly had spent many miles trying to befriend Kid, and that it gave him a certain satisfaction to force a smile onto the stoic face.

I stayed with Chilly and Kid until mid-afternoon, when they decided to stop for a break. I didn't want to stop. It was 4:00 PM, and Moot was nowhere in sight. This was it. I was free! All I had to do was hike hard until sunset and I would once again be on my own.

I lowered my head and began to stride down the trail like an Olympic speed-walker. With great enthusiasm, I hiked up a mountain, past a shelter, up another mountain, over a bridge, and into the woods, until the sun finally disappeared. It grew darker and darker and darker, and when I could no longer make out the trail, I took out my flashlight, traveled twenty yards into the woods, and set up my tent.

Inside the tent, I changed clothes, and wrote in my journal about how glad I was to no longer be with Moot. And finally, I turned off my headlamp and laid down to sleep. Then I heard a noise...

At first I thought I was dreaming, but then I opened my eyes and discovered I could still hear it—a melodic whistle traveling down the trail. The tune was accompanied by footsteps, and then, peeking under my tent cover, I saw a light beam through the trees. I lay motionless, like an escaped convict trying not to be recaptured.

The footsteps and whistling grew louder until they were right near my tent. I hoped that in a few seconds I would hear them fading away as they continued up the trail, but suddenly the sound stopped, and all I heard were crickets. When my tent walls lit up, I knew I had been caught.

"Odyssa, are you awake?"

"Hi, Moot."

"I'm beginning to get the feeling that you're trying to lose me."

Really? Because I'm beginning to get the feeling that you're trying to stalk me! Mumbling obscenities under my breath, I listened to Moot's ramblings as he set up his tent next to mine and prepared his dinner.

I stayed relatively quiet inside my tent, but Moot talked throughout his dinner and hardly seemed to notice my lack of response. At one point during his monologue, Moot suggested, "You know, Odyssa, since you haven't had sex, if you ever have any questions, feel free to ask me, because I would be happy to answer them. I'm really open, and I think you might find the information helpful down the road."

I still didn't respond, but I was quite certain I knew more about the subject than he thought I did, and furthermore, the last person I would ever want to consult on the issue was Moot.

Despite my silent treatment, after he finished dinner, Moot had the gall to conclude his monologue with, "So, do you think that hiking partners can be cuddle buddies too?"

What!? I don't know what bothered me more: the phrase "hiking partners" or the term "cuddle buddies." I knew that I didn't want to hike with Moot, and the concept of spooning with him made me cringe. Even if it was ten degrees outside and I didn't have a sleeping bag, even if my only chance of making it through the night was to rely on Moot's body heat, I *still* wouldn't have cuddled with him. A shudder traveled down my spine, and instead of responding to him, I pretended to be asleep.

The next morning, I didn't even try to be quiet and sneak away. I knew I was trapped.

I angrily packed up my belongings and thrashed through the brush back to the trail. I had progressed from resistence to resignation, and I spent all morning trying to come up with coping mechanisms.

At first I tried to rationalize my fate. I mean, was Moot really that bad? After all, he had been relatively interesting for the first twenty-four hours that I'd known him. He was outgoing, he was a strong hiker, and most importantly, he said he had a girlfriend, so there could be no way he was looking for more than friendship. But then why would he ask if we could be cuddle buddies?

When Moot caught up to me a few hours later, I laid down the final card in my hand, hoping that it would be enough to win some solitude.

"Moot," I said. "I'm having girl problems this morning, and it's best if you just go ahead."

I wasn't really, but typically the topic was guaranteed to cause men to distance themselves. Not Moot.

"That's okay," he said. "I have a sister, so I understand. I don't mind hiking slowly and waiting for you."

"No, *really*," I replied. "I'll probably have to stop and do some maintenance, and you don't want to hang around for that."

"Don't worry, it doesn't bother me. It's natural."

"Well, I'd really just prefer to be by myself right now."

"Okay, I'll just hike a little bit in front, in case you need me."

Need him? I didn't need him. What I desperately needed was to get rid of him! I had tried everything I could think of to free myself of Moot, except being brutally honest—which probably would have worked, but it wasn't in my repertoire. I had tried to hike fast, but Moot was faster. I had tried to hike really far, but Moot kept up. I had tried to hike painstakingly slowly, but Moot decelerated. And when I told him I really liked hiking solo and could not imagine having a hiking partner, he agreed!

The small gap between us that morning served as a temporary respite, but soon Moot was waiting for me every few minutes to make sure I felt okay. He also decided to alternate hiking just a little ahead of me and a little bit behind me so he didn't create a large gap.

Once, when he was hiking behind me, I had the idea to hide in the woods and force him to pass me unknowingly.

I began to speed up. I needed to gain some distance if I was going to be able to dash off the trail unnoticed. After a quick burst of speed, I noticed a well-covered grove a few dozen yards off the trail. This was my chance!

I shimmied up underneath the branches of a broad rhododendron. There, covered with leaves, with my chest against the ground, I waited.

I peered up with anticipation, knowing that Moot would soon be passing just a few hundred feet away and hoping he wouldn't see me.

But what if he did? What would I say? I cowered even farther beneath the cover of the rhododendron, then stilled everything but my heavy breathing and my anxious heart.

As the seconds slowly passed, I began to wonder how a reasonable twenty-one-year-old girl could find herself hiding under a rhododendron tree to escape the only human companionship for miles around. Lying there with my nose pressed close to the organic smell of the earth, I didn't feel clever or elusive, I just felt pathetic. I didn't know which was worse, not being able to honestly tell Moot that I didn't want to hike with him, or trying to hide from him under a bush. My body felt warm with nerves and shame. I wanted to get rid of Moot, but this didn't feel right. I hadn't come out here to hide from my problems, but to face them.

I decided that instead of playing the victim, I was going to stand up, walk back to the trail, and when Moot arrived, I would tell him that I no longer wanted to hike or camp with him.

Ten seconds after I returned to the trail, Moot rounded the corner behind me.

I tried. I really did. I even got out most of the words. "Moot, I don't want to hike with you anymore . . . "

But then I paused. The look on his face suggested that I had just run him through with my hiking stick. I couldn't handle the guilt or his pathetic attempts at sputtering out a response. So I interrupted.

"Moot, I don't want to hike with you anymore . . . *today*."

When he heard the word "today," the gleam reappeared in his eyes.

"That's okay," he said, ready to compromise. "I know you're having a hard day so I'll hike ahead and hitch into Pearisburg to find the hostel. I'll save you a bunk and see you when you get to town."

Staring at the ground, because I couldn't look Moot in the eyes, I replied, "Okay, I'll see you in town."

I knew I would have to go into town that evening to resupply, but I was determined to make it back to the trail before nightfall and elude Moot. There was no way I was stepping foot inside the hostel!

So now I was lying. Why was it so hard for me to be honest? I should have just stayed underneath the rhododendron—I'd rather be a coward than a liar.

As I hiked slowly toward the road, I came across Chilly, who had passed us both that morning. He said Moot had leap-frogged him an hour ago and was more than likely already in town at the hostel.

When we arrived at the road, Chilly stood a bit behind me, and I stuck out my thumb for a hitch. Guys always love hitching with girls, because it considerably increases their odds of getting a ride.

We climbed into the first truck that passed us and dismounted five minutes later on the outskirts of Pearisburg. I quickly thanked our driver, then raced across the street to the Dairy Queen that had caught my eye.

Pearisburg was a big town, at least compared to Hot Springs and Damascus. Then again, if a town had a fast-food restaurant or a super-market other than Dollar General, I now thought of it as a big town. Even if Pearisburg did look a little rundown, it still felt great to be in a big town, especially one with a Dairy Queen.

I dropped my pack at the door and ran to the counter, where I ordered the most decadent Blizzard on the menu. As I walked back to my pack to fetch my wallet, I felt a strange uneasiness, as if something were missing. Looking down at my belongings, I realized I had forgotten my hiking stick in the back of the pickup truck.

I ran out of the Dairy Queen and sprinted toward the gas station where Chilly and I had been dropped off. I looked at the pumps, in the parking spots, and behind the building, but the truck was gone, and so was my stick.

I couldn't go back to the trail without my stick! The constant ups and downs with thirty pounds on my back were very hard on my knees, and without a stick they would be unbearable. My hiking stick had become an extension of my hand—I was lost without it.

I started to tear up at my loss, not so much over the stick itself, because unlike most hikers, I hadn't spent $100 on hiking poles; instead, I used an old ski pole that Warren Doyle had given me at his Appalachian Trail Institute. He bought single ski poles at thrift stores, typically for about a buck, and handed them out as mementoes at his workshop. It was more the situation that upset me than the loss of the stick. If I couldn't find a replacement stick tonight, I would have to stay at the hostel—with Moot—and try to find an outfitter and a new hiking pole the next morning.

Chilly reappeared from inside the gas station and came over to check on me. He walked me back over to the Dairy Queen, helped me collect my pack and my ice cream, and reminded me that if there was anything that would make the situation better, it was an Oreo, brownie, and chocolate chip Blizzard. I nodded in agreement and, ice cream in hand, we walked together to the nearby grocery store to buy rations for the next few days of hiking.

The two of us bought provisions for supper as well. We were enjoying an evening picnic outside the rundown shopping center when I noticed a Magic Mart at the end of the strip mall. I had never heard of a Magic Mart before, but I asked Chilly to watch my belongings while I went to see if they had a sporting goods section.

The Magic Mart looked like a small, dilapidated Kmart. I was disheartened to discover that they did not have a sporting goods section, but on my way out the door, the store earned its name when something magic caught my eye. To my right, I noticed a broom—which, minus the bristles, resembled a sturdy, albeit heavy, walking stick. Then I spotted a more viable lightweight alternative.

Three dollars and one bright yellow mop stick later, I had my new hiking pole.

I walked out of the store, unscrewed the gathered rope on top of the shaft, threw it away, and walked back toward Chilly. As I approached, he clapped his hands and laughed approvingly. With my problem solved, I threw my pack on my shoulders, said good-bye, and headed off into the setting sun.

Instead of hitching, I walked the mile and a half back to the trail on the shoulder of the highway, holding my bright yellow mop stick in one hand and my recharged cell phone in the other. I was such a spectacle that I actually caused rubbernecking on the highway. But I didn't care how absurd I looked, because I was on my own once again.

I enjoyed a new sense of liberation and continued on in the dark. I hiked several miles until I found a level camping spot underneath a brilliantly lit sky. It was the first night on the trail that I was able to fall asleep without wearing my winter hat and gloves, and it was the first night in almost a week without Moot camping nearby. My escape was hardly honorable; I regretted not being able to be up-front with Moot, and vowed that in the future I would be clear with potential stalkers from the start. But at last I was free!

DALEVILLE

TINKER CLIFFS

ROANOKE

MCAFEE KNOB

DRAGON'S TOOTH

VIRGINIA
WEST VIRGINIA

PEARISBURG

10

DISCOMFORT

OUTSIDE PEARISBURG, VA, TO
TROUTVILLE, VA—92 MILES

The stretch between Pearisburg and Roanoke is surprisingly rocky. It's like a small sampling of Pennsylvania stuck in Virginia. The first mountains outside Pearisburg greet you with extended rock fields, and the rocky spine of the Dragon's Tooth requires some novice bouldering moves. The finale of the section includes scenic McAfee Knob and Tinker Cliffs, which both feature rocky ledges, rocky views, and rocky footing.

A fter being smothered by Moot for six days, I went the next thirty-six hours without seeing anybody. I saw more than fifty deer, but not a single, solitary person. I think very few people have a day in their life when they don't see or interact with anyone else. It's kind of weird and disorienting not to see anyone for that long. I did a lot of singing, I talked to God for company, and I wondered if there had been some catastrophe that had caused everyone to go into hiding.

Because of the not-too-distant memory of 9/11, there had been several times on the trail when I had wondered what would happen if the country suddenly went to war, or an epidemic started, or the stock market crashed. How would I find out? What would it mean for my hike . . . for me?

As for everyday news, I didn't miss it at all. Politicians running smear campaigns, erratic Wall Street trends, the demigods of professional sports, celebrity gossip—even though I hadn't paid much attention to mainstream media when I was still at home, I began to realize how much it had pervaded my life.

I started to realize how what was important in my life had changed. Out here I wasn't worried about the government or the economy, fashion or pop culture. Instead I was concerned about whether or not I had enough food to make it to the next resupply point, where my next water source would be, and whether my clothes would keep me warm and dry.

For the first time in my life, I was experiencing real hunger and thirst, freezing nights, and prolonged physical weakness. For the first time in my life, I was experiencing real pain. And even though it hurt, it made me feel more alive than I did in the controlled comfort of society.

That afternoon, I felt painfully alive with every step.

After traveling on dirt trails through the woods and across the trodden grass of vast meadows, I arrived at my first rock field. I had heard about rock fields, but I didn't really know what they were, or what to expect.

It turns out that a rock field is a section of earth completely covered with big, jagged stones, with no soil to walk on. It is a minefield of potential injury. Each step could lead to a fall or a sprained ankle. And if your feet don't start to hurt from the sharp, pointed topography, your neck will ache from constantly looking down.

That afternoon, both my feet and my neck hurt, but especially my feet.

While I was conscientiously focusing on foot placement, I noticed a burning irritation on the bottom of my feet. My soles felt hot and sore from stepping on the uneven rocks, and while it was annoying at first, the pain soon escalated to an unbearable stinging sensation. With each step it felt as if the skin on the bottom of my feet was ripping apart.

If I could have stopped and set up camp in the rocks, I would have. The ache was so overwhelming that it caused me to tear up, which made it even harder to focus on the uneven tread. Although the rocky obstacle course was only two miles long, it took me nearly two hours to make it through.

I have never been so happy to see dirt. When the rock field ended and I could place my feet on soft earth, I stopped to set up camp. There were still several hours of daylight left, and I was four miles from the shelter where I had planned to spend the night, but I couldn't travel any farther on my battered feet.

After setting up my tent, I took off my shoes and socks to inspect my feet. As soon as I slid my wet, mud-stained socks off, I was assaulted by an overwhelming smell of mold coming from my feet. I admit that I had experienced foot odor on the trail before, but now the stench suggested that my feet were rotting off. It was one of the worst things I had ever smelled, much worse than the diapers I'd changed as a babysitter, and on about the same level as the hog farm and sewage-treatment plant that I had visited on school field trips.

Examining my feet was only slightly more tolerable than smelling them. The flesh was wrinkly and white, the top layer flaked off when I touched it, and the skin between my toes was cracked and bleeding.

Worst of all, the soles of my feet were covered with strange Dippin'
Dot–sized indentions.

I knew that some of the pain was from the rock field, but I also
determined that the damp, putrid socks I had been wearing since
Damascus were part of the problem.

With so much time on my hands before sunset, I built a small fire
and burned my socks. I had a clean pair in my pack, so I offered the
non-wicking, sadistic foot coverings up as a sacrifice. I thought that
perhaps if I burned my socks, I would also burn away the pain that
afflicted me. And while I wasn't physically healed, it was emotionally
gratifying to watch the synthetic threads melt into the hot embers.

The sacrifice worked. The next morning my feet felt better, and thankfully, instead of traversing another daunting rock field, the trail spent
much of the morning hugging farmland, wandering through hay fields,
and traveling through paddocks.

There are places in southwest Virginia where the trail travels across
private farmland. The landowners are very generous to allow hikers on
their property, and there are signs posted regularly that make it clear
that hikers are at no point supposed to wander off the trail.

I loved being near livestock. Without people around, I tried to talk
to the animals with moos, neighs, and brays, but when they didn't
respond I reverted to speaking in English.

I was caught off guard, however, when I came to a pasture full of steers.
So far, I hadn't encountered any animals with a reputation for goring
people, but now I found myself locked in a staring contest with a mam-
moth black steer with sharp white horns. Now my words were rooted in
fear instead of a need for socialization.

"Nice steer, good steer. You just stay right where you are. No need
to get up for me."

I kept telling myself he was a steer. I grew up close enough to the
country to know that steers had been castrated and were less aggressive
than bulls.

The enormous creature sat exactly in the middle of the trail. So much
for land easements. There was no way I was staying on the path if a

horned animal that weighed seven times as much as I did was sitting in the way. I made a wide semicircle off the trail and around his flared nostrils. He turned his head to follow me with his eyes, then when his neck could go no further, he stood up . . . and he was definitely not a steer!

For the next four hundred yards, the bull followed close behind me. I walked, looked back, then sped up, again and again. I was trying not to make any sudden moves, but I didn't want the bull getting any closer either. I felt like an unwilling rodeo clown or an innocent bystander on the streets of Pamplona. I rationalized that if I kept my back to him and he did charge me, at least he would gore my pack, which might keep me alive.

When I finally reached the fence, I quickly climbed over the stile to safety. Once I was out of range, I turned to the bull and stuck out my tongue. He responded by pawing at the ground with his right front hoof. All of a sudden the fence didn't look quite so sturdy, so I turned and kept hiking.

I really liked hiking in Virginia, but besides the bulls, there were three other drawbacks to the rolling farmland of the southern Appalachians.

The first was cow patties. Lots of big farm animals meant lots of big cow patties. I knew I had too much time on my hands when I started trying to accurately date them. I decided that the harder, drier, and lighter the cow patty, the older it was. Some of the really old ones— I'm guessing three to five years—looked less like manure and more like flat white rocks. On the other hand, dung that was distributed within the past three years had more of a yellow color, it could be easily be broken apart with a hiking stick (or mop handle), and it distinctly showed undigested blades of grass and hay. The stinky, mushy brown piles that were covered in flies and sucked my shoe off when I accidentally stepped in them—well, those were the recent additions.

As if dodging aggressive animals and feces weren't difficult enough, the hardest trial was getting in and out of the pastures. Most fields were surrounded by barbed wire or an electric fence. In order to climb over the fencing, hikers had to walk over an A-frame-shaped set of steps, known as a stile. The stiles were old and wooden, several had missing boards, and most of them shook and swayed when I passed over them. The biggest problem was that when I turned around at the top of the stile to climb down the opposite side, my pack would become wedged in the space where the two ladders connected. When I tried to use my momentum to free my pack, I would lose my balance and tumble down the descending ladder, often landing on my knees.

The third downside to the gentle terrain of Virginia was the water quality. So far the water on the trail had been great: copious, clear, and coming up from natural springs or running off the sides of undeveloped mountains. But after Pearisburg, the water wasn't quite so appealing. The water sources for this part of the trail were creeks and rivers that bordered rural farmland. I worried about pesticide runoff from the crops, but the bigger deterrent was the animals grazing on the banks of the rivers or drinking from the creeks. Unlike hikers, animals did not follow the rule of relieving themselves a hundred yards away from a water source, which might have been why, after heavy rains, the rivers looked like chocolate milk.

I hadn't anticipated the decrease in water quality, and since I didn't have a filter, I went thirsty for most of the morning. In the early afternoon, the trail left the rolling countryside and began to climb up the ridge of a nearby mountain. As soon as I had hiked above all visible livestock, I stopped at the first stream I came to and immersed my water bottle in the cool, clear current. I filled it to the brim and was about to bring it to my lips when something in the creek bed caught my eye.

A bone.

A large white bone the size of my forearm was nestled among the rocks a few inches from where I had filled my bottle. As I looked closer, I began to notice several other bone fragments scattered throughout the stream. It looked like some animal had died right in this spot. I gagged and quickly dumped out my water bottle. I decided to continue hiking up the mountain, hoping there would be more water closer to the top.

A few miles later, I still hadn't passed any water sources when I reached the narrow mountain ridge where the trail transitioned from a dirt path into a sloping rock face. The slant of the trail was relentless, and soon my ankles began to ache from climbing the severe incline.

As I hobbled across the slick granite, time moved more slowly than it had in my high school pre-calculus class. Since this morning, I had traveled sixteen miles, and only consumed one liter of water. My mouth and throat were so uncomfortably dry that I started coughing involuntarily. I kept praying that the trail would descend the slope into a watershed.

After several more miles, I was still on the ridge and still had no water. My thirst grew with every step. I began to feel dizzy and light-headed from dehydration, and my body's core was filled with a dull ache. I imagined my lungs, heart, liver, and intestines all withering to the size of a softball within my body.

My senses started to deceive me. The wind through the leaves sounded like a rushing creek, and any time something moved or glistened in the forest I would see water before realizing that it was the sunlight reflecting off a low-lying bush or a swaying branch.

Just when I decided to no longer trust my eyes or ears, I saw a small brook lining the trail. I ran up to it and plunged my hand into the gurgling current. It was real!

I began scooping up water with my hands while filling up my water bottle. When the bottle was full, I drank the entire thirty-two ounces, refilled it, then drank another thirty-two ounces without pausing.

Within seconds, I felt like I was going to throw up. My stomach was queasy and my head started to spin, but I didn't care because my organs were expanding.

I laid against my pack for several minutes so my stomach could settle and the water could disperse itself throughout my body. Occasionally I would dip my fingers in the clear water beside me and press my chilled wet hands against my forehead and neck. I was so thankful for this brook! It was humbling to realize how dependent I was on water sources during this journey. At home, I never appreciated water because it is always available, but lying beside the brook and listening to the water splash over the earth, I realized how precious and important clean water is. When I left the stream, I carried as much as my water bottles would hold.

Twenty minutes later, it rained.

Half an hour before, I would have done anything for a drop of water, and now the storm left water streaming down my face and cascading over the crevasses and gullies that lined the trail.

I looked up to the sky and laughed. At home, I was god. Water depended on me: I could turn it on and off with the twist of a knob. Out here, I was dependent on nature. The rain shower reminded me that I was not in control; I was part of something much bigger than myself.

The rain continued into the evening, and I was thankful to reach Sarver Hollow Shelter just before dusk. I was about forty yards away when I heard a scuffle from under the wooden roof. I looked up in time to see a big black-and-white dog leap out of the shelter in my direction. He barked ferociously as he sprinted toward me, and I instinctively held my mop stick in front of me to fend him off. He stopped a few feet away from me, dug in his paws, lowered his shoulders, and bared his teeth as he growled.

Then I heard laughter. A female hiker emerged from the shelter, yelling, "Katahdin, Katahdin, you silly boy. Get back here!"

The dog immediately turned, wagged his tail, and trotted back toward the shelter.

The woman called out, "Hey there! I'm out hiking for the weekend and I always bring my dog, Katahdin. He's just trying to protect me."

She named her dog Katahdin? Dogs aren't even *allowed* on Mount Katahdin!

I took a deep breath and approached the shelter. Ten steps later, the dog charged back at me, sounding a death bark.

"Katahdin, quit that! Stop it! Don't worry," she called to me. "He's friendly, he just needs to get to know you."

When I finally made it to the shelter, the woman called her dog over to sniff me so that we could be "friends." Katahdin's version of making friends involved startling me with a low growl, then circling me with his teeth bared and drool strands hanging from his mouth.

"There now," the lady said with an oblivious smile. "Now everyone knows each other!"

I love dogs. At least, I thought I did. But the trail was causing me to seriously reconsider that stance. Pets are supposed to be leashed on almost half of the Appalachian Trail, but I had yet to see a single dog owner obey the leash laws. Instead, I saw dogs barking and growling at people, chasing wildlife, mucking up water sources, and taking up room in shelters. I had met several wonderful dogs on the trail, but unfortunately the poorly behaved ones left the more lasting impression.

And I didn't blame the dogs, I blamed the owners. I didn't feel safe around Katahdin, and by bringing him on the trail and into the shelter without a leash, this woman prioritized her own comfort and safety over my well-being. Despite my lack of human contact the past few days, I was too put off by the shrill tone that the woman used when she addressed her slobbering beast to join in their discussion. Instead, I rolled out my sleeping bag and said good night.

"Oh, have a good night," she said cheerfully. "And don't worry about bears. Katahdin won't let any animals near the shelter."

Worry about bears? I was hiking the Appalachian Trail to *see* the bears!

I fell asleep quickly, but then woke up again, and again, and again, as Katahdin spent all night pacing the shelter and barking at noises coming from the dark woods.

I was not sad to say good-bye to Katahdin the next morning, or to see the woman hike south when she left the shelter.

It had rained all night, and it was still drizzling when I started hiking. After four miles, the trail reached yet another rock obstacle: the Dragon's Tooth.

I didn't know what the Dragon's Tooth was, but it sounded mean. And when I arrived at the jagged rock outcropping, my fears were validated. The Dragon's Tooth was a rock field on a granite slope. It required some novice-level bouldering skills to traverse which, in my opinion, jumped to intermediate in the rain, and advanced-intermediate with the addition of a pack and mop stick.

I wish I had been hiking in the opposite direction, because climbing up through the Dragon's Tooth would not have been nearly as difficult. As I hiked down the Tooth and off the ridge, I struggled to lower my fully extended six-foot body to each descending precipice.

At one point, I was wiggling my lower body backward off a rock ledge to the path four feet below, and I felt a rock underneath my left foot. I thought I had made it to solid ground, so I pushed off the ledge to transfer my weight to my feet. But with my full weight on the rock, it came loose, and I tumbled off the ledge to the path below, landing hard on my back.

The fall knocked the wind out of me and I panicked for a moment. I quickly propped myself up on my elbows, and after a few seconds, my lungs once again filled with air. I wiped the raindrops off my face and examined my stinging left elbow. It was dirty and scraped. Next I felt for my hip, which was sore to the touch, and although my hip belt had protected it, I was sure it was bruised.

I wanted to cry. If there had been anyone else around, I probably would have cried, but without an audience, without sympathy, I just whimpered and took a few deep breaths. Then I stood up and kept hiking.

On the backside of the Dragon's Tooth, the trail started a long, steady ascent up to the neighboring ridge. The climb itself wasn't too difficult, and my elbow and hip began to feel better, but my feet started to feel tender, and soon the tenderness grew into raging discomfort.

I could have endured the pain in another part of my body, but hiking on hurting feet was awful. The pain was so overwhelming that I couldn't feel my toes. I also couldn't tell when my weight was on the ball of my foot and when it had shifted to my heel. I was miserable.

At one point, the ridge took a short dip to cross a highway. There was an empty parking lot next to the road, so I stopped to rest my feet. The morning's drizzle had begun to clear, and I took my socks off to air out my feet.

I had the same symptoms that I'd suffered two days before on the rock field outside of Pearisburg. I had no clue what could cause my feet to hurt this much and smell so bad.

Maybe it was just a process that they had to go through in order to toughen up for the trail. But I had hiked nearly seven hundred miles— my feet should be tough by now!

I had switched socks in Damascus and wondered if that could be part of my problem, but socks were socks, right? Surely a slight change in the padding and material wouldn't cause polka-dotted holes to appear on the soles of my feet.

Perhaps it was the rain? At the ATI, Warren Doyle had told us to expect rain every fourth day on the trail, but I couldn't remember the last time I had hiked three days without rain. And I had definitely hiked with wet feet more than dry feet.

"Hey, pretty girl."

I stopped diagnosing my feet and looked up. I didn't know where the voice had come from, but it sounded much more deliberate than a drive-by catcall.

Then I noticed the blue SUV slowing to a stop at the edge of the parking lot. When the door opened, Chilly stepped out. I hardly recognized him, since he was clean-shaven and wearing khaki pants, but his smile and warm eyes were the same on and off the trail.

I loved Chilly. Honestly, I had a crush on him. Not the type of crush that I actually wanted to act on, because that would have ruined it. I just thought Chilly was perfect. He was kind, handsome, funny, a good listener, and definitely not overbearing—basically the opposite of Moot. Whenever I saw Chilly, he made me laugh, he made me feel special, and he gave me butterflies in my stomach. He probably had that effect on most girls, but that just made him all the more crushable.

"How are you?" he asked as he approached.

"Hurting." I showed him my feet and he grimaced.

"I'm taking a break from the trail to visit family. We're headed into Roanoke right now. Why don't you come with us and we can take you to a doctor."

I took a moment to think about his offer. Common sense said that I should go with him and seek help.

"No thanks. I just have to make it until tomorrow morning, and then I'm staying with a family friend who can help me." The pain must have been clouding my judgment.

"Are you sure? That looks pretty bad."

"Don't worry. I'll get help first thing tomorrow."

Chilly shook his head in disapproval, then consented. "Okay, but take these with you." He reached into his pockets and brought out a piece of fresh fruit and a bag of homemade cookies. His hand brushed mine as he handed them over, and a shock of excitement raced through my core. Then he turned to walk back to his car, and with one last glance over his shoulder, he called, "See you down the trail, Odyssa."

I could only hope.

Chilly had not just given me food, he had given me the morale boost I needed to continue hiking.

I put my wretched socks and wet shoes back on and walked across the highway.

The trail continued to climb, my feet still hurt, and the butterflies in my stomach eventually turned to nausea. After several miles, the trail leveled out but my stomach didn't. I felt like I was going to vomit.

I hadn't thrown up since third grade. I had a thirteen-year retention streak going, and I didn't want to blow it now. Even the day before, after drinking sixty-four ounces of water at once, I had felt queasy but I knew that I could keep it down. Today I wasn't so sure.

I came across Campbell Shelter and stopped to rest. I took out my sleeping bag, curled inside, and then brought out my cell phone to call my mom. No matter how old I was, if I was sick or hurt, I wanted my mother. The irony was, she wasn't very good at sympathy. I knew that if I called her I would hear something along the lines of, "Well it's your own fault for wanting to hike the trail, and now you're stuck out there all alone with hurt feet because you don't know how to take care of yourself." But in my heart I knew that it was just her way of saying she loved me.

When I picked up the phone to call, I braced myself for her response. I didn't have the opportunity to tell her about my ailment before she anxiously inquired about the weather.

"Are you stuck in a thunderstorm somewhere? Do you need to be rescued off the trail?"

"Rescued off the trail? No, Mom, I'm fine. I'm in a shelter and I had cell phone reception. so I just wanted to call and tell you that I—"

"Oh, you're in a shelter. With a roof, right? Well, stay there and don't go anywhere. The Weather Channel is showing a huge green blob with a red and yellow core pounding Roanoke right now."

"Mom, it rained this morning, but it's totally stopped now."

"It's not safe. Just stay put and I'll call you when the storms have passed."

Mom was anxious enough about the weather; I didn't want to add illness to her hysterics. And even though she had completely overreacted about the rainstorm, the call had served its purpose. At least I knew that she was thinking about me.

In a strange way, it almost felt as if the pain in my feet and my nausea were connected, as if my stomach was having a physical reaction to the pain. But after an hour and a half of lying in the shelter, they both felt better.

I called my mom again to see if it was okay to hike to the next shelter. She said no.

An hour later I tried again. She still said no.

Finally, after four hours of waiting and resting, my mom called and said that the rain had passed and I could continue hiking.

Ten minutes past the shelter I heard thunder, and within the hour I was caught in another torrential downpour.

I decided that despite our advances in technology, sometimes in life and on the trail, I was simply better off with the information at hand. I traveled six miles and arrived at Lambert's Meadow Shelter at dusk, soaking wet and cold. I resolved not to let my mom perform any more armchair meteorology.

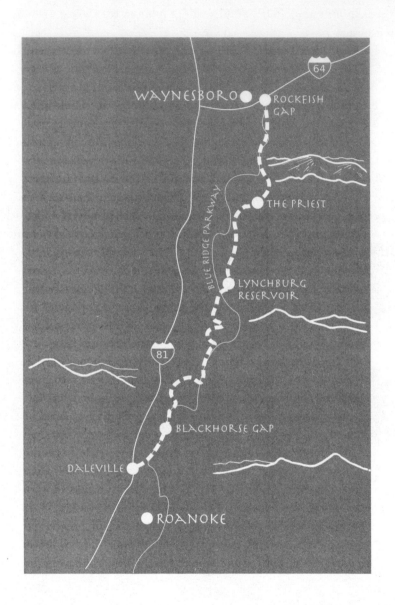

11

INSPIRATION

TROUTVILLE, VA, TO ROCKFISH GAP, VA—132.3 MILES

The Appalachian Trail leaves Roanoke and crisscrosses the Blue Ridge Parkway on its way to Rockfish Gap. People who drive on the Blue Ridge Parkway like to pull over to check out scenic overlooks and then keep driving. Thru-hikers work harder for the same views and know them more intimately. For a hiker, the prominent peaks are not connected by a road, they are woven together with hardwood forests and meandering creeks. Cold Mountain, The Priest, and Three Ridges each provide glimpses of the lofty Blue Ridge Mountains to the south and the green Shenandoah Valley to the north.

I couldn't wait to get to Roanoke. The trail doesn't actually go through Roanoke, it skirts the city on a high ridge and then dives down into the outlying town of Troutville. Pastor Leslie lived in Roanoke, but she was going to pick me up at the post office in Troutville around lunchtime.

I arrived at the post office earlier than expected and immediately went inside to collect a resupply box that I had sent. The mail clerk handed me the box of provisions I had prepared at home, plus another box that was twice as large and oozing something out of the bottom left corner.

I took both parcels outside. I hadn't anticipated a second package, and when I saw that it was from my college roommates, I didn't know what to expect—especially since it was dripping orange slime and they had paid thirty dollars to overnight it to Troutville.

When I tore through the wet cardboard, I found one shoebox full of homemade cookies and another full of individually wrapped orange mush that had created a puddle of sticky goo inside the package. Even in their melted state, I still recognized Katie's sweet potato bars, and I immediately started eating and licking the orange goo off of the plastic wrap.

I loved my college roommates, and I knew that I always would. There was something about surviving such a transitional four years together that made me believe we would always be friends. My mom must have felt the same way, since Pastor Leslie had been her college roommate.

As I took another bite of my sweet potato bar and licked the dripping goo off my hand, I decided that my mom must have been relatively cool growing up, because she had some pretty amazing friends.

When I was a child, I was convinced that Pastor Leslie—which is what I grew up calling her—was just as much my friend as my mother's. She would play sports with me in the yard, tell me stories that were usually reserved for the older kids, and let me drink Sprite at dinner. As I grew older, I saw Pastor Leslie less, but she remained an influential part of my life. I always wanted updates on what she was doing, and I was captivated by the mission trips she took to serve the sick and poor in Africa.

I never thought it was weird that Pastor Leslie was a white pastor at an African-American church. I had gone to her church once as a child and loved it. What I loved most was leaving the service and eating donuts and watching Bible cartoons in the basement with the other kids, but I also remember the singing. For the first time in my life, I'd heard people willing to sing above a whisper in a church service. I remember looking up at men and women swaying and singing with their eyes closed. Some clapped their hands, some danced, and the sound of their voices coming together . . . I didn't just hear it. I *felt* it.

I arrived in Roanoke on Saturday, so I spent the day relaxing and doctoring my feet with over-the-counter first aid treatments. And the following day I went to church.

When I woke up on Sunday morning, I put on my nicest outfit, which consisted of clean, black rain gear. On the way to church, Pastor Leslie asked if I would be interested in speaking to the children's Sunday School class and telling them about my hike. Her offer caught me off guard. I wasn't sure what I would talk about, but I agreed, mainly because I love kids (and I was secretly hoping for some donuts).

When we arrived, I was ushered into the small sanctuary where the children gathered for Sunday School. There were just over a dozen kids in the room, ranging in age from four to twelve.

I asked them to raise their hands if they had ever heard of the Appalachian Trail, but no arms went up. Then I asked if any of them had ever been backpacking—still no hands. Finally I asked if they had ever been on a hike, and three children shot their fingers toward the ceiling.

I started with an overview of the trail. I told them how far I had come, what a typical day was like, what I carried in my pack, and how I resupplied. Then I opened the floor up for questions.

Instantly every hand went up. I called on the children one by one, and even after answering the first ten questions, there were still twelve hands in the air. I was a veteran at fielding inquiries about the trail from adults, but I was taken aback to hear an entirely new set of questions from these children.

Adults usually asked questions rooted in fear: Was I scared? Did I carry a gun? What did I do about snakes and bears? What if I couldn't make it? What did my parents think?

The children, on the other hand, asked questions rooted in curiosity: What was my favorite part of hiking? What did I like about sleeping outside? What were my favorite animals? What was I going to do when I got to the end? Would I ever want to do it again?

Their interest was so great that even after our hour together had ended, there were still kids propping their hands up on a pew or holding up one hand with the other, hoping I would call on them. Our session ended abruptly when the adults flooded into the sanctuary and Pastor Leslie directed me to a front pew, where I sat waiting for the service to begin.

After starting with announcements, the congregation was called to their feet, and for the next hour, the small sanctuary was filled with heartfelt song.

Much like I remembered, this was not the praise music of contemporary churches, nor was it the bellows of traditional hymns. It was the music of a community overtaken by joy. Soulful harmonies filled the chapel, and I was amazed by the freedom of expression. The congregation swayed, danced, stomped, clapped, and raised their hands in the air, but it wasn't for show, it was in celebration.

At most churches, the noon hour would mark the end of the service. At this Assembly, 12:00 marked the end of the music hour and the beginning of a period where people who were filled with the spirit could speak in tongues.

I had never heard anyone speak in tongues, and my home church treated it as taboo, so I was filled with curiosity when the first groans and mutterings filled the room. The congregation mumbled and uttered in ways I could not comprehend, but I knew that this was important to them, and I could tell that it made them feel connected to a higher power.

It occurred to me that hiking allowed me to experience God in a way that others might not understand. In many ways, I felt a direct communion with God through the trail: I saw His glory in the mountains, His presence in the clouds, His peace in the rivers, His power in the weather, and His ingenuity in the animals of the forest. Maybe hiking the trail was my version of speaking in tongues?

After the Holy Spirit had passed through the congregation, men and women walked up to a microphone at the front of the church and spoke the words that God had placed in their hearts. And, as it turns out, God had convinced several people to talk directly to me.

The first woman who stood up was middle-aged, round, and dressed in all purple. She said, "God has a purpose for your hike. He is with you, and He will never leave you or forsake you."

The congregation agreed: "Amen." "Hallelujah." "Mmmm, mmmm, mmmm."

Next, an older man with glasses and dark freckles on his wrinkled cheeks walked up to the microphone, looked me in the eyes, and said, "Sister, don't ever think that you are alone in your journey, for even in the deepest valley and on top of the highest mountain, there God is, walking beside you."

The crowd responded, "Yes, Lord!" "Preach it brother!"

I was embarrassed at being directly addressed, but I believed the words were true, and whether from God or man or both, I needed to hear them.

I was relieved when the time of sharing came to an end, but I wasn't prepared for what came next.

The next part of worship began once again with gospel music, which I loved, and the singing led to dancing, which I liked, but then the dancing led to shaking, and I wasn't so sure about the shaking. One by one, I saw men and women seized by convulsions that they couldn't control.

Then one of the women stopped shaking and fainted. She really fainted! Then another man passed out . . . and then another! The only time I had ever seen anything like this was flipping through TV channels and watching televangelists yell and scream and then heal people with their hands. I had always thought that it was fake, but the people in front of me were really passing out! They even had spotters poised to catch the limp bodies before they hit the floor.

Speaking in tongues was one thing, but this was another level of crazy. I wasn't prepared for it and didn't know whether to believe my eyes.

And that's when I began to feel it.

I felt lightheaded—really lightheaded. My knees grew weak, and then I had a head rush, and even though my eyes were open, everything around me went dark and I felt dizzy. As the darkness continued to close in, I felt for the pew with my hand and quickly sat down. Once I was seated, my vision and strength returned. I was the only person in the church not standing, but that was okay, because I hadn't passed out.

I had never been overcome by such a powerful weakness in my life. If I had remained standing, I'm sure I would have fainted. I wanted to believe that it was low blood sugar that caused my dizzy spell, but I knew it was more than that. It felt like something had passed through me. I was scared to stand up again, so I was thankful when, a few minutes later, the entire congregation sat down to listen to the sermon.

I had grown up in a church where we weren't even allowed to clap, but that morning I was convinced that the Holy Spirit could make people shake and faint. I didn't want to shake or faint as an act of worship, I wanted to hike 2,175 miles.

It probably would have been a whole lot easier to just pass out.

Pastor Leslie sent me back to the trail with salve, powder, bandages, and, most importantly, moisture-wicking socks. Considering the shape my feet were in when I arrived in Roanoke, it was amazing how much better they felt after keeping them dry, clean, and rested for two days.

I didn't just feel rested, I felt renewed. I couldn't believe that I had hiked over seven hundred miles. I was proud of my accomplishment, but the distance had also taken a toll on my spirit, especially when I thought about the fourteen hundred miles I had left to hike.

The people at the church in Roanoke inspired me because they believed in a God Who could do anything, and Who wanted you to ask Him for everything. They were people who allowed the Holy Spirit to work in and through them without shame. They spoke words that were uplifting, they gave me hugs and handshakes that felt healing, and they prayed that God would protect me and provide for me. Their love, their fellowship, and their prayers gave me strength.

I felt like God had been sending me encouragement throughout my time on the trail. He had sent me sunsets, wildflowers, wildlife; He had sent kind words from strangers, or trail magic when I needed it most. But my time in Roanoke was His biggest gift yet. I no longer cared how crazy it seemed or what other people thought: I believed I had been called to the trail.

When Pastor Leslie dropped me back off at the trail on Monday morning, it was the middle of April and I was in central Virginia. That meant I was well ahead of most thru-hikers, so I only encountered a handful of people on the trail. It also meant that I was able to watch one of the prettiest stretches of the trail wake up from winter and bloom into spring.

Spring was timid in arriving. During the day, she would show her presence through a deer next to her fawn, the excited chirping of a songbird, or an early flower such as a bright orange Indian paintbrush poking up through the heavy, wet fall leaves. But at night, she surrendered herself to the cold temperatures and snow flurries that still gripped the darkness.

I decided that if spring needed encouragement to hang around, then I was going to be her biggest cheerleader. I thanked her each time the sun greeted me with a blanket of warmth, I laughed with the wafting breeze when it carried a scent of honeysuckle to tickle my nose, and I hiked late into the evening so that I could dance down the trail to the crickets' serenade.

Like the weather, the trail had also become more kind. The path no longer presented grueling half-day climbs, but it did keep me busy with constant ups and downs that alternated their views between mountain vistas, expansive valleys, rolling meadows, and winding countryside.

Yes, it was a good time to be a thru-hiker in central Virginia. With so much beauty, so few people, and such mild terrain, I found myself unintentionally hiking thirty miles a day. I wasn't hiking any faster than before, but the days were longer, the trail was less difficult, and I always wanted to go a little farther to see what pleasant surprise awaited me around the next turn.

I loved waking up to hike, but for the first time since starting the trail, I no longer loved to eat. Leaving Roanoke, I had filled a third of my pack with just food. But on this stretch, I didn't want to eat any of it. I don't know if I was distracted by the splendor of the trail or if I required fewer calories in spring's warmer weather. Perhaps I was just tired of trying to consume four thousand calories every day. But whatever the reason, my appetite had vanished.

One night, I had a lollipop for dinner—that was all. The next day, instead of lunch, I just sucked on multicolored, sour neon gummy worms for energy. This seemed to be working, until I tripped over a rock and got one lodged in my throat.

I could barely breathe. I hunched over, hacking to try and dislodge it, but the worm remained. The sour coating burned the back of my throat.

Finally, red in the face and reduced to my knees, I dislodged it with a convulsive cough. It had been a freak incident, but I was traumatized by the thought of choking with no one around to help. And that did nothing to help my appetite.

Even though I wasn't eating, my energy level stayed constant—until I reached Cold Mountain.

A lot of hikers love maps; they love to carry maps, they love to look at their maps throughout the day, and they love to figure out the specific distances and elevations separating different points on the maps.

I don't particularly care for maps.

The trail is clearly marked, the mountains are clearly there, and the elevation is not going to change no matter how many times you pull out the map and look at the climb in front of you. If I am going to summit regardless of elevation, then I would rather determine the difficulty once I arrive at the top of the mountain and am able to look down, as opposed to standing at the bottom and looking at a map.

I was glad there were no maps warning me about the climb up Cold Mountain from Brown Mountain Creek. If I had known what I was getting myself into, I think I might have just stayed in the valley. It took several hours to reach the top, and the ascent was so steep that I had to walk on my tiptoes because my heels couldn't reach the angled tread.

At the start of the climb, I felt lightheaded and dizzy, then after an hour I began to feel a slight pain in my stomach. Initially, I thought it was a cramp, but then I realized it was a hunger pain. My body needed nourishment. The problem was that I was so lightheaded and nauseated from not eating that I couldn't stomach the thought of food.

Originally, eating had been one of the biggest draws of thru-hiking. Being able to eat whatever I wanted and still lose weight was revolutionary. It was a no-fail diet. I never dreamed that I would get tired of it. But just like filling up a gas tank, keeping up with my caloric needs had become a chore.

I knew I wasn't going to make it much farther if I didn't stop to refuel, so I sat down and started gumming a granola bar. I sucked on it until it became soft, and then rolled it around with my tongue until I could swallow it. I didn't want to chew. I was tired of chewing.

One hundred and fifty calories was enough to get me to the top of Cold Mountain. Unfortunately, climbing down the mountain wasn't much easier than going up it. My body felt horrible hiking, but when I stopped to take a break, I felt even worse.

When I came out to a dirt road, I was tired, weak, and still unwilling to chew. There was a pickup truck nearby, and beside it stood a woman who was probably in her mid-thirties. Granola, as she introduced herself, had braided pigtails and wore a cute athletic tank-top and sport skirt. She was a vision of cleanliness and beauty—except for her legs, which looked like they hadn't seen a razor in over a year.

"Are you a thru-hiker?" I asked.

"I was last year," she said. "I made it to Katahdin in July, but I liked the trail so much that I just turned around and started hiking back to Georgia."

The trail had a term for thru-hikes completed back-to-back in the opposite direction. "So you did a yo-yo?" I asked.

"Yep, and when I got to Springer Mountain, I still didn't want to go home, so I headed farther south and hiked the Florida Trail."

"I didn't even know there was a trail in Florida," I said.

"Yeah, it's great," said Granola. "It's fourteen hundred miles long and goes from the Everglades to the Panhandle. But it's pretty flat and doesn't have clean water. That's one of the reasons I was so eager to get back to the AT. This year I'm just hiking my favorite sections and visiting old friends."

Granola walked over to the pickup truck. "I have some food in here. You want something?"

"No thanks, I'm not really hungry," I replied.

Granola looked stunned. "I never thought I would hear a thru-hiker say that."

"I know, it's weird."

"Well, what about a drink? I have a cooler in the back with sodas." Hmm. I didn't have to chew soda. "Yeah, that'd be good. Thanks."

Granola handed me a cold Pepsi. As I opened it, I asked, "How much longer are you going to be on the trail?"

She laughed. "Until my life savings are gone."

I guess, for her, hiking was a different form of life savings.

I stayed at the road with Granola while the cold drink infused my veins like an IV drip. The sugar and caffeine rejuvenated me, and after thirty minutes I was ready to keep hiking.

After leaving Granola, I surfed the sugar wave for about an hour until I once again crashed into a state of physical exhaustion. My body was overcome with weakness, and even though my muscles cried out for energy and my stomach screamed for food, my mind said that I still wasn't hungry. I traveled the next three miles so slowly that I barely made it to the shelter before nightfall.

The Priest Shelter was perched on top of a lonely mountain, and I was the only hiker there. When I arrived, I still didn't want to eat, I just wanted to lie down.

I curled up in my sleeping bag, ready to fall asleep. In my famished state, I wasn't really aware of the thoughts that were running through my head. At one point, I thought about having to quit the trail because I was too weak to finish. My eyes shot open.

Had I really just thought about quitting the trail? Up until this point there had been no correlation in my mind between not eating and not hiking. Could I really sabotage myself like that?

I sat up quickly and grabbed my food bag. I didn't care that I wasn't hungry, I didn't care that I felt sick and hated chewing. I was going to make it to Maine even if it meant I had to force-feed myself to get there. I pulled out one food item after another and ate as much as possible. I gorged myself on nearly two thousand calories. But I didn't feel sick. Instead, my body seemed to absorb every bite immediately. When I was finished, I set my watch alarm for 9:00 AM, twelve hours away and two hours past sunrise.

I was not going to quit. I was going to eat and sleep as much as I needed to remain healthy and stay on the trail.

It's amazing what food and rest can do. It was a drizzly morning with heavy fog, but I felt much, much better, and after a big breakfast I set out to test my new strength.

I knew that my recent turn toward self-destruction was my own fault, but I also don't think I grew up with a very good model. The majority of our culture believes that we can operate with very little sleep as long as we supplement it with enough caffeine and processed food. My college friends treated caffeine pills like candy and Red Bull like water.

None of us really thought about how what we put into our bodies would affect their outputs. But the trail was teaching me that if I wanted to make it to Maine, I was going to have to take care of myself. I was going to have to eat often and vary my diet to include more than snack cakes, candy, and energy bars. I was also going to have to rest and maybe not hike thirty-mile days back to back.

During my leisurely descent down The Priest, I saw a man in running shorts pierce the mist and sprint up the mountain toward me. He looked exceptionally healthy and strong. I stepped to the side of the trail to let him pass, but surprisingly he pushed a button on his monstrous wristwatch and stopped to talk.

"Ya' thru-hiking?" he asked in an enthusiastic Southern accent.

"Yep, I'm going to Maine. Are you a runner?"

He laughed. "Yeah, you could say that. I like to run. And I *really* like to run on trails."

"Have you done any races?"

He laughed again. "A few."

"How far do you go?"

"Oh, thirty, fifty, or a hundred miles, usually."

Wow! I couldn't imagine running fifty or a hundred miles at once and was in awe of the discipline (and masochism) it must take to complete such a race.

"Well, don't let me hold you up," I said.

"All right." He pushed a button on his enormous watch and started running up the trail. But before he turned at the next switchback, he looked back and yelled, "By the way, my name's David Horton. Have a good hike!"

"I'm Odyssa," I called back. "Good luck with your running!"

Then I turned and continued walking.

David Horton? David Horton? DAVID HORTON!

My jaw dropped. I knew I had heard that name before, and now I remembered why. Even with my limited knowledge of trail culture, I knew who David Horton was—he was one of the most famous trail runners in the world. He had won countless races and been featured in numerous running magazines. And in 1991, he had set the speed record on the Appalachian Trail by doing it in fifty-two days. Fifty-two days—that meant he averaged over forty miles a day. How was that humanly possible?

I was so excited to have had an unexpected celebrity encounter in the middle of the woods that my mood only suffered slightly when I realized that I had just met the Michael Jordan of trail running and I didn't have a picture to prove it. I know it's pathetic, but as a substitute, I took a picture of his truck in the gravel parking lot at the base of the mountain. At least I think it was his truck; it was the only one there, and it had several ultra-trail-marathon stickers on the back, so I figured the odds were pretty good.

I ducked out of the rain at Harpers Creek Shelter. Someone had left a *Backpacker* magazine near the shelter register, and unpacking my sleeping bag to cozy up and stay warm, I read through every single page. A few months before, I had read *Backpacker* magazine with dreams and ambitions, but now it was my reality. I read every page with authority. I disagreed with gear reviews, related to the survival stories, and read about the featured trails and hikers with great interest.

I had almost reached the end of the magazine when I saw an article that mentioned David Horton. Ha! I knew he was famous. (Or else he planted this here to make people think he was.)

The simple pleasures of a warm sleeping bag and rain on a tin roof made it hard to leave the shelter, but I wanted to hike a little farther before nightfall, so I continued up the long incline of Three Ridges.

I was busy taking baby steps up the long ascent when I heard the sound of feet quickly approaching behind me. I turned to see David Horton running up the trail once again. He had run thirty miles in the time it had taken me to walk eight!

I knew he was in a hurry, but I didn't want to botch my second chance, so I quickly expressed my admiration and requested a photo. A willing subject, he smiled and put his arm around my shoulder. I extended my outside arm, clicked a button, and captured our encounter.

I thought he would run off again after the photo, but instead he looked at me with a funny expression and said, "You're brave."

"Brave? Why?"

"You're hiking the trail alone. Aren't you scared?"

"No. Would you be scared to hike alone?"

He grinned. "I'd be scared to carry a pack, and I'd be especially scared to do it alone. Runners don't make good hikers, but they do smell better."

He leaned over to sniff me, then held his nose and laughed. This guy had just run thirty miles and he was making jokes! He was so full of life and energy, and though we hadn't talked for long, there was something about him I connected with. Even though he did seem a little crazy.

"I like you," he said. "You're special. You're gonna make it to Katahdin."

"I hope so."

"NO!" he exclaimed. It was the first time I had seen him look serious. "You *will* make it to Katahdin."

"Yeah, I *will* make it," I said. He nodded his head with satisfaction. Then I asked, "So, are you just out here running for fun or are you training for something?"

"Both. I'm having fun, but I'm also training for the Pacific Crest Trail. I'm gonna try to set the record on it this summer."

"How far is it?"

"Two thousand six hundred and sixty-three miles."

"That's four hundred miles longer than the AT!" I exclaimed.

"You're right. And I'm gonna finish around the same time that you'll finish. And you *will* finish! So you have to look me up afterward and say hi."

"Okay, I'll do it. I *will* look you up this fall."

David laughed. "Okay, girl, I'll talk to you soon." Then he once again activated the machine on his wrist and continued running up the mountain and out of sight.

If I had been on the streets of Los Angeles and seen a movie star, it wouldn't have meant as much to me as my run-in with David Horton.

Meeting David Horton was amazing, but the one thing I really wanted to see while I was on the trail was a bear. I wasn't scared. I didn't think it would eat me. I just wanted to see one in the wild. The three places on the trail where bear sightings are most common are in the Smokies, the Shenandoahs, and New Jersey. I hadn't seen anything but rain or snow in the Smokies, so now that I was so close to Shenandoah National Park, I was extra vigilant.

Nearing the park, I noticed lots of little orange lizards. Maybe they were technically newts or salamanders, but whatever they were, they littered the trail. They were bright orange with dark spots on their backs. They were about the size of my pinky finger, and they were really slow. In fact, they hardly moved at all. I could stoop down within inches of them and they wouldn't budge. Even after I named them and started petting them, they only took a step or two.

I had to walk very gingerly down the trail to make sure I didn't step on them. Despite being almost neon orange, they blended in amazingly well with the remaining fall leaves that were decomposing on the ground.

While I was looking down at the trail for the little lizards, I heard a rustling noise ahead.

A bear? No, not a bear.

It looked like a turkey—but it wasn't a turkey.

A peacock! It was a female peacock with funny antennae sticking up out of her head! She ran several yards down the trail and then stopped to look back. I followed, and when I was within a few feet, she once again sprinted down the trail. She probably stayed on the trail for a quarter mile, running ahead and then waiting for me to catch up before running a little farther. Finally she veered off the trail and ran through the woods until I couldn't see her anymore.

I laughed at the absurdity of seeing a peacock in the woods. I'm sure peacock sightings on the Appalachian Trail weren't very common— probably far less common than seeing a bear. I remembered from my classical studies that peacocks were considered the bird of Hera, queen of the gods. Maybe this bird was a good omen? Maybe good things were about to happen!

I smiled as I thought about the many pleasant surprises I'd had recently. I loved central Virginia. I loved the trail. Spring was making herself more known each day, and I felt full of love, laughter, and life. Even by myself, even in the middle of the woods.

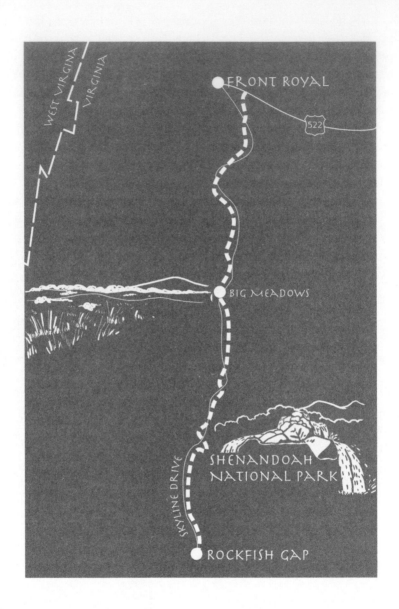

12

GENEROSITY

ROCKFISH GAP, VA, TO US 522 (FRONT ROYAL), VA—107 MILES

Shenandoah National Park is a favorite section for many thru-hikers. There is enough wilderness in the park to satisfy the longings of any outdoor enthusiast, but there are enough amenities to keep a hiker clean, fed, and happy throughout the hundred-mile stretch. It is a place where beauty and convenience meet, and where gentle climbs and gradual descents lift your spirits. It is a place that makes you feel like maybe thru-hiking isn't so difficult after all.

On my first day in Shenandoah National Park, I came across Nightwalker and Mooch. I had met them just outside Roanoke at Apple Orchard Shelter. They were friends from Connecticut who had been Boy Scouts growing up, and now that they were out of college, they were on the AT together.

I had taken to them immediately because Nightwalker had shared his dried fruit with me at the shelter—and sharing food on the trail is a *big* deal. I also remembered them fondly because Mooch's thick sarcasm kept me entertained and laughing well into the night, long past when I usually fall asleep.

The only strike against them came when the rain started blowing inside the shelter and onto the bottom half of our sleeping bags. Nightwalker convinced us to put trash bags around the ends of our sleeping bags to keep them dry. It seemed like a great idea. But when we woke up in the morning, our sleeping bags were dry up top and soaking wet underneath the trash bags. Both boys marveled at the outcome like it was a science project that revealed something new and amazing about the laws of condensation. All I knew was that my sleeping bag was wet and heavy.

Now that we were in the Shenandoahs together, and there wasn't any chance of rain, I was happy to see them.

"Odyssa!" they called as they hiked toward me. (*Toward* me? That was weird.)

Nightwalker was the proverbial tall, dark, and handsome type. By this point on the trail, he had a thick black beard that made him look like a rugged cowboy or a rider for the Pony Express. Mooch was even taller than Nightwalker, gangly and topped with a huge smile and out-of-control curly hair. He reminded me of a good-looking Gumby with a 'fro.

"I'm sorry again about your sleeping bag," were the first words out of Nightwalker's mouth.

"Don't worry about it." I laughed. "Why are you guys headed south? I *am* still hiking north, right?"

"Yeah, you're good," said Mooch. "Nightwalker's mom is here and she's slackpacking us through the Shennandoahs. It was easier to start near the lodge and have her pick us up at the park entrance, so we're hiking south today."

"We have extra snacks. You want some?" asked Nightwalker.

I nodded enthusiastically. Mooch gave me cookies and Nightwalker handed me fruit snacks. If I hadn't already forgiven them for the wet sleeping bag, this would have done it.

"Hey, we need to keep hiking, but my mom's doing trail magic all week, so when you come to a road crossing tomorrow, keep an eye out for a pretty, dark-haired lady with snacks and drinks."

"I will definitely keep an eye out for your mom. But don't let me keep you from getting to your showers and warm, soft beds. After all, I still have a few miles to the dirty, hard floorboards waiting for me at the next shelter."

The boys laughed.

"You know, Odyssa, the thought of you out there in the cold on the uncomfortable floor of the shelter is just going to make my bed feel that much better," replied Mooch.

I brandished my mop stick at him like a martial arts weapon.

"Okay, okay," said Nightwalker, as the two laughed and stumbled farther away from me. "We'll look for you tomorrow, Odyssa."

"Yeah, and maybe I'll bring you some of the leftovers from my delicious continental breakfast," shouted Mooch as they disappeared around the turn.

The Appalachian Trail has more road crossings per mile within Shenandoah National Park than in any other section of trail. And the weird thing is that it's always the same road. The Blue Ridge Parkway becomes Skyline Drive at the park's southern boundary. Skyline Drive touches the AT forty-five times in Shenandoah National Park.

It was late afternoon, and I had already crossed the road nine times since leaving the shelter that morning. At each stretch of pavement, I carefully surveyed the area, hoping to spot Nightwalker's mom. But it wasn't until my final road crossing of the day that I discovered her trail magic. There was a cooler filled with sodas, and beside it was a cardboard box overflowing with cookies, crackers, and fruit snacks.

I had already helped myself to a drink and was busy selecting my snacks when an attractive lady with short, black hair shut her car door and began walking toward me.

"You must be Odyssa. The boys told me about you," she said.

"You must be Trail Magic Momma," I replied. I didn't know her name, or her son's real name, and "Trail Magic Momma" just kind of came out.

"Ha! I love it," she said. "Maybe that can be my trail name—Magic Momma. I'm glad you're here," she continued. "I've been parked here all day, and you're the first thru-hiker I've seen. You haven't seen the boys, have you?"

"Nuh-uh," I said, with graham cracker crumbs falling out of my mouth. "Where are they?"

"They should be here soon, I hope."

I finished my snack and grabbed a second helping from the cardboard box. I sat in the grass, laughing and talking with Magic Momma in between mouthfuls. She and I quickly discovered that we both loved books, tennis, and red wine. She told me about her work, her husband, and how much she loved being here with her only child. (Well, that is, if you don't count the black lab that she'd left at home.)

I believe that there are only a handful of people in life that a person will meet and immediately feel deeply connected with. I had imagined this immediate bond was usually reserved for a best friend or the love of your life, but I found myself experiencing it with a fifty-year-old woman.

After a long visit that seemed to have lasted only a few minutes, Magic Momma concluded the conversation with an offer. "We're staying at the lodge that's just a mile up the trail. You can eat dinner with us there if you like."

"I'd love it!"

Magic Momma gave me the key to their rooms and told me that I could have a shower and take a nap on one of the beds until the boys arrived.

Hiking toward Big Meadows Lodge with Magic Momma's room key, I realized that this was like a slackpack in reverse. When I slackpacked, I had to trust someone with all my gear and belongings, but now Magic Momma was handing over the key to her hotel room to someone she had just met.

When I arrived at the lodge, I entered Magic Momma's room and the adjacent room where Nightwalker and Mooch were staying. Next to the beds there was a laptop computer and a wallet, and on the floor there was an open bag of beef jerky. I stole a piece of jerky.

Then I took a long shower and a quick catnap before the boys arrived and woke me up.

"What is this, *Goldilocks and the Three Bears?*" Mooch asked.

"Yeah, we said you could have some trail magic, not our beds!" Nightwalker followed.

Their sarcasm was a welcome wake-up call.

At dinner, Mooch spent most of the meal entertaining us with crude jokes. I thought it was hilarious. Not so much because of the jokes themselves, but because I don't have any friends who would be willing to use such profanity and sexual innuendo in front of my mom, or their mom, or anyone else's mom. But Mooch kept cracking himself up, and Magic Momma just kept shaking her head and smiling.

Magic Momma refused to let me pay for my meal, which was very generous because a hungry thru-hiker is not a cheap date. Nonetheless, she insisted on treating everyone to appetizers, entrees, desserts, and drinks.

When we were finished, I was full, I was content, and I was ready to hike back down the trail to find a camping spot. That was, until we walked outside and into snow flurries.

"You've got to be kidding me," said Nightwalker. "It's May and it's still snowing?"

Turning to me, Magic Momma pleaded, "You can't go back to the trail in this."

"Well, she can't have my bed," Mooch quickly interjected.

"Yeah, I'm not sharing mine, either," agreed Nightwalker. "But you're more than welcome to sleep on the carpet."

Mooch relented. "I might give you a pillow . . . if you're lucky."

It was settled. I was clean, fed, and now I was staying in a hotel room—even if it was on the floor.

One of the best parts about spending the night with Mooch and Nightwalker was that I got to slackpack with them the next day.

You'd think a slackpack would be substantially easier than hiking with a heavy pack. But for me, that day, it was hard—and it would have been miserable if I'd been carrying my pack.

Some people think it is inappropriate for me to discuss women's issues on the trail, and I don't think that's really fair. I don't think it's fair because it's natural, it's unavoidable, and it's highly disruptive to everyday activities—especially hiking. (Moot understood.)

Menstruation is a fact of life. And the only way to describe how tough the day was is to mention that my lower back hurt, my stomach was cramping, I suffered a slight headache, a wee bit of nausea, escalated hunger, and fatigue. Combine that with having to hike thirty miles (with or without a pack), and that just makes it a hard day. But the one thing that made my day better was that Mooch was in even more discomfort.

Intimacy is not just fostered on the trail, it's required. If you're hiking as part of a group, you have to be vulnerable. When you're hurting, even if it's embarrassing, you have to communicate that you're not feeling well, that you need to slow down, or that you need help.

When Mooch needed help, he turned to Nightwalker.

"Nightwalker. Hey, Nightwalker," he said.

"What's up, Mooch?"

"I need a favor. I need you to slap me across the face as hard as you can."

"What?"

"Seriously, I need to take my mind off my butt rash, and if you slap me really hard, that might do the trick."

We erupted with laughter. Well, Nightwalker and I erupted, but Mooch still looked serious. I'd noticed that Mooch had been waddling uphill, but, not knowing him that well, I thought it might just be the way he hiked. And even though Nightwalker never slapped him, I think just confessing his symptoms made Mooch feel a little better.

We devised a system to help Mooch make it to the road where we planned to meet Magic Momma: Every thirty minutes we all took a break to let Mooch step into the woods to apply Gold Bond powder. In addition, we all agreed to walk slowly up the inclines so Mooch could waddle up with wide steps to avoid any further rubbing or irritation. And when we reached the top of the climb, Mooch would hand me his hiking sticks and run downhill. He said it hurt the worst on the down-hills, so running was a way to shorten the duration of discomfort.

Mooch was pitiful. I knew he wasn't faking it or exaggerating. But one thing that made it more tolerable for all of us was that Mooch was a master at making fun of himself. I never thought it was possible for someone to expound upon the concept of chafing with the language and detail that Mooch used. If you're not the afflicted party, then a butt rash is pretty much always funny, but on Mooch it was hilarious.

I was so entertained by Mooch's rants that I had almost forgotten about my own ailments when we reached our final road and met Magic Momma. Much to my delight, I was invited to spend another night at the lodge.

That night we enjoyed another delicious meal, complemented by more of Mooch's offensive humor. Back at the room, we weren't quite ready for bed, so we ended the evening with a few rounds of sleeping-bag wrestling.

I was new to the sport, but the rules were easy: all limbs must stay inside the sleeping bag, there is no standing allowed, and the first person to say "uncle" loses.

I may not have been the best wrestler, but I never said "uncle." None of us did.

The next morning, the three of us set out together, this time to reach the northern park boundary. The morning hike was enjoyable and lighthearted, because that's how it was hiking with Nightwalker and Mooch—it was fun. But as I listened to their banter, I also began to feel a little sad.

I knew that around lunchtime we would reach the road where Magic Momma would be waiting for us, and at that point, Nightwalker and

Mooch would join her for two rest days off the trail, and I would continue hiking—alone. I liked hiking alone—no, I *loved* hiking alone—but I had also loved hiking with Nightwalker and Mooch.

They had invited me to spend their rest days with them and then continue as a group, but I didn't want to take two rest days, and more importantly, I didn't want to be a part of a group. My pride made me want to hike the trail alone, and my insecurities meant that I didn't want the constant company. But at the same time, I was going to miss those two, and Magic Momma. My time in the Shenandoahs was the most fun and lighthearted I had experienced on the trail.

On the surface, I didn't have much in common with Mooch or Nightwalker. Mooch had descended from a long line of New Yorkers, and he had the cynicism and humor to prove it. Nightwalker, on the other hand, was more of a cultural mutt, who was very interested in science and related closely with nature. I was, of course, Southern and Christian, which would count as at least two strikes against me to most New Englanders. But it seemed like it was because of our differences that our group worked so well together and the chemistry felt so strong.

While I was thinking about how much I would miss Mooch and Nightwalker, I felt something wet on my leg. I looked down and saw a bright yellow stream running from my inner thigh down my calf and into my sock.

I didn't feel like I had to use the bathroom! I'd just stepped into the woods ten minutes ago. I was in shock, and without thinking, I blurted out, "But I just went!"

Nightwalker and Mooch, who had both been hiking behind me, overheard me and started cracking up. I was peeing on myself, and they were laughing! I was deciding whether to lash out at them or run into the woods and hide when Nightwalker finally said, "Odyssa, check your pack."

My lemon-lime Gatorade, a present from Magic Momma, had leaked out of my day sack and down the middle of my legs. I was so relieved that I started laughing too. Then I stopped and looked at the boys very sternly.

Then I started to laugh again.

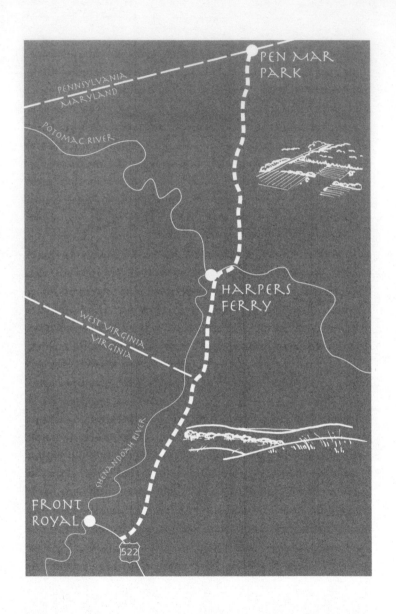

PEN MAR
PARK

PENNSYLVANIA
MARYLAND

POTOMAC RIVER

HARPERS
FERRY

WEST VIRGINIA
VIRGINIA

SHENANDOAH RIVER

FRONT
ROYAL

522

13

DIVERSITY

US 522 (FRONT ROYAL), VA, TO
PEN MAR PARK, MD/PA—95 MILES

The transition from rural Virginia to the mid-Atlantic is drastic. The trail continues to level out as the roads, attractions, and amenities increase. After hundreds of miles of remote farmland, this stretch feels overstimulating, but the historical landmarks that line the trail are a welcome addition. For close to one hundred miles, the trail feels more like an outdoor museum than a long-distance foot path as the land tells of the great triumphs and tragedies of American history.

I already had a bias against most weekenders, but after my night at Manassas Gap Shelter, I decided I didn't like section-hikers much either.

A common piece of advice on the trail is "trust your instincts." I heard people talk about instincts concerning weather, animals, and ability, but I thought the most important time to trust your instincts was with people. And although my mood was already tainted after parting ways with the boys and Magic Momma, my gut clearly said that I was not going to like the couple I met at Manassas Gap Shelter that evening.

As I approached, they were so wrapped up in themselves that they barely acknowledged my presence.

"Hey there," I said.

The man just turned and nodded his head.

"Are you two thru-hiking?" I asked.

"No, we're section-hiking," he replied gruffly.

A section-hiker, by definition, is only doing a portion of the trail. They may piece together all the sections to eventually complete the entire trail, but usually they just fall into a strange purgatory of doing more than weekenders but less than thru-hikers.

It seemed to me that, as a thru-hiker, I should be able to pull rank over a weekender or section-hiker. But I was discovering that the weekenders and section-hikers thought they were just as important as me, if not more so.

For example, the couple I met tonight—on this, their second night out—decided to tell me that I was doing everything wrong. They criticized my gear, my miles, and my diet. Granted, that last one might have been deserved.

"Is that your hiking stick?" the woman asked in a condescending tone, pointing to my mop stick.

"Sure is," I said. "It cost three dollars and it's made it almost two hundred and fifty miles so far."

"Well, I doubt it provides much support," said the man.

"Actually, it's great. You should try one sometime."

"And you wear an external-frame pack?" asked the woman.

"Looks like I do." I was beginning to feel less polite.

"Why are you wearing running shoes?"

"Because boots are too heavy and they hold in moisture."

"Boots are better for ankle support."

"Yeah, but they're not designed for thirty-mile days."

"You're doing thirty-mile days?" she asked with surprise in her voice. I knew that would impress her. "Yup," I said proudly.

"That's stupid! There's no way you'll make it to Maine doing thirty-miles days."

"Well, I made it through Virginia doing them—and I liked it."

"What do you eat, then?"

"Snack foods, mostly. Peanut butter and jelly, cheese, salami, Nutella, trail mix, granola—basically anything."

"Yeah, but what do you cook for dinner?"

"I don't."

"You don't cook?"

"Nope. Don't like doing dishes." I said this as they were wiping down their dishware to prepare for supper.

I would have been less annoyed with the section-hikers if they'd been doing it right. I mean, at least I knew what I was doing wrong. I realized that my gear was old and far from top-of-the-line, and that my diet could have been healthier, but that said, I had still hiked a thousand miles. These two were on their second night, and they were carrying a bear canister. Who carries a bear canister?

It was the first one that I had ever seen, but I immediately knew what it was. Its barrel shape and high-tech, indestructible material designed to keep bears from eating the food stored inside made it unmistakable. No one on the AT carried a bear canister. Everyone hung their food from trees or from the bear cables near the shelters. If you carry a bear canister on the AT, you might as well have a big IDIOT sticker pasted across it because they weigh about ten pounds and take up half your pack. They are great for open expanses out West, but unlike the Sierras and the Rockies, the Appalachians always have trees to hang food from.

The couple, who were no longer talking to me, cooked their dinner and then took turns feeding one another with their one spoon. (They brought a ten-pound bear canister, but only one spoon?)

The woman spoon-fed her husband right in front of me. For twenty minutes, she used baby talk and *choo-choo*ed and airplaned each bite into the fifty-year-old man's mouth. Even if I wasn't doing everything right on the trail, at least I could feed myself!

To make matters worse, after dinner, they didn't even use their bear canister. They just left their food around the shelter where I was sleeping and camped twenty yards away, directly beside the water source—another hiking faux pas.

The next morning I got off to a very early start to avoid any further run-ins with the couple.

On the trail, I was soon confronted with one of Virginia's most tumultuous thirteen miles. It was nicknamed "the roller coaster" and involved a constant pattern of inclines and descents. Although I had heard that this section was challenging, my legs and mind were now well accustomed to PUDs—pointless ups and downs—and I traveled through the undulating green tunnel with little difficulty.

When the trail is referred to as a green tunnel, it means that the only view is of tree branches beside and above you. Much of the Appalachian Trail is a green tunnel. Most of the time I enjoyed the tunnel, but today I was a little bored with the limited scenery, and I wanted some excitement.

I had just sat down for a snack when I found it.

I saw a little black bag on the side of the trail. I went over, picked it up, and opened it to see what was inside. Imagine my surprise when I found a beautiful ceramic pipe!

Then consider my astonishment when I dug a little deeper and found the contents that were supposed to go inside the pipe!

Now, my knowledge of narcotics is a little fuzzy, but I was pretty sure I had discovered what the Latins would have called *cannabis*. I couldn't recall meeting anyone on the trail who had a terminal illness or who hailed from Amsterdam, but I was sure that there had to be a valid reason for my discovery.

Not wanting to leave my findings to someone who might put it to ill use, I decided to pack it out and figure out what to do with it later. Within five minutes, I regretted my decision. I mean, what was I going to do with it? I wasn't going to smoke it. My countless Little Debbies were bad enough for my system. Combining that much refined sugar with an illegal substance certainly couldn't be good for my health.

I didn't want to carry it. I wasn't even willing to carry a hairbrush because of the extra weight, and now I had a bag of non-caloric plant by-products in my pack?

Turning it in to the authorities wasn't an option. How would they know it wasn't mine? What if I had to do a ton of paperwork? Does this kind of thing go on my record?

No way was I sending it home. My mom would kill me.

The little black bag hung like an albatross around my neck.

At the height of my indecision, a sprightly kid just a little younger than myself bounded down the trail. Panting and out of breath, he politely asked me if I had come across "anything" on the trail.

"What do you mean, 'anything'?" I asked.

"I dropped a black pouch somewhere," he said.

"A black pouch, hmmm . . . What was inside?"

I had him cornered, but the look on his face was too much to bear, and I started laughing. I was relieved to return the black bag to its rightful owner, seeing as I had no clue what to do with it.

Pluto, as he introduced himself, graciously thanked me and then bounded back up the trail. Once he disappeared, my amusement once again turned into paranoia. Did this make me a drug trafficker?

When I finally arrived at David Lesser Memorial Shelter, I was greeted by Pluto, as well as several other weekenders and section-hikers.

The short-term backpackers greeted me warmly, made room in the shelter, and offered me food. There was a ten-year-old girl out for an overnight with her mom and aunt. She was a sharp kid who asked me some great questions about thru-hiking, and even volunteered to refill my water bottle at the spring so that I wouldn't have to walk any farther.

It had been a very redemptive evening, until I laid down for bed and started to smell something funny. I propped myself up to look around the shelter, and a few feet away, I saw Pluto lighting up. Right next to two old men, just a few feet away from a little girl, her mom, and her aunt! I couldn't believe it.

These weekenders and section-hikers were going to *hate* thru-hikers. They were going to think we were all pot-smoking hippies who lit up at night in the shelters near impressionable children. Pluto caught my eye and offered me a hit. I simply shook my head and lay back down.

Thru-hikers can be so inconsiderate.

The state of Virginia encompasses almost one-fourth of the entire Appalachian Trail. After hiking over five hundred miles in the state, it felt strange but gratifying to be in West Virginia, which covers less than twenty-five miles, or about one percent of the trail.

I had been looking forward to West Virginia for two reasons: to get out of Virginia, and to see my cousin Wendy.

Wendy was a great friend, a respected nutritionist, and a phenomenal mother. Her daughter Lila was my favorite two-year-old on the planet. But above all, Wendy was family. And after a thousand miles of hiking, I was ready to see some family.

It's funny how being isolated on the trail had made me feel more connected to friends and family. My off-trail visits felt like aid stations along a race course. They provided the help, encouragement, and rest I needed to make it to Maine.

Wendy was fifteen years older than me, so along with being my cousin, she was also a little like a mom or a cool older sister. And like any good older relative, she wanted to make sure that I was taking care of myself on the trail.

"So what have you been eating?" she asked.

"You wouldn't approve," I replied, trying to avoid the lecture that I knew was coming.

"What do you mean I wouldn't approve? You're eating fruits and vegetables, right?"

"Honestly, Wendy, I can't remember the last time I ate something I didn't have to unwrap."

Wendy looked at me with wide eyes and an open mouth.

"Let me see your eyes," she said.

"What?"

"Let me see your eyes."

Wendy held my chin and stared into my eyes.

"Well, your pupils don't look cloudy, so that's good. You're probably burning off most of the toxins before they can settle into your system."

Even though my eyes passed her test, Wendy refused to drive home until we had stopped at a grocery store to load up on fresh produce for the weekend, and hiking foods that were healthy, high-energy, and all natural.

For me, the over-stimulation started in the parking lot, where cars beeped and honked and positioned themselves for prime parking spots. I had hiked one thousand miles to this grocery store, and these people got upset if they had to walk one hundred yards to the front door?

I had never been to a Wegmans before, and judging from the outside of the building, it was going to be a memorable trip. Wegmans was the size of Wal-Mart, but it didn't have a home goods section or clothing, it was just a grocery store—the biggest grocery store that I had ever seen.

I was completely disoriented when I walked inside. It wouldn't have been so overwhelming if I hadn't just come from the woods. However, after a month and a half on the trail, it was hard to process the tsunami of scents, sounds, and colors that crashed down on me beyond the automatic doors.

To my left there was a large bakery, a floral department, a hot food buffet, an international food buffet, a salad bar, and a sushi station; to my right was a line of cashiers that extended into the horizon; and in front of me was an olive bar the size of a trail shelter.

I watched men with shopping carts experience road rage in the aisles, I saw grandmothers speeding around the store in a race to be the fastest and most efficient shopper, and I saw petite, well-groomed housewives bicker about who was first in line at the meat counter.

At one point, Wendy sent me on a mission to pick out four ears of corn from a bin overflowing with produce. After I made my selection, I wandered to the opposite end of the display, where Wegmans had provided a large trash receptacle for husking corn. I had peeled back the green shell of one ear when a pint-sized woman in high-heels and designer clothes elbowed in front of me and monopolized direct access to the husking station.

Like animals around a kill, three women hovered around the trash bin, unwilling to relinquish their positions, tearing the husks and silk strands off their corn so frantically that discarded remnants flew through the air. Talk about living in the wild! Lacking the killer instinct, I placed my four unshucked ears in a clear plastic bag and resigned myself to doing the chore at Wendy's house.

Skulking back to seek my cousin's protection, I followed Wendy to a section within Wegmans, comparable to the size of an average grocery store, dedicated entirely to organic and all-natural foods. I reluctantly chose my favorite combinations of seeds, nuts, and dried fruit, and hesitantly pointed to which organic rolled-oat bar looked the most appealing.

I was relieved to finally make it safely back to Wendy's home, where Lila greeted me with a huge hug, followed by, "Jen-Jen, you stinky!"

Her vocabulary had increased since my last visit.

After a long shower, I spent the rest of the afternoon acting out *Dora the Explorer* with my baby cousin. *Dora the Explorer* is an animated show that features a young, bilingual adventurer climbing mountains, crossing oceans, and surviving educationally valuable dilemmas with her trusty backpack, map, and monkey sidekick. Lila and I spent hours replicating Dora's adventures, pretending to hike, camp, and read a map.

I loved Dora. I wanted to *be* Dora, except I wanted a bear as a sidekick, instead of a monkey. I was now well aware that most people thought it was dangerous for a woman to be in the woods by herself, but obviously they had never watched *Dora*—or been to Wegmans.

It was important to me that Lila felt that the wilderness was safe, and that it was a place she would want to go. She didn't have to be a hiker; I didn't care if she ever hiked the Appalachian Trail. I just didn't want her to be afraid of the woods. And whether she learned that from Dora or me didn't matter, as long as she got the message.

For two days, my cousins nourished me with food and love. When it was time to return to the trail, I was sad to leave Wendy and Lila, but I was ready to say good-bye to suburbia. I was ready to leave behind the endless maze of housing developments. I was ready get away from the busy roads where "driving" consisted of accelerating to sixty mph, then braking to a screeching halt. And I was ready to leave a place where everything you could ever want was available for purchase, and return to a place where I was content to carry only the items that I needed.

I was surprised at how close the trail came to the nation's capitol. Hiking through northern Virginia, West Virginia, and Maryland, it was strange to think that I was in the middle of the woods and, at the same time, just an hour's drive away from the President of the United States.

I was constantly reminded of the region's historical significance, since the trail frequently opened up into fields where a preserved building, historic monument, plaque, or war memorial was located. I had always loved studying history in school, but on the trail the lessons felt more personal. When the trail passed through Harpers Ferry, West Virginia, I thought about John Brown's raid that had taken place there. I wondered, if I had been a slave, or if I had been white and lived 150 years ago, whether I would have had the courage to fight against slavery.

Hiking beyond Harper's Ferry, it occurred to me that only in the past hundred years had walking long distances evolved from necessity to recreation. I was walking because I chose to walk, but I imagined how hard it must have been for slaves escaping the South on the Underground Railroad who were walking for their freedom—and their lives.

I thought about the Native Americans who used to live here with little to no impact on the land, the originators of "leave no trace" ethics. But because the European settlers wanted to own the land, the Native Americans had been corralled into small territories and forced to walk thousands of miles west.

Passing near Gathland State Park at Crampton's Gap, I thought of the Civil War soldiers who walked from the North and the South to arrive at nearby South Mountain Battlefield. A plaque by the side of the trail said that six thousand men died at the Battle of South Mountain. Six thousand fathers, husbands, and sons had walked a really long way to get here, never to return home.

Near Boonsboro, Maryland, the trail passes the original Washington Monument. It's not like the towering phallic obelisk on the Mall in D.C., but a thick stone pillar that looks like a two-story milk bottle. It was built in 1827 by men who would have known Washington or been alive during his presidency, perhaps even by men who had served under him in the Revolutionary War.

I remembered from my American history classes that Benjamin Franklin had given George Washington a walking stick as a gift. I looked down at my yellow mop stick and smiled. How different America would be if sixteen-year-olds received walking sticks instead of cars.

As I traveled farther away from the nation's capitol, I was grateful that I could walk for pleasure, instead of for my freedom, and that I could carry a mop stick instead of a gun.

In a short stretch, I was reminded how diverse and unique our country is, and how our history is one built on triumph, tragedy, and a lot of walking.

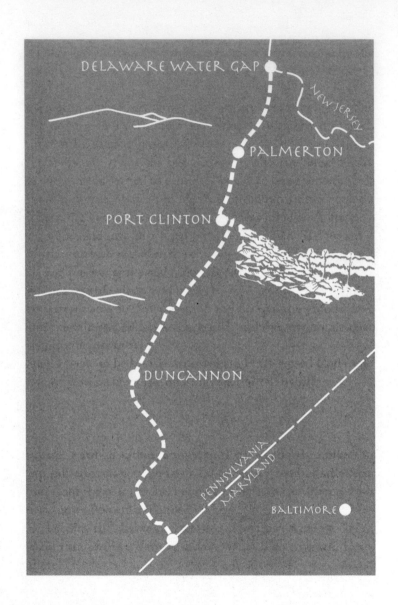

14

ABNORMALITY

PEN MAR PARK, MD/PA, TO
DELAWARE WATER GAP, NJ—260 MILES

The trail passes the half-way point near a quiet state park in southern Pennsylvania, and from there it travels through the scenic farmland of the Cumberland Valley. Then, when you reach Duncannon, everything changes. The trail's neighboring towns feel mysterious and forgotten, and the path becomes rife with rocks: big rocks, small rocks, sharp rocks, and snake-ridden rocks. It's as if all the other states collected their rocks and dumped them on the trail in Pennsylvania.

I was both excited and nervous to cross the Mason-Dixon Line. There was a part of me that was apprehensive about leaving the South and walking farther away from my friends and family, but I was also proud to have hiked all the way from Georgia to the mid-Atlantic, and I was looking forward to exploring a different part of the country.

I had hiked several miles into the state of Pennsylvania without seeing anyone. I enjoyed the solitude and the warm spring air that surrounded me. The trail was relatively flat except for some sporadic boulders that lined the sides of the trail. Some of the large rocks were the size of a small house, but most were comparable to a compact car. I was rounding a large rock about the size of an SUV when I was startled by two men on the other side.

I only glanced at them for a split second, but it's amazing how clearly the image was impressed on my mind.

They were only about five feet away, and one of them was definitely *not* wearing any clothes. He was an older man with a long yellow beard and a big round belly, but no clothes—not even socks.

The other man had red hair and looked fairly young, with freckles on his face and on his bare chest. He was wearing a pair of shorts (thank God) but no pack. Neither of the men had a backpack or any other gear to suggest that they were hikers.

"I'm sorry!" I gasped, and quickly hiked away, shielding my eyes with my hand.

The two men laughed. It didn't seem like embarrassed laughter, but laughter at my expense, as if they didn't care if I was offended. Then the older man shouted out proudly, "Bet you're gonna write home about this one!"

If only he knew.

I steadily hiked my way through shock and denial, but when I arrived at anger, I wasn't just mad at the two men, I was mad at myself.

Why on earth had I felt compelled to say that I was sorry? *I* didn't need to apologize!

You say, "I'm sorry," when you're at a public restroom and you open a stall door that wasn't locked properly and there is someone already inside. You say, "I'm sorry," inside a changing room when you pull back a curtain without realizing that the space was already occupied. But you don't say, "I'm sorry," when you pass an old man stark naked and grinning on the side of a national long-distance trail.

I was the one who now felt unsafe and unsure about what was around the next turn. Those guys should have apologized to me!

Later that afternoon, I was walking through the woods when I saw a type of snake I didn't recognize. It was black, but not consistently black—more of a dark gray, with bands the color of dusk circling its outstretched body. At first I just saw its head lying on top of a fallen tree, but then I traced its body through the leaves and found its tail almost six feet away.

The snake wasn't just long, but fat too. I don't know if it had just eaten, but the middle of its body was as big and round as a grapefruit.

I slowly began to pull out my camera, but as soon as I brought my hand in front of my body, the animal sprang into a tight coil. Then, with its tongue flickering and its tail poised, it rattled!

A rattlesnake? The tail was dark and hard to define, but now I could see a narrow honeycomb rattle. I had never seen a rattlesnake in the wild before!

I was already ten feet away from the creature, but I respectfully backed up several more yards before taking a distant photo.

I was becoming a lot more comfortable with snakes, or perhaps just inured to them. And I decided that I liked rattlesnakes the best, because they could communicate their location, their emotion, and whether or not they wanted their picture taken, with a shake of the tail.

Sounds are so important on the trail. When it came to animals, roads, people, and water, I would usually hear them before I saw them. Toward the end of the day, I heard a noise that I couldn't quite pinpoint. It didn't sound like a human, more like an animal, but whatever was making the noise was clearly in distress. As the sound grew louder, I became more apprehensive with every step. I don't know why I kept walking forward, except that I had decided to follow these white blazes wherever they led.

When I finally came out of the forest and into a grove, I saw where the sound was coming from. Twenty yards away, in the middle of the field, a man wearing a black hooded cloak was reaching his stiff arms heavenward. His body looked tense and rigid, and his groans were deep and indecipherable.

My brain said to keep moving, but my eyes and feet remained glued where they were. I was lost somewhere between fear and fascination. Could this man be a monk performing a Gregorian chant or a Wiccan conducting an outdoor ceremony? Did I even want to know what he was doing?

Suddenly the chanting stopped and my spine stiffened. The man's body remained motionless except for his neck, which he slowly turned in my direction. The way his head turned independently from his torso, it seemed like his neck could screw off his body. Looking in my direction, I knew that he could see me, but I couldn't see his face under the shadow of his hood. Was there even a face in there?

Like a wizard raising his staff to ward off evil, I raised my mop stick in the air to acknowledge the encounter. Then I put it in my hand closest to the shrouded figure and kept hiking.

The man didn't acknowledge my presence, but once he identified me, he rotated his head back to the front of his body and began to cry out to the sky in the same possessed groans as before.

Once I was out of sight, I hiked as quickly as possible away from the field. It was already dark, and I had planned on camping soon, but I continued hiking until it was completely dark and then set my tent up far off the trail.

That night in my tent, I felt uneasy. In one day I had seen a naked man, encountered my first rattlesnake, and passed a dark figure moaning to the sky. I was all about adventure, but this was too much for one day. One of the encounters by itself would have been humorous, a good story, but the three of them together left me feeling restless and afraid.

The next day, I still felt uneasy. I was busy looking at the ground and trying to place my feet on rocks that wouldn't move when I heard laughter coming up the trail. When I discovered the source of the giggling, I thought I was dreaming. Two teenage girls were hiking down the trail in long-sleeved floor-length blue dresses and bonnets.

The rocks didn't seem to bother them at all. Even though they couldn't see their feet underneath their flowing skirts, they glided easily down the trail.

The heat didn't seem to bother them, either. I was in a tank-top and running shorts and I was sweating, but they looked cool and comfortable with everything covered but their faces and hands.

They said hello and smiled as they passed, then continued gliding down the trail, immersed in their lighthearted conversation. The image of their carefree grins stayed with me. It was the most genuine and innocent expression of joy that I had seen since playing *Dora the Explorer* with Lila.

I guessed the two girls must be Amish. I knew that Pennsylvania had a large Amish population, and I couldn't think of any other sixteen-year-old girls who would dress that way. They seemed happy and full of life. I wondered what they were talking about. Maybe they were giggling because the boys they liked were just starting to grow out their Amish beards? Or because they were planning to catch one of the plentiful Pennsylvania snakes and play a prank on one of their brothers?

The encounter felt welcome and redemptive, but still seemed completely out of the ordinary. I felt like I must have gotten off the trail somewhere past Maryland and entered an alternate universe. The thru-hikers had disappeared, the terrain was different, and I was beginning to expect the unexpected.

The eeriness of Pennsylvania continued when I reached Duncannon. The trail winds right through downtown. I was tired and my feet hurt, but I didn't stop because Warren Doyle had said that the one town that I shouldn't stay in if I was hiking alone was Duncannon.

I didn't know the history of the town, but I did know that there was a hostel/bar in town called The Doyle. It stood out in my memory because Warren had said that he wouldn't want his daughter to stay there and he didn't think I should either. I thought it was funny that the one hiker service that Warren warned me about bore his last name. But it did make it easy to remember.

I followed the white blazes on telephone poles through a residential neighborhood. The two-story homes and fenced yards that lined the street looked lifeless. The doors were locked, the windows were drawn, and several yards had tall grass and weeds that came up to my knees.

I heard a noise as I passed by a wooden house that looked exposed under a peeling coat of white paint. In the backyard, I saw a rusted swing set; the empty swing swayed back and forth in the breeze and creaked eerily.

The neighboring house had a wraparound porch with several pieces of railing missing, like gaps between teeth. The open slats revealed a wooden porch swing with one end suspended from the ceiling and the other resting on the floorboards. On the other side of the porch sat an elderly man in a rocking chair. His eyes were closed, and he was so still that I couldn't tell if he was sleeping or dead.

In Duncannon, wherever I expected to see life, there was decay.

The trail turned out of the neighborhood and toward a large bridge over the Susquehanna River. To my left there was a gas station, and looking ahead beyond the potholes in the road, I could see a looming mountain. I wanted to stop at the gas station to buy some candy or a soda before I kept hiking, but the entrance was blocked by a man in a flannel shirt smoking a cigarette and drinking from a brown paper bag, so I turned toward the bridge and kept walking.

When I reached a rocky overlook on the other side of Duncannon, I peered down on the town. From the cliffs I could see the expansive Susquehanna River, and Duncannon gridlocked on the other side by highways and railroad tracks. The valley felt secluded and forgotten, as if Duncannon were a town holding on to secrets and clinging to the past. Perhaps I would have had a more favorable impression of the town if Warren hadn't warned me not to stay there, but everything inside of me said that I had made the right decision.

People told me that Pennsylvania was rocky, but I thought that the large boulders and rock formations in the southern portion of the state had been what they were referring to. It wasn't until I left Duncannon that I knew what people had *really* been talking about. After Duncannon the trail was absorbed by rocks. There was no longer any dirt; there were just rocks. Rocks and snakes.

I had seen my first two black snakes in North Carolina and encountered about a dozen more in Virginia. But since entering Pennsylvania, I had seen at least two or three snakes every day. And they weren't all black either.

Besides seeing my first rattlesnake, I had also come across a green snake slithering through the grass, a gray snake swimming in a river, and a brown snake hiding in the leaves. Leaving Duncannon, I saw ten snakes in three miles, and they were mostly camouflaged with patterns of brown, tan, and yellow.

I think that there were so many snakes on the trail in Pennsylvania because they loved the warm rocks, and also because it was mating season—at least, I think it was mating season, since several of the snakes I saw were coiled together in tight, wriggling balls.

That afternoon, I traveled on a long, sunny rock field that spanned the mountains above the Susquehanna River. Hiking across a scalding, unending rock field full of jagged edges, loose footing, and snake beds was brutal, and I rapidly transitioned from slightly uncomfortable to utterly miserable.

I thought my feet had become accustomed to rock fields, but now on the serrated ridge, a familiar burning sensation accompanied every step. In my mind, the uneven rocks had morphed into primitive weapon tips designed to pierce my flesh.

There was no dirt tread to rest my feet, and the trail was so narrow and overgrown that there wasn't anyplace to sit and rest my body. I had to stop! I took my mop stick and spent five minutes poking around a large rock in the middle of the trail. I was prodding to see if there were any snakes, but in retrospect, poking them with my mop stick probably wouldn't have made them very happy.

I sat down and immediately took off my shoes. As I stripped off my socks, I could see that the pus, inflammation, and polka dots had come back with a vengeance.

I had worn a new pair of socks since leaving Harpers Ferry, and my feet obviously didn't like them very much. I took off the suffocating masks, put my bare feet back in my shoes, and kept walking. I made it about half a mile before I determined that removing my socks did nothing for the pain, but it did allow the dust and dirt direct access to the infected portions of my feet.

I again looked for a rock to sit on, checked it for snakes, then sat down to put my socks back on.

I made it another hundred yards before the shredding sensation in my feet became overwhelming, and without checking for snakes, I collapsed in the middle of the trail.

I had no intention of getting up. I could feel the tears welling up in my eyes. But as the first drop began to slide down my face, I smeared it away with the back of my hand and took a deep breath. I already felt a little dehydrated, and I decided that losing more liquids wouldn't help the situation.

Instead, I sat there and thought about things that were worse than foot pain: I thought about cancer and malnutrition, slavery and women's servitude. I thought about civil wars and terrorism, homelessness and genocide.

I know it seems dramatic, but it was like Mooch wanting to be smacked across the face to take his mind off his butt rash. When the hurt becomes too much to bear, sometimes the best way to work past it is with more pain. My feet screamed in agony, but they were just feet. By comparing them to realities that were far more serious, I was able to suck it up, stand up, and walk.

The rest of the day was wretched. My feet were killing me, and I have never been so depressed about the social injustices in the world. For five hours, I did nothing but focus on suffering.

When I arrived at an empty campsite that evening, I cleaned my feet and laid down in my tent to try and end the day as quickly as possible. However, as soon as I went horizontal, the pain that had been concentrated in my feet started to spread. It leaked into my legs and then filled my stomach with nausea, it permeated through my arms with stinging pricks, and then it seized my head in a throbbing migraine.

It hurt to open and shut my eyelids. I was entirely alone, and I was afraid something terrible was happening to me. I thought about trying to describe the overwhelming pain in my journal, in case someone came along later and found me unconscious, but the thought of moving to collect my pen and pad seemed torturous, so instead I remained rigid.

The pain never went away before I fell asleep. I just remember thinking I was experiencing a medical emergency, and then waking up the next morning and feeling fine.

My body had become totally unpredictable. After being seized with unbearable pain at the campsite, the next day I completed thirty miles with little discomfort.

Then the following day, I once again wanted to gnaw my ankles off.

It was a planned resupply day, and my goal soon became very clear: hike twenty-three miles to Port Clinton and seek immediate medical attention.

In general, I had a severe aversion to going to the doctor. However, at this point, the soles of my feet were infected, bleeding, and they reeked of sour putrescence. I was determined to find a doctor or emergency room before the day was over. I worried that if I didn't, my ailing feet would force me to end my hike, and that thought was even more unbearable than the shredding sensation in my soles.

The path to Port Clinton was lined with rocks and every step felt like I was walking barefoot over hot coals. If I had been able to come up with any other means of effectively moving down the trail besides walking, I would have done it.

When I arrived at an overlook above Port Clinton, I honestly wondered what would happen if I just rolled my body down the remaining descent. Then, turning away, I gritted my teeth and descended, one flinch after another, into the valley.

The base of the mountain marked the start of the town—and also the end of the town. With one quick glance, I lost all hope of finding a doctor's office or urgent care center. Like Duncannon, Port Clinton looked deserted. I didn't see a traffic light, I didn't see any businesses, and I didn't see anyone walking down the sidewalk or driving down the street. It was an abandoned mountain town with litter-strewn railroad tracks running beside it. Port Clinton and Duncannon both seemed like they had once been thriving places of industry and trade, but as time passed, these places had been neglected and eventually left behind.

In despair, I plodded down the empty drag looking for a sign of life. When I passed a closed door with an old FIRE STATION sign on it, I thought my prayers had been answered. Surely someone here would have the knowledge and first aid supplies to assist me.

The door was locked, so I knocked loudly.

The hinges creaked, and through a small crack in the door the sound of loud eighties rock music escaped. I peered in the vertical opening and saw what looked like a small sports bar in the background.

Then the door opened more, and a tan, gaunt, dark-haired man stepped into the entrance. Before he could say anything to me, a gruff voice from the bar yelled, "It's a girl! Let 'er in!"

The man looked me over for another few seconds, then ushered me into the building. As I passed, he said, "This is a locals' bar. You're lucky we let you in."

The man made me sign something like a guest log before I could sit down at the bar.

"Do you guys have a first aid kit?" I asked the bartender.

She shook her head and said, "Nope, but we have plenty of Jägermeister."

I didn't want to drink with this crowd. "Maybe I'll start with a soda," I said.

One of the patrons overheard me ask for a first aid kit and kindly went out to his car to retrieve a travel medical kit. He brought it back, sat right beside me, and started asking me how old I was and if I had a boyfriend.

I don't know if you can classify residents of the mid-Atlantic as rednecks or if those only reside in the South, but these men proved to be close relatives of the Southern species. At 3:00 in the afternoon, most of them were inebriated and yelling at the TV, and the Pittsburgh Pirates—down by three runs—weren't helping the situation.

Excusing myself from the bar, I found a separate table and began to nurse my wounds with triple antibiotic ointment, gauze, and a second soda. Surprisingly, the travel first aid kit had a great selection of cleaning pads, medicated ointment, and bandages. After twenty minutes of work, I had decimated its inventory, but had managed to soothe the burning irritation in my feet.

As I began to reorganize what was left of the supplies, I heard another knock at the door over the din of clanking glasses and men shouting at the TV.

The same man that let me in walked to the door and opened it just a crack, but it was a big enough crack for me to see Raptor.

"He's with me!" I shouted.

I had met Raptor at the last shelter, and although I didn't know much about him, I knew he was a thru-hiker, and I knew he had grandkids because he had showed me their pictures. The way he had teared up as he looked lovingly upon his family's faces had made me like him immediately.

The doorman gave me a cold stare and let Raptor in.

Raptor signed the guest log and then sat beside me. He was a strong hiker, and I thought he looked too young to be a grandpa. When I asked, I found out he was the same age as my father. Raptor kind of reminded me of my dad, and I was glad to have him here to protect me from the other men—also my father's age—who were trying to hit on me.

It turns out that Port Clinton does have one restaurant. The locals at the "fire station" gave us directions, but when we arrived, we were told that hikers weren't allowed to eat in the main dining room. We were only allowed to sit at the bar.

I found an empty stool, but I was not happy. This was not an especially nice restaurant, and there were certainly plenty of empty tables available. Then, partly due to the circumstances and partly because of my low blood sugar, my annoyance soon grew into rage. This was discrimination!

All the thoughts of social injustice from the last section of trail came flooding back. So *this* is what it felt like! This was segregation. At least the prejudice I faced was based on the concrete fact that hikers are filthy and smell bad. But underneath the dirt and grime, hikers are still people!

I couldn't believe that, within my parents' lifetime, parts of this country had had separate restaurants, restrooms, and water fountains simply based on skin color. On *skin color*!

I was reminded of John Brown's raid, which had taken place in Harpers Ferry. Maybe this was my time for revolt? I was about to stage a walkout, really I was, but then a plate of battered chicken fingers piled high on a stack of golden fries was placed in front of me.

I relinquished my stance and asked for the ketchup.

I told myself that if it had been racial, sexual, or religious discrimination, I would have stood up and left. But this was just about being a hiker, and God knows I was a hungry hiker.

After dinner, Raptor and I traveled to a pavilion at the edge of town where hikers could spend the night. We claimed different corners of the open-air structure, crawled into our sleeping bags, and tried to fall asleep. The attempt proved unsuccessful. Before I drifted off, I started to hear voices approach the shelter. Drunk voices.

There was a trio of voices: one happy female soprano, one angry male baritone, and another female who just sounded belligerent. The entourage sat on the pavilion steps, lit a joint, and started passing it around. At first, they were oblivious to our presence, and neither Raptor nor I moved a muscle. But when they spotted our sleeping bags, the hazing began.

"Damn thru-hikers coming to town," the man said, raising his voice.

"Stinkin' hippies!" shouted the woman, followed by an unsettling laugh from the other female.

Then they started whispering, and actually succeeded in not letting us hear what they were saying—except the woman who couldn't control her laughter.

"He he, yeah, we should do it. Ha ha ha."

Then there was silence.

The three of them stood up and stumbled away, the woman's laughter occasionally flaring up in the distance.

I heard a noise coming from Raptor's end of the shelter.

"*Psst*. Raptor, are you okay?"

"Yeah, I'm just getting my pocketknife out of my pack."

"Do you think they're coming back?" I asked.

"I don't know."

I lay awake, listening for any unusual noises. The wind was blowing hard, which made it difficult to hear anything else, until the thunder started. It grew louder and was followed by heavy rain and bright lightning. I was thankful for the storm. I hoped that if the Port Clinton residents had made any plans to come back to the pavilion, the weather would deter them.

The rain lasted a long, long time. The downpour washed away some of my fear, and before the end of the storm, I was asleep.

I awoke later that night to a noise in the distance. At first I thought it was more thunder, but as it grew louder, it seemed more like a churning sound. It grew louder and louder, and then I could feel the floorboards of the pavilion begin to vibrate through my sleeping pad.

I was anxious and frustrated because I couldn't figure out what was happening. I slept so heavily on the trail that waking up in the middle of the night always left me disoriented. It seemed that if I couldn't figure out what was coming toward me, it would consume me. Then I heard the whistle—a train.

I hadn't seen the railroad tracks when we set up in the pavilion, but they must have been close, because even though I covered my ears to muffle the sound, I could still hear rocks from the tracks hitting the side of the building.

After the roaring freight train passed, I didn't go back to sleep. I just lay on my back with my eyes open, waiting for the sky to lighten.

As soon as the dawn greeted the darkness, I packed up and walked over to Raptor. He was still asleep, with his pocketknife clutched in his hand.

"Hey, Raptor," I whispered.

He awoke immediately, his eyes wide open, as if he had tried to be vigilant even in his sleep.

"Hey, I just wanted to let you know I'm leaving. I wanna get out of this town."

"I'm right behind you," he said.

I wanted to leave Port Clinton as quickly as possible. Originally, I had planned to take a rest day to care for my feet, but now I just wanted to get back on the trail. However, I knew I couldn't leave without new socks.

It amazed me that socks were such an important piece of equipment. I had experienced enough discomfort by now to know that it wasn't my shoes causing the pain, it was my socks—or, really, the combination of my socks and the weather. The wicking socks I bought in Roanoke were great, but switching back to a synthetic pair made me miserable. And whether it was from rain, sweat, morning dew, or a river crossing, it seemed that my synthetic socks were always wet. Wet feet in wet socks led to stinky, bleeding, crumbly white feet with polka dots. The rocky terrain in Pennsylvania just exacerbated the situation.

I knew I wouldn't find socks for sale, let alone wicking socks, in Port Clinton. I had asked at the restaurant the night before, and a man sitting at the bar told me there was an outdoor store ten miles down the road. I needed to get to that store, and that meant I needed to hitch. I was still hesitant about hitching alone, but I was sure that if my mother had seen my feet, she would have understood. That, or she would have yanked me off the trail.

I stood at the side of Port Clinton's main road and held out my thumb.

A few cars passed, splashing stagnant rainwater up onto the sidewalk. It's easy to tell when people are not going to give you a ride, because they don't even look at you. It's like they justify not picking up hitchhikers by pretending that they aren't there. I'd rather someone smile and nod their head or even look at me in disgust as they drive by than act as if I didn't exist.

In a few minutes, a large eighteen-wheeler roared down the road. As it passed me, it started to slow down, and I heard its brakes screech on the wet asphalt. The truck pulled off the road and finally came to a stop about a hundred yards down the highway.

I wasn't sure whether or not he had stopped for me, but I cautiously jogged down the side of the road and approached the driver's side of the cab.

Staring up inquisitively, I saw an older, bearded man stick his head out the window and ask, "Well, honey, you need a ride or not?"

I had always wanted to hitchhike on the back of a motorcycle, but this was so much cooler!

As I climbed into the shiny blue cab, it seemed like I was staring out of the top window of a two-story house. I could not believe how high above the ground I was.

When the driver cranked the engine and the truck lurched forward, I was overcome with a feeling of power. My stomach dropped, my adrenaline rose, and the entire acceleration process felt more like a roller coaster than a ride down the highway.

The truck driver was extremely nice and eager to help me find new socks. During our ten minutes together, he told me a little about being a trucker—which sounded like it was even harder than being a thru-hiker. I always knew that truckers worked tough shifts, but the driver told me that the hours were so demanding that most truckers used drugs to stay awake and alert.

I didn't understand how drugs helped drivers stay awake—or focus on the road—but the guy insisted that for many it was part of the job description.

"You almost have to do hard drugs if you want to keep your job," he said. "There's so much pressure not to stop and to make good time that most truckers don't even take bathroom breaks. They just pee in a bottle, or they cut a hole in their floorboards."

I casually began to look around for holes, or bottles, or white powder.

"It's also hard to have a wife and family," he continued. "You're on the road most of the year, and when you're at home, your kids hardly know who you are. Sometimes at the truck stops there will be prostitutes hanging around. I never saw why men would want a hooker . . . until I became a trucker."

At that, he suddenly became quiet. I wanted to change the subject, so I quickly asked, "Do you pick up many hitchhikers?"

His tone lightened. "Oh yeah, I used to always pick 'em up. I like the company, and hitchhikers always have good stories. But I don't pick up as many as I used to. A few years ago I picked up a guy who seemed okay at first. But after riding together for a little bit, he told me I looked like this man his girlfriend had cheated with, and he started attacking me while I was at the wheel."

"Were you hurt?"

"I wasn't hurt too bad, but I could have wrecked. I left that maniac on the side of the interstate, ten miles from the nearest exit, and since then I've been carrying this in the backseat."

The driver reached behind my seat, pulled out a metal baseball bat, and placed it between us.

If I hadn't already been on my best behavior, now I was.

The truck driver said he knew right where the outdoor store was and mentioned that it was a Cabela's.

"I've never heard of Cabela's," I said.

The driver laughed. "Well, sweetie, I'm sure you'll be able to find some socks there."

When we exited the highway and drove toward a building so large that it could have housed the entire town of Port Clinton, I was shocked. Cabela's was as big as Wegmans!

Taking my gear, I thanked the trucker, climbed down the ladder from the shiny blue cab, and waved good-bye as I walked away. My descent from the cab of a semi with a pack on my back and a yellow mop stick in my right hand probably seemed preposterous to the onlookers who stared at me as they filtered into Cabela's, but to me, the entrance felt regal, as if I had just departed a chariot with a golden scepter in my hand.

As I paraded into Cabela's, I was overwhelmed with aisles upon aisles of outdoor "essentials." I honestly didn't know there was so much outdoor gear. Granted, in this store, "outdoor supplies" referred mostly to hunting and fishing gear. I looked to my left and saw a section of the store that looked like an indoor marina, and to my right there were aisles of camo clothes, guns, fishing rods, lures, and beef jerky. After entering Cabela's, I decided that, yes, there *are* rednecks in the mid-Atlantic.

It seemed ironic that all these man-made goods were designed to help folks enjoy the simplicity of the outdoors, when the more stuff I carried on the trail, the more uncomfortable I felt.

I don't want to sound ungrateful, because Cabela's did provide me with the moisture-wicking socks and foot-specific first aid kit that I needed. But though the products were supposed to help people enjoy the great outdoors, it seemed like many of them, like the four-hun-dred-square-foot tents, blow-up camp beds, and solar-powered radios and TVs, would prevent people from truly experiencing nature.

My hitch back to Port Clinton wasn't nearly as exciting as the tractor-trailer ride to Cabela's had been. As soon as I reached town, I headed straight for the trail and by mid-afternoon, I had caught up with Raptor. We spent the night together at Allentown Hiking Club Shelter, and the next morning we hitched into Palmerton to spend another night in town.

Palmerton gave off a better vibe than Duncannon or Port Clinton. In other words, there were people there. We saw men and women walking along the street and going in and out of stores. And although the town did not have a hiker hostel, it did allow thru-hikers to sleep in the city jail.

It wasn't a real prison, in the sense that it no longer housed convicted criminals. It was the town's old jail, located underneath City Hall. The large holding cell had metal bars on the outside and wooden bunks on the inside. It felt safe and secure, especially with Raptor there.

It seemed strange that jails punished people by isolating them from the world. As I looked out a small window that was covered with bars and gave a ground view of the outdoors, there was something appealing about being removed from society.

After picking out my bed in the slammer, I went to take a shower. It was the best shower of the entire trail.

The women's bathroom had open shower stalls with water pressure so hard that it hurt. The water was really hot, but never too hot, and the steam made the entire bathroom feel like a sauna. There were three showerheads right next to each other, and at one point I turned them all on and ran back and forth through them like a kid running through sprinklers. I smiled the entire time and occasionally laughed out loud. At home, I usually reserved smiles and laughs for other people, but on the trail I was learning to smile and laugh just for me, even if no one else was around.

When I finally finished my shower, I had completely fogged up the women's bathroom and was the cleanest I had been since leaving Georgia.

Refreshed, I dug out my cell phone to call my mom. I couldn't wait to tell her I was spending the night in jail!

My mom didn't have much time to talk. She was at my grandfather's eighty-seventh birthday party. Everyone was there: my parents, my brothers, my aunts and uncles, and cousins. I was the only one missing.

The trail didn't mean more to me than my grandfather did. Still, I had chosen to be out here instead of at his birthday party. I started to second-guess my decision not to go home for it. What if this turned out to be his last?

The cell phone was passed around, and with each family member I spoke to, I felt a little more guilty for not being there.

The last person I talked with was my granddad.

The first thing he said was, "I love you, and I am so proud of you." He continued, "You just keep hiking. I love the outdoors, and out of all my grandchildren, I think you're most like me in that way."

I was stunned. I'd never known my granddad felt that way. I mean, I knew he loved the outdoors, but I thought it was the Cabela's type of outdoors—hunting, fishing, and beef jerky. I had never realized that he saw a connection between my time in the woods and his love of outdoor sports.

After I hung up the phone, I no longer felt sad that I had missed my granddad's party. I knew I was where he wanted me to be.

Raptor and I spent the remainder of the evening eating pizza and talking in our cell at the jailhouse. It was like having a slumber party with a fifty-seven-year-old man.

The more I found out about Raptor, the more I liked him. I learned that he had worked in a factory for thirty years, and that he was an avid cyclist, which is probably what made him such a strong hiker. But my favorite story he told me that evening was about running off and eloping.

"So you really did it?" I asked. "You just went and got married without telling anyone?"

"Yep."

"Why?"

"Well, I knew that I loved her and wanted to marry her. It's like the trail. I hear a lot of people say they want to hike the Appalachian Trail, but they never do it. When I want something, I'm gonna do it. I love my wife, and marrying her was the best decision I ever made."

"So was the trail a good decision too?"

"Ha. We'll have to wait and see, but I think so."

At that point we heard a door slam, followed by heavy footsteps descending the stairs.

A short, agitated older man entered the room, turned on the lights, and looked at Raptor and me. Instead of introducing himself to us, he started talking to himself.

He walked over to an empty bunk, threw down his pack, and rummaged through it for his sleeping bag. Once he was situated, he stopped talking to himself and started asking us rapid-fire questions.

"When did you two leave Georgia? Are you hiking together or separately? Who's the better hiker? How many miles do you average per day?"

Raptor and I looked at each other in disbelief. It was like this man was playing some obnoxious trail version of Twenty Questions. Most of the time, he didn't even wait for a response before asking the next question.

Eventually, we learned that this man's name was Neon, which was appropriate, considering he was like an irritated blinking light that screamed incessantly for attention. He had chosen a bunk near Raptor and eventually focused his interrogation on my friend. Since they were close in age, Neon probably viewed Raptor as his primary competition. I pulled out the earplugs that Raptor had given me to block out his snoring and placed them in my ears. Then I pulled my sleeping bag over my head and tried to fall asleep. I didn't feel obligated to say good night or offer an explanation for going to bed early. At this point, I felt like Pennsylvania owed *me* an explanation.

The next morning, I awoke to Neon's boots stomping past my bed. Then I heard him curse at the light switch as he flipped it on. I stayed motionless in my bunk, pretending to be asleep. But I did stealthily remove my earplugs so I could better understand Neon's rants. Apparently, he had been woken up by Raptor's snoring, and since Neon couldn't sleep, he decided that we shouldn't be able to rest either. He complained out loud to himself about his poor night's sleep, while at the same time stuffing a large pizza into a one gallon Ziploc bag. He had brought the pizza with him to the jail cell the night before but hadn't eaten any of it. This morning, he picked up whatever would fit in his hands and mashed it into the bag, showing no respect for the integrity of individual slices. After he secured the bag, he licked the sauce off his fingers, packed up his gear, and left.

I sat up in my bunk and looked at Raptor. He just shook his head, and we both laughed. There was so much absurdity about the mid-Atlantic that it made me appreciate Raptor's normalcy all the more.

We took our time getting ready that morning, knowing that an early departure for the trail would put us in close proximity to our cellmate.

The climb outside of Palmerton was unlike anything else I had experienced on the trail. We had to use our hands and feet to scramble up a rocky mountainside, only to arrive at a desolate wasteland on top of the ridge. There weren't any trees, there weren't any animals, there weren't even any weeds. It was completely barren.

"Did you know this was a Superfund site?" asked Raptor.

"Super fun? What makes it super fun?"

Raptor laughed, "No Odyssa, *Superfun-Duh*."

"Oh. What does that mean?"

"It means someone screwed up, did something really harmful to the environment, and then the government spent our tax dollars trying to clean it up."

"What happened here?"

"There used to be zinc plants in and around Palmerton, and the emissions they let off killed the vegetation and polluted the river. If you think it looks bad now, think about what it must have looked like twenty years ago, and think about how bad those emissions must have been for the lungs of the people who lived here."

I tried to take shallow breaths until we climbed off the ridge and back into the forest.

After making it safely past the Superfund site, Raptor and I decided to hike separately, but we agreed to reconvene at Delaware Water Gap. Delaware Water Gap was a source of confusion for me because the term "water gap" made me think it might be a river crossing, but the words were printed in bold in my Data Book, which meant it had to be a town. In addition, the phrase had me erroneously convinced that the trail went through the state of Delaware.

The one thing I did know about Delaware Water Gap was that there was pie there. Warren Doyle had given us lots of trail pointers at the institute, and I had made plenty of notes in my Data Book. Beside Duncannon, I had scribbled, "DO NOT STAY THERE!!!!!" But beside Delaware Water Gap, it read, "Mmmmm . . . pie!"

I was excited about the thought of pie, and I hiked quickly toward its promise. That's when I had my second encounter with Neon.

"Hi, Neon," I called.

He didn't respond, but he did increase his pace.

I hiked up behind him. Instead of stepping to the side of the trail and letting me pass, he started walking faster. I kept up.

"Excuse me, can I get by?"

He pretended he couldn't hear me.

I shifted to the left and then the right, trying to pass, but he shadowed my movements and wouldn't allow me to go around him. It felt like I was being boxed out underneath a basketball net.

Finally I faked left, spun right, and hiked past him. Score!

Neon was the first person I had met who was actually trying to race people to Katahdin. It was fine if he wanted to hike fast, I didn't have any problem with that. But he should do it because he wanted to hike fast, not in an attempt to race other people.

The next time I saw Neon, I was sitting on the patio of a bakery eating apple pie in the town of Delaware Water Gap, above the Delaware River, but definitely not in the state of Delaware.

Neon did not stop for pie. He just kept hiking. I hoped that he would beat me to Katahdin so I wouldn't have to see him again.

That night, Raptor and I stayed in Delaware Water Gap at a church hostel, where the congregation had converted the sanctuary's basement into a bunkroom and common area for hikers. The hostel had a great shower, a comfy couch, and it was stocked with pie that I had brought back to share with Raptor.

After reducing my daily miles and spending several nights in towns, my feet felt much better. I also had started to carry pink flip-flops with red hearts on them, which I had picked up for three dollars in

Palmerton. When I wasn't hiking, I would put on the flip-flops to let my feet air out. They also made me feel pretty, which helped my morale.

That evening, I told Raptor that I wanted to start hiking more miles and spending more nights on the trail since my feet were feeling better.

"Yeah, right," he said. "You just want to race Neon!"

"How'd you know?" I laughed.

We stayed up talking and eating pie well past my normal hiker-bedtime. There was a lot to celebrate, after all. This was our last night in Pennsylvania, and I couldn't wait to leave.

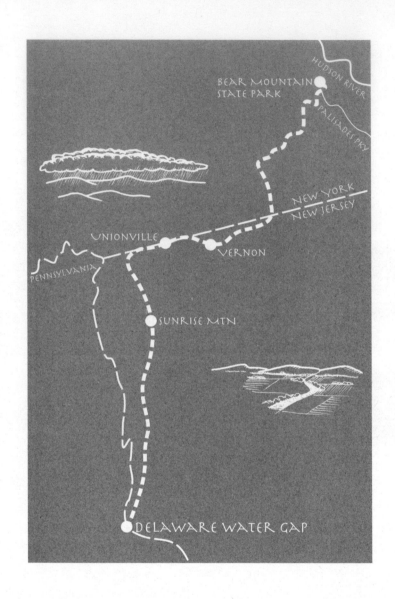

15

MORTALITY

DELAWARE WATER GAP, PA, TO BEAR MOUNTAIN STATE PARK, NY—107.9 MILES

The rocks continue into New Jersey just past the glacier-formed Sunfish Pond to High Point and then begin to disperse. The soft earth is a welcome transition, but during a heavy rain, the path quickly turns to mud. There is an enchanting mile-long boardwalk that spans a mile of protected wetland near Vernon, New Jersey, and a scenic dirt path that leads through a marsh and bird sanctuary in Unionville, New York. Thirty-four miles north of New York City, the trail crosses the Palisades Parkway and climbs up Bear Mountain before descending to the Hudson River—at 124 feet above sea level, this is the lowest point of the trail.

After 230 grueling miles in Pennsylvania, I had made it to New Jersey. I expected the rocks to disappear immediately when I left Pennsylvania, but they didn't. I also thought things would suddenly get better in New Jersey, but I was wrong.

For one thing, I didn't think I would miss Raptor as much as I did. But my first night in New Jersey, when I found myself in Gren Anderson Shelter alone with Neon, I felt like I had made a mistake by hiking ahead.

Neon insisted on setting mousetraps throughout the shelter. I don't know if he carried the traps in his pack or if they were already in the shelter when he arrived, but he baited the devices and encircled our quarters with them.

"I don't want any mousetraps around me," I told him.

"The mice are going to get your food."

"A mouse hasn't gotten into my food so far. Plus, I move around a lot in my sleep and I don't want to roll onto a trap. And I always have to pee in the middle of the night, so I'll probably end up stepping on one too."

Neon rearranged two traps to give me an aisle out of the shelter if I needed it. But I still wasn't appeased.

"It's not the mice's fault, you know. It's our fault. If we wouldn't lure them here with our crumbs and dinner smells, then they would never be here. They're just trying to survive."

Despite my aversion to rodents at the beginning of my trip, they now seemed kind of cute. After all, I was in their world, and I had no more right to a shelter than they did. Perhaps in a house I would have felt differently, but after living and walking in these woods, I believed the trail was not a place to kill for convenience, but a place to respect life, to watch it and learn from it.

I had not quite fallen asleep before a trap snapped, and I heard a brief squeal.

"Gotcha," Neon gloated.

The next morning, I awoke and left the shelter before 6:00 AM to put distance between Neon and me.

It was a beautiful, warm morning, one of the first days on the trail that I could hike in shorts instead of pants. The grass had changed from faint lime green sprouts to dark green clusters dotted with small purple flowers. The promise of new life abounded.

I was about eighty feet from the top of Sunrise Mountain when I pulled out my camera to capture the stunning vista below me. True to its name, the mountain framed a rising sun, whose majestic ascent highlighted the mist-filled valley below in a glowing light.

I embraced the stillness and tranquility of the moment. Even after packing away my camera and continuing to climb, I remained mesmerized by the expansive valley to the east. It wasn't until I came upon flat terrain and the open-air pavilion that marked the summit that I looked away from the valley.

I froze.

My stomach lurched, and I felt sick.

It couldn't be . . .

I stood frozen, and the seconds felt like minutes as I tried to process what my eyes were telling me.

There, twenty feet away, a limp and motionless body swayed gently from a rope tied to the rafters of the pavilion.

I saw the rope tied to the rafters, tautly connecting to the neck of a young man. His face was pale and framed by smooth, black hair. His eyes were closed, and his head was cocked to the side above his gruesome collar of rope.

He was wearing a maroon shirt and loose green khakis. His hands were tied behind his back. His fingers were clasped together, and the thin twine was cutting into his skin. His black shoes pointed to the cement floor, with nothing between them and the ground but three feet of air.

I couldn't breathe; my stomach churned and my eyes watered. I turned and ran. I tried to run as fast as I could, but everything seemed to be happening in slow motion, and my feet stumbled over the rocks.

The scene I had just witnessed was preserved in perfect detail in my mind, but my thoughts were moving too rapidly to provide answers.

What had I just seen? Was it a suicide? Was it a murder? Were there other people around? Was this a sick joke? Why were his hands tied? Had I really just seen what I thought I saw, or was my mind playing tricks on me? What do I do?

What do I do? That question stopped the stream of inquiries, and when I was about four hundred yards from the pavilion, I stopped, pulled out my cell phone, and called 911.

I spoke with a dispatcher, who immediately patched me through to the local police. I choked out the details to the police officer. He began to reassure me and give me instructions—and that's when I lost him. My cell phone had dropped the call.

Frantic, I again dialed 911 and began to talk to a different dispatcher. I told her the same thing that I had told the first dispatcher and the cop, but she refused to reconnect me with police.

"I need to know where your car is," she said.

"I don't have a car. I hiked here."

"Well, where did you park your car?"

"I didn't park anywhere. I'm an Appalachian Trail thru-hiker."

"What county are you in?"

"I don't know what county I'm in. I'm at Sunrise Mountain in New Jersey."

"So where do you live in New Jersey?"

"I don't live in New Jersey."

"Then where is your car?"

"Please, I just came across a dead body, I need to talk to the police. I was just talking to them and I got cut off. Please connect me to the police."

"First tell me where your car is. Then I will connect you to the police."

I was scared, I knew I would probably lose cell reception again, and all I wanted to do was talk with the police. Losing my composure, I begin crying into the phone and asking over and over if I could talk to the police. The woman insisted that I calm down and refused to patch me through. But her chiding simply increased my hysterics.

Finally, I took a deep breath and began mumbling an explanation of thru-hiking.

The woman interrupted my second sentence and asked how hiking some trail that started in Georgia was relevant to a death in New Jersey.

"Who are you talking to?" I heard a man's voice in the background addressing the dispatcher, and then I heard him say, "Patch her through to the police *now*."

When I was reconnected with the police, they seemed to know more about the body and the pavilion than I remembered telling them. It didn't make sense until they called me Susan.

"My name's not Susan," I replied.

"You're not Susan? Have you spoken with the officers at the pavilion?"

"There aren't any officers at the pavilion."

"Yes, there are."

Twenty minutes must have passed since I talked with the initial officer, and within that time another woman, a local day-hiker, had approached Sunrise Mountain pavilion from a parking lot on the north side of the mountain and witnessed the same sight that now haunted me.

The police had been alerted by my initial call, but after I lost the connection, Susan called, and from that point on, they assumed we were the same person. It wasn't until I assured them that I was not Susan and did not have an officer standing beside me that they sorted out the confusion.

The voice on the other line then asked me to approach the pavilion and talk with an officer.

With a weak and shaky voice, I responded, "Is the body still there?"

"Yes, the body won't be removed until the crime scene investigation is complete."

With gasping breaths, I said, "I . . . I don't want to see it again."

The officer understood, and he instructed me to approach the summit while staying on the phone with him, and to call up to the pavilion when I was within earshot. He would instruct an officer to come down and meet me.

Within a few minutes, two officers were standing beside me. Gently and informally, they began to ask me questions—first for my sake, then for their own.

They asked me where I was hiking from, who I was hiking with, and if I had any friends or family in the area that they could contact.

Then they eased into the mandatory questions: whether I knew the victim, if I had seen anyone else this morning, whether I had noticed anything unusual the night before, and when I had first arrived at the scene.

Then one of the officers asked, "Do you have any questions for us?"

I looked up and sputtered, "Wa–was it a suicide?"

"We won't know for sure until after the investigation, but all initial signs point to suicide."

"Why were his hands tied?" I asked.

"Sometimes when people hang themselves, they'll tie their hands behind their back. That prevents them from struggling and pulling at the rope."

The answer gave me a pain in my chest and I suddenly felt nauseated. Why would a person try to kill himself if he knew that he would struggle against it? What the officer was saying, what I was hearing—it sounded so unnatural.

When the officer continued to explain the details of asphyxiation, I quickly asked him to stop. He did. Then he asked, "Is this your first stiff?"

At sunrise, this young man had had a story, a family, a lifetime of contributions and interactions. And now, only a few short hours later, he was simply a "stiff"?

My disgust must have been apparent, because without waiting for a response, the other officer quickly changed the subject.

"We can take you into the station to talk to a counselor if you want."

"Yeah," said the first one, "or we could help you find a motel room if you want to spend a night off the trail."

"If you want us to contact friends or family for you, we will."

The cops were trying to be helpful, but none of the options they presented seemed like the right choice. I was having a hard time making decisions. I didn't want to speak with a counselor, a hotel room would be too expensive, and I definitely didn't want to tell my parents. My mom would never let me keep hiking after this.

"You don't have to decide right now. Why don't you just think about it?" suggested the first officer.

Then the second officer tried to change the subject again.

"Have you seen a bear yet?" he said.

"Um . . . no, but I want to."

"Oh, you're bound to see a bear here. This is New Jersey. We have bears everywhere, around every turn. Trust me, you're not going to leave the state without seeing one."

Bears were a point of common interest that kept me from crying. And not knowing how else to comfort me, the officers mumbled about bears for ten minutes until the chief officer walked down the hill and asked me: "Have you decided what you want to do?"

"I want to hike," I said.

He silently looked at me and nodded his head.

It was the hardest day of my life.

The only hiker I saw after leaving the pavilion was Neon, and I was in no mood to answer his questions about why the trail had been rerouted and what all the police were doing at Sunrise Mountain.

I had tears in my eyes for most of the day. I wanted to call someone, but I didn't want my parents to find out what had happened, and I didn't know what to say to my friends. At one point, I wasn't paying attention to the trail and I became lost on a spur. It took almost an hour for me to find my way back.

Despite my sadness and confusion, I was glad that I was hiking. I felt like if I had gone into town with the officers, I wouldn't have wanted to get back on the trail. It would have been good to talk to a counselor about what had happened, but the trail provided its own sort of therapy.

There was something about hiking, something about making forward progress that felt healing. In a way, it was good to be processing the death alone on the trail. I could deal with it in my own time and think through it completely. I didn't have to repress thoughts of the suicide and try to go on with everyday life. Instead, I was forced to face it head on. I was forced to think about what had happened, what I had seen, and then I could start to work my way through it, one step at a time.

I have never been through a day where I experienced such a vast array of emotions. At first, I was angry with the victim, but then I was moved with sympathy for his family. I questioned why God had put me in this situation, and how the smallest of choices could have changed or prevented the morning's events.

Mostly, I was upset over how premeditated the victim's death seemed, and how he had tied his hands so he wouldn't struggle. I think the twine around his hands bothered me most, even more than the rope around his neck. Tying your hands is admitting that every natural instinct is to fight and live.

I wondered why he had chosen to do it here, in nature. Why couldn't he have done it in a dark room somewhere? And why did he choose hanging? Why such a dramatic death?

Eventually, the questions began to fade, and the sense of physical illness and tension started to subside. I began to sense something larger and more powerful at work in me. And although I didn't come to an understanding of that morning's events, I was filled with gratitude for the joy, hope, and love that filled my life. I thanked God for the warm breeze that caressed my skin, the chirping birds that sang to me in the woods, and for my family and friends back home. I was thankful for my life, and for the life all around me.

That afternoon, the sky opened up and flooded the ground, but that evening the rain stopped, the sky cleared, and the sunset cast a flaming orange glow across the sky.

When I went to bed, I was still shaken, but I sensed God's presence and felt very aware of all the blessings that filled my life.

At sunrise, I awoke and began hiking. I had planned to hike through the day, but after an hour and a half, I came to a road. A stile separated the trail from the road, and as I climbed over it, a car driving down the highway slowed down and pulled off beside me.

The lady in the driver's seat rolled down her window. "Hey, I'm headed up the road to Vernon. If you want to go to town, I can take you there."

It's rare to be offered a ride without hitchhiking, and I didn't want to pass it up. I didn't need to resupply, but I figured that a hot lunch might raise my spirits.

Upon arriving in the small town and climbing out of the car, I heard church bells ringing. I had totally forgotten that it was Sunday. As I looked around, I could make out four churches within a quarter mile.

It was strange that the woman had dropped me off here instead of at a grocery store or restaurant.

As I continued to listen to the bells, they seemed to chime with the promise of comfort. I followed the music to an Episcopal church that had a hiker hostel in the basement, and I decided I would attend the service there. However, as I approached the front door of the Episcopal church, a neighboring Methodist church caught my eye. I had no preference between Methodist and Episcopal churches, but a sudden inexplicable urge, like a strong wind, built up inside my body and drew me to the Methodist chapel.

I left my pack by the side of the building and slipped inside the sanctuary to claim a seat by myself in the back pew.

The service started with the hymn "In the Garden." I could remember my grandmother humming this song around the house when I was little, but I didn't remember all the words. That morning as the congregation sang, "*And He walks with me, and He talks with me. And He tells me I am his own,*" the lyrics returned to me and flooded my heart.

The scripture reading that followed was Psalm 23, a chapter I had heard so many times that it had lost its meaning. But that morning I recited the passage as if I were speaking the words for the first time.

"*He makes me lie down in green pastures, He leads me beside quiet waters, He restores my soul. He guides me in paths of righteousness for His name's sake. Even though I walk through the valley of the shadow of death, I will fear no evil, for You are with me.*"

The pastor used those words to preach a sermon on comfort. He talked about allowing God to comfort and heal us, and how we have a responsibility to try to comfort others. At the end of his message, he concluded with a story.

"There is a woman in our congregation who came across a suicide yesterday," he began.

What? I looked to my left and my right and then grew red in the face. How did he know I was here?

"She has stayed in contact with the police and the family of the victim, and she has several ways that we can pray for them and serve them this week. If you have time to make them a meal or serve the family in other ways, meet Susan at the choir pew after church."

Susan? That was the name of the woman who had approached Sunrise Mountain pavilion from the north while I was on my cell phone. She was here?

After the service, in a congregation of less than forty people, thirty miles away from Sunrise Mountain, I met Susan.

My conversation with her gave me more details about the young man and the investigation. While I had set off hiking into the woods after my brief talk with the officers, Susan had spent much of the day with the police.

"So was it really a suicide?" I asked.

"Yes, he left a note for his family at home before he did it."

"How old was he?"

"Twenty-four. He grew up just a few miles down the road. He was a graphic designer and a musician. He had moved to the city to work, but he had come back home recently. His parents and sisters are taking it very hard."

As sorrowful as it was, learning about the young man's life helped me to focus on what he had contributed to the world, as opposed to what he had taken away. He was more than the "stiff" that the officers referred to; he was a brother and a son, an artist, and a gifted instrumentalist.

Then, more for comparison than compassion, I asked Susan, "How are you? Are you okay?"

Susan teared up. "Yesterday was a hard day. But it made me appreciate my faith, my family, and my life more. It made me realize how much I take for granted. It also makes me want to help people who may be struggling and don't know where they can turn. I'll never forget what I saw at the pavilion, but I hope I can use my experience to become more understanding. I promised myself that I would try to be a better friend and family member, and a better listener."

After my talk with Susan, I felt empty—in a good way. It was like I had been carrying this heavy load, and being able to share it with someone who understood, who *really* understood, made me feel lighter.

I wish that I could say things got better over the next few days, but they didn't. I still had times when I enjoyed being on the trail—like when I saw a woodpecker knocking on a tree, or a patch of wildflowers lining the trail—but overall I was not doing well.

I was frustrated that even though it had been more than two days since I left Sunrise Mountain, the scene I witnessed for just a few seconds remained present in acute detail in my mind. I couldn't remember the name of the officers I had spoken with or what they looked like, but every aspect of the victim was still vivid, especially his pale face and swollen hands; hands that had struggled and bled against the rope that bound them.

As I hiked around turns in the trail, I would experience flashbacks to Sunrise Mountain. My mind would trick me into thinking that every loose limb hanging from a tree was a dangling body. And I became uneasy at any shelter that had rafters in it. The weather didn't help either. Ever since leaving Vernon, New Jersey, I had been hiking in a cold, steady rain. New York was stuck in a nor'easter, and I was stuck in New York.

I began to feel rundown, not because of the event of two days before, but from the lingering effect it was having on me. I realized that the incident would always be a part of who I was, and the vivid image of a man hanging from the rafters would always be stored away in my subconscious. Although I had left New Jersey and entered New York, I knew that it didn't matter how fast I hiked or how many miles I put in. I could never outrun the events at Sunrise Mountain pavilion. The suicide had happened, and although I knew the pain would ease, I still agonized over the permanence of the act.

When I arrived at the top of Bear Mountain, I found myself completely alone. The helpful tip I had left myself in my Data Book read "Bear Mountain—Very CROWDED." Since Bear Mountain State Park was just forty miles from New York City, I figured it must be crowded most of the time—just not in a nor'easter, and not when I needed company.

The precipitation permeated my clothes and soaked my skin, and as the sun sank towards the horizon, the temperature dropped. I could see my breath in the air, my nose was cold to the touch, and my fingers looked white. I was in the midst of a twenty-six-mile stretch of trail that didn't have a shelter, and I was inside a state park that didn't allow tent camping. I hiked to the end of the park, where I thought I could stay in the Bear Mountain Lodge, but when I arrived, I found it was closed for renovations.

I tried to get back to the trail from the lodge, but I became disoriented and wandered over to Bear Mountain Lake's paved pedestrian trail. I felt out of place; I was no longer on the trail, but I couldn't find civilization either. Shivering and trying to hold back tears, I stopped under a covered park information kiosk to try to regain my composure. I looked down to the lake and saw a mother goose sheltering three goslings under her wing.

I couldn't hold back my tears any longer, and I pulled out my cell phone to call my parents.

My dad, hearing the tremors in my voice as I told the story, insisted that I get to a road and find the nearest lodging, promising to pay for several nights of rest. My mom, in the meantime, had looked online and found that Bear Mountain Lodge was operating an alternate inn during the renovations.

My parents stayed on the phone with me as I wandered around the lake and up a neighboring hill to find the obscure, dimly lit inn.

The rooms were dark, the attendant was inept, and the only food available was in a fifty-year-old vending machine in the lobby, but in exchange for an outrageous $100 fee, I had a clean, dry bed, a musty room, and a warm bath with brown water.

After treating myself to a $1.50 dinner from the vending machine and a long, murky bath, I was ready for bed, so when my cell phone started ringing, it took all the emotional energy I had to pick it up and talk with Magic Momma.

I had exchanged numbers with Nightwalker's mom in the Shenandoahs, and she was calling to check on me. She had read about the suicide in another hiker's online trail journal. I knew that news traveled quickly down the trail by word of mouth and shelter logs, but I hadn't thought about people finding out through blogs and internet journals.

"Oh my God, I'm so glad you picked up," Magic Momma said. "I've been worried sick about you. How are you?"

"Oh, I've been better, but I'll be okay," I said.

"Well, where are you? I'll come pick you up."

"I'm at Bear Mountain State Park, but I've paid for my room already and it's almost midnight. Don't worry, I'll be all right. Really."

"Well, I'm just an hour away in Connecticut, so if you need anything tonight, or tomorrow, or the next day—if you *ever* need anything, call me. Okay?

"Okay."

I had no intention of calling Magic Momma back, but I knew that she wouldn't hang up unless I left it as a possibility. It was nice of her to call, but I was fine. Really, I was fine.

I called Magic Momma at 9:00 the next morning.

After sleeping for six hours, I dressed in wet hiking clothes, put on my pack, walked through the lobby and out the front door. That was as far as I got.

It was forty degrees, pouring down rain, and the wind was bending even the strongest trees. I waited under the hotel awning for five minutes, trying to find the motivation to start hiking, but it never came.

I decided to stand under the awning for another five minutes, then force myself to hike. But as I looked at my watch to mark the time, I noticed it was May twenty-fifth.

It was my birthday.

There was no way I was doing this on my birthday.

I went back to the front desk to reclaim my room key and returned to bed, where I slept for another two hours. And when I woke up, I called Magic Momma.

She was thrilled to hear that I wasn't hiking in the nor'easter, and she offered to pick me up after she finished a half-day at work. I agreed, and I was excited to see her, but it still felt odd accepting help from someone I had only met once.

When Magic Momma arrived, she greeted me with a warm hug and reassuring words. I don't know why I had hesitated to call her or accept her help, because after fifteen seconds in her presence I already felt much better.

I put my gear in her car, which didn't smell quite so much of hikers as it had in the Shenandoahs, and together we drove over the Tappan Zee Bridge to her home in Stamford, Connecticut.

We talked and laughed the entire way. Magic Momma was the

kindest, warmest woman I had ever met, and for the first time in a long time, I felt at ease. When we arrived at the house, Magic Momma positioned me on the couch in her living room with a selection of movies and snacks, and then stationed Tazzy, her affectionate black lab, on the floor beside me. I spent the rest of the afternoon watching romantic comedies and letting Tazzy lick my hand. There is no better medicine than the unconditional love of a black lab.

That night, when Magic Momma's husband came home, the three of us went out to dinner, and they treated me to a meal at one of the best restaurants in Stamford. Together, we celebrated my birthday with a bowl of pasta, a bottle of red wine, and a chocolate lava cake. There were no tangible gifts to unwrap, but their unexpected kindness and overwhelming hospitality were the best birthday presents that I had ever received.

After dinner, I returned to a strange house in an unfamiliar part of the country with people I hardly knew, but I felt completely at home. My opinions of humanity had traveled on a roller coaster that week, but because of Magic Momma's compassion, my faith in people had not only been restored, it had been improved.

The next morning, Magic Momma asked me if I wanted to go back to the trail, but she wasn't talking about Bear Mountain State Park. She was talking about driving down to northern New Jersey to surprise Mooch and Nightwalker.

Magic Momma and the newly named Mr. Magic both decided to take a day off from work, pack up the car with food and drinks, and drive down to find the boys. Magic Momma knew the boys' location because they planned to receive a mail drop that day. Mooch and Nightwalker didn't have a clue we were coming, and they had no idea that Magic Momma had picked me up off the trail. So when we jumped out from behind the car to greet them, they were surprised to see us all, especially me.

They had heard about what happened at Sunrise Mountain, but they didn't mention it. And they never asked why I was with the Magics; they both knew Magic Momma well enough to figure that out on their own. Instead, they each gave me a huge bear hug, and then we picked up right where we left off.

"Odyssa, I've been meaning to tell you this since we split up, but you stink!" Mooch said. "In fact, I think you smell worse than most of the guys out here. I mean, you smell okay now, but when I gave you a hug at the end of the Shenandoahs, it nearly knocked me out. And I'm glad you're here, because I've been waiting four hundred miles to tell you that."

"Thanks, Mooch," I said. "I'll try to work on that. How's the butt rash?"

Everyone laughed. It was the first time I had felt lighthearted in days. Together at the roadside, we ate and recounted our stories from the mid-Atlantic. Then, when the boys were full, I hiked six miles with them to the next road crossing.

In general, I held it as a principle not to walk more than I had to on this journey. And although I had already hiked these six miles, and they in no way helped me get any closer to Maine, it just seemed like I needed to take a few steps back before I could go forward.

I needed to remember what the trail was like before the mid-Atlantic and before the suicide. I needed to remember the adventures I had in North Carolina and Tennessee, the confidence I had gained in Virginia, and the fun I had with the boys in Shenandoah National Park. I needed to reflect on all the good memories from the trail, because that made me want to keep hiking.

Hiking with Mooch and Nightwalker made it easy to focus on the good. During the first few miles, Mooch sang us a few songs and told us a few jokes before he was forced to separate himself from the group and take a long bathroom break in the woods. I was left walking alone with Nightwalker.

"I was really worried about you," he said. "I can't imagine what that would have been like."

"I've had better days. But your mom helped a lot, and so have you guys."

"Well, if you ever want to talk to us about it, or if you want to hike with us for a while, we're here for you."

"Thanks."

Even though six miles was a relatively short distance compared to what I had been hiking, I made more progress that afternoon than at any other point on the trail. It had been a hard, sad week, but after those six miles, I knew that I was going to make it to Maine.

I knew that I was going to make it to Maine, but restarting the trail from Bear Mountain State Park took me longer than I thought it would.

Magic Momma held me captive with the lure of food, a bed, clean clothes, and multiple trips to the trail to visit Mooch and Nightwalker. She thought I should take a few days off to rest and spend some time hiking with the boys before setting out on my own again. And she didn't have to work too hard to convince me.

When I was truly ready to return to the trail, my mom decided I couldn't get back on until I first visited my aunt and uncle in Wallingford, Connecticut. She said they wanted to see me, and it would be rude to be this close and not pay them a visit, but I knew that she really wanted a mental health checkup. She needed a family member to make sure I was okay before I got back on the trail, so I obliged her and took the train from Stamford to New Haven, where my aunt picked me up.

I love my aunt. If I had her energy, I would probably be in Maine already. After a day spent following my aunt around central Connecticut, I was convinced she had more endurance than anyone I had met on the trail.

The first stop we made that morning was a grocery store, where she insisted on buying every food item I might want for my next resupply. Then we went to the house where my wonderful uncle was making a breakfast of scrambled eggs, smoked salmon, fresh berries, and muffins. I enjoyed the food and needed the energy, because as soon as I placed the last berry in my mouth, my aunt and I were off again.

She wanted to give me a walking tour of the prep school where my uncle taught, a driving tour of their hometown of Wallingford, and a multi-modal tour of nearby New Haven. Somewhere in between hearing about the prep school's annual fund and architecture, looking for cows in the fields of Wallingford, and visiting the libraries and museums at Yale, I decided that I would be less tired if I'd simply spent the day hiking thirty miles on the trail. Sure, I had just gotten to see two volumes of the Gutenberg Bible at the Beinecke Rare Collections Library, but all I wanted to do was sit down to eat something.

About the same time that I decided I couldn't set foot in another museum, my aunt decided that she had fulfilled her quota of cultural enrichment for the day, and we finally stopped for a snack, followed by a visit to the local outfitters.

After fifteen hundred miles of shoulder pain, I decided that maybe I didn't need to toughen up; instead, maybe my brother's hand-me-down backpack just didn't fit. And although I'd had visions of standing on Katahdin with my external-frame pack and mop stick, I was ready to replace my borrowed backpack with something a little less sadistic.

A nice young man named Jeremy, who looked outdoorsy but probably wasn't, helped me pick out a pack. I told him specifically what brands and models most thru-hikers used, and even went so far as to suggest certain weight and capacity specifications, but somehow he managed to talk me into one of the heaviest and most expensive packs.

At this stage of the trail, a comfortable pack was worth any cost, even $360, which was the price of the new pack I bought.

After receiving a passing mental health grade and replacing my pack, I was finally ready to get back on the trail. It was time to finish what I started.

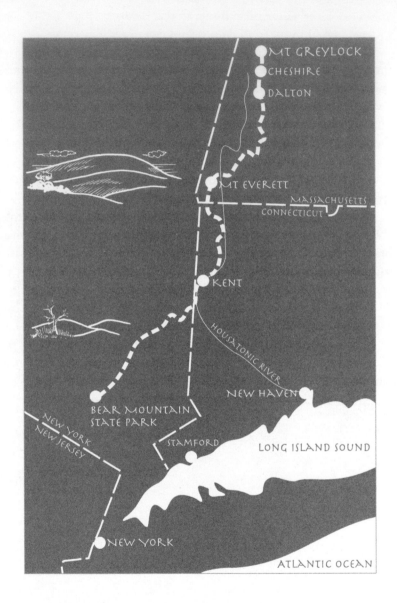

16

PERSEVERANCE

BEAR MOUNTAIN STATE PARK, NY, TO MOUNT GREYLOCK, MA—183.9 MILES

Connecticut has a little of everything: beautiful rolling farm-land, a long stroll along the Housatonic River, a steady boulder climb outside Kent, and an untouched ravine just before Massachusetts. Plus, a determined hiker can walk through the entire state in two days. Massachusetts, on the other hand, is like Connecticut's less attractive half-sister. It has some nice features that run in the family, but it also has bogs and bugs—lots of bugs.

My transition back to the trail wasn't as smooth as I would have hoped. While I was mentally ready to be back, my body had forgotten how to hike. Up until this point, hiking twenty to thirty miles a day had been routine, but after five days of rest, my muscles felt like they had atrophied, and now I had to work much harder for my miles.

Even more frustrating was the fact that my new $360 pack was not an improvement over my old one. Though the majority of the pack weight no longer rested on my shoulders, now it dug into my haunches. There were two metal pack supports, called "stays," which ran the length of the pack, and their pointy ends dug into the outside of my butt cheeks. They rubbed hard against the top layer of skin, giving me open blisters that were aggravated with every step. The waist belt also hugged a little tighter than I would have liked, and at one point it pinched a nerve that sent a numb feeling shooting down my thigh to my knee. And while that wasn't a good feeling, at least it didn't hurt.

One positive was that the weather was amazing, much better than it had been at Bear Mountain several days before. My first day back was pleasantly warm and complemented by a cool breeze.

After spending my first day back on the trail alone, I was surprised the next morning to come upon a crowd of thru-hikers. A crowd?

I hadn't seen any thru-hikers besides Mooch, Nightwalker, and Neon in weeks. And now there were five thru-hikers who were just getting back on the trail after a town stop in Kent, Connecticut. The group included four boys and one girl. The girl, named Rainbow, had hiked the southern half of the trail last year and was finishing the section from Harpers Ferry to Katahdin this summer. She wore a long, earthy skirt and a cotton shirt, neither of which were traditional hiker apparel. She also carried a blow-up pink flamingo in her pack, and that wasn't exactly normal, either.

For my part, I didn't care what she carried or what she wore; she was a thru-hiker, she was around my age, and she was a girl! Although I enjoyed the presence of all five thru-hikers, I was drawn to Rainbow above the rest.

Male thru-hikers always talked about how there weren't enough women on the trail. I completely agreed. The guys said that after a few hundred miles of hiking, they actually develop "trail goggles." Trail goggles are much like beer goggles, meaning that after a while on the trail, almost any woman looks good.

One male thru-hiker elaborated on the concept, telling us, "I was in a town for a resupply and I saw a woman walk into a grocery store. I realized that I hadn't seen a woman in five days. I wasn't very close to her, but I could tell that she was a female, and she moved, so I liked her."

The strange thing was, I had trail goggles too—and it wasn't for the boys. The boys looked worse the farther I traveled down the trail. They were the only hikers I saw, and they appeared less human and more like wild animals the longer they were on the trail. Their facial hair grew over everything but their eye sockets, and they would spend time at the shelters in the evenings picking the bugs and crumbs out of each other's beards. It was evidence for the theory of evolution and a sign that we might in fact be able to devolve back into chimpanzees.

Rainbow was beautiful, and I missed the company of other women, so I walked and talked with her for the rest of the day. I listened to her describe the organic chicken farm where she worked in the Southwest, and tried to console her when she mentioned how much she missed her girlfriend—that must have disappointed the goggle-eyed boys.

That evening, the two of us decided not to stop and spend the night at a shelter with the rest of the hikers. Instead, we hiked a little further and found a campsite next to the sprawling Housatonic River.

The water was golden as the setting sun hit the surface, and tall purple wildflowers lined the grassy banks. I felt full, happy, and at peace. I had a new friend, I was in a new place, and everything around me was beautiful.

Before I went to bed, I decided to bathe in the river. It was the first time on the trail that I was able to completely submerge my naked body into a water source. It felt so good to be surrounded by the flowing water. I would take a breath and then sink under the surface of the water and feel the current wrap around me, holding me lovingly until I had to go back up for more air.

So far on the trail, either the water had been too cold for bathing or I had been in the company of male thru-hikers. I decided long ago, while hiking with Moot, that I wasn't going to skinny-dip when there were boys in the vicinity. But tonight it was just Rainbow and me, in my first and only all-girl campout of the entire trip.

The Housatonic River is beautiful, and it's level. Ninety-nine percent of the trail fell into the categories of "difficult" or "more difficult," but along the river the walking was actually easy.

I traveled along the soft riverbank and then back into the rolling Connecticut countryside. I didn't see Rainbow after leaving camp that morning, but I did stop to eat lunch with Texas Ranger at a shelter. Texas Ranger was a thru-hiker who I had met back in Virginia. He was friendly, outgoing, and aside from Raptor and Neon, he was one of the few fifty year-old hikers who was still at the head of the pack.

Texas Ranger hadn't seen me since I'd bought my mop stick almost nine hundred miles ago, and he couldn't get over what a wonderful accessory it had become.

"It's great," he said. "I love it! A mop stick? Who would think about using a mop stick as a hiking pole? That's gotta be the best piece of gear I've seen all trip. You know what would be funny? You should change your trail name to Mop 'n Glow. You're always so happy, and now you hike with a mop stick. It couldn't be more appropriate."

I laughed. "Texas Ranger, you can call me whatever you want. But I was Odyssa on top of Springer Mountain, and I want to sign Odyssa at the Katahdin register, so I think I'll stick with what I've got."

When I first learned about trail names, I thought they were just a fun tradition that provided anonymity, but now they were so much more. Odyssa wasn't just a nickname; it was a second identity. Thinking back to pre-trail Jen, there was no way that she could have hiked this far. There was no way she could have gone through all the good and the bad, the hard and the ugly, that Odyssa had experienced. Jen would never have crawled into the cab of a semi-truck with a man she didn't know, Jen wouldn't have been able to deal with seeing snakes every day, and she wouldn't have been able to cope with a suicide or rely on complete strangers for help. But Odyssa was a totally different person.

It was funny to think back to Springer Mountain, where I had chosen "Odyssa" on a whim, as a way to avoid unflattering names that drew attention to my long legs and lack of curves. But now Odyssa felt completely appropriate. I had experienced enough obstacles, magical encounters, and diversions to feel like an epic Homeric character. And like the legendary Odysseus, I was on a journey home. But maybe home wasn't a physical place at all, but rather a state of truly knowing myself and feeling at peace with who I was.

Maybe that was the point of trail names: to recognize the person that you would become on the trail. For me, the distance between Jen and Odyssa marked the journey between naïveté and experience. I knew that when I reached Katahdin, Odyssa would be a person far removed from the girl who started the trail. I just hoped I could take Odyssa back home with me, and that Jen would get along with her.

That night at the shelter, I felt a little less like Odyssa and a little more like Jen.

It had been a great day, a beautiful day, but as night approached and I hiked off-trail to nearby Riga Lean-To, I discovered that I was the only one there. I hadn't spent the night alone since the suicide.

A few weeks ago, spending the night alone wouldn't have bothered me. I had slept on my own in shelters and on the ground many times on the trail. But now it was different. I wasn't ready to be alone at night.

I hesitantly ate my dinner and prepared my sleeping bag. I prayed that another hiker would come and join me, but then when the sun disappeared, I prayed the exact opposite. I was scared that I would be hurt or threatened. The fear was making me feel sick, and I would have given anything to be somewhere else. But there was nothing I could do. The darkness had trapped me.

I lay awake that evening in fits of terror and insecurity. I tried to keep my thoughts positive, but thinking about my family and friends only made me feel more alone.

I felt unsafe on the trail and foolish for wanting to hike it alone. My mind kept flashing back to the negative encounters in Pennsylvania and the suicide in New Jersey. My current isolation and fears had stripped me of the confidence that I felt during the day. I started to sniffle, and tears began to slide down my cheeks. I looked up toward the rafters and started talking to God.

"God," I said, sniffling, "I'm scared. I don't know why I'm out here. When I started, I was so strong and healthy and confident. But now I feel weak, I feel broken. There is so much hurt and heartache out here. I don't know why I wanted to do this alone. That was stupid.

"At one point I felt like You wanted me here, like You were calling me to the trail, but why would You make me go through all this?

"I don't feel like I'm loving people well. How could I? I'm not even hiking with other people. And I don't feel like I'm glorifying You, so if You did want me out here, then I don't see why.

"But I *am* out here, okay? And whether it's Your fault or my fault, I just need You right now. I need You to protect me. I don't want to feel scared, and I don't want to feel alone."

There is never any doubt in my mind that God hears my prayers. And that night more than ever, it wasn't about whether or not He was listening; it was about how and when He would respond.

Lying in the darkness, I never felt comforted. I continued to feel scared and alone, and I slept in fits of fear. But in the morning, things were different.

I awoke to discover the sun rising above distant mountains and green fields below. I was still in a daze when I saw it, but I immediately tried to find my camera. It was so beautiful; I wanted to save it.

The shelter faced east and offered an expansive view above the tree cover. The entire sky was glowing with radiant, rose-colored hues and bright orange highlights; everything around me seemed painted with an artist's touch. The scene reminded me of standing alone and watching the sunset on Roan Mountain in Tennessee. I felt like God had designed this moment just for me.

He was communicating to me through the sunrise. He was talking—no, He was singing to me with colors. It was like being woken up with a lullaby. The pink said, *I am here*. The orange said, *I am going with you*. And the gold, the bright gold, said, *Trust in Me*.

It took me two days to hike the fifty-two miles through Connecticut—two wonderful days filled with rolling hills, verdant farmland, lush riverbanks, and rocky cliffs. I was sad to leave Connecticut, especially since it was directly followed by Massachusetts.

Massachusetts started with a descent; a steep, slick, rocky descent off of Mount Everett. I needed to use both hands, both feet, and both butt cheeks to navigate the course.

Since I couldn't use my mop stick on the downward rock scrambles, I would javelin it off the top of a rocky decline and then use all four of my limbs and my booty to lower myself down the trail and retrieve the yellow pole.

The trail was not marked well in spots, and I was frustrated at how long it was taking me to climb safely down the mountain, but it was fun to watch my yellow mop stick bounce off the large boulders on its way to a resting place farther down the trail. It was like watching Plinko or a pinball machine.

I must have thrown my stick a dozen times during the descent, and because it was a three-dollar mop stick and not a hundred-dollar hiking pole, I didn't feel bad about it. It sure was nice to have use of both my hands when I needed them. As it turned out, I would need to use my hands for the rest of the day, but not for climbing.

When I reached Jug End Road at the base of Mount Everett, I entered what seemed like a lost circle from Dante's *Inferno*. The dark, wet shadows of the thick bog-forest were home to the highest concentration of mosquitoes that I had ever seen.

The tiny, black insects attacked me in swarms, landing all over my body. By the time I had smacked one of them off, five others had bitten me somewhere else. I was completely miserable, and I didn't have any bug repellent.

I didn't think I needed bug repellent! I had hiked hundreds of miles and only suffered two bug bites. But in Massachusetts, I counted 137 mosquito bites the first morning.

Without bug repellant, my main line of defense was sprinting. I ran with my pack bouncing up and down on my back, rubbing deeper gashes into the sides of my hips. I used my right hand to wave away the mosquitoes in front of my face so I could see, and my left hand to smash the bugs on my skin.

I fought a valiant fight, and I'm sure I looked ridiculous, but the flailing did little good, and the swarms continued to attack. They encompassed me, and if at any point I had stopped to rest, I would have been eaten alive. The bugs were in my ears, up my nose, under my shirt, and covering every inch of exposed skin. I had done fast miles on the trail before, but those miles paled in comparison to the "10K for Life" that I did at the start of Massachusetts. It took me about an hour to complete six miles, which would have been a decent time even without a pack on my back.

When I exited the marsh, I was covered in bumps from the bug bites and bruises from smacking myself. To make matters worse, I was exhausted and dehydrated. I hadn't been able to stop even for a second, and as I left the swamp, I realized that my water bottle was empty. Now at the edge of the forest, the only water was the thick brown sludge that served as a mosquito breeding ground and larvae incubator.

I followed the murky headwaters to higher ground, and as I rounded a turn on a wooden boardwalk, I saw a hiker butt (fully clothed) sticking up in the air. There was a backpack lying beside the swaying bottom, and I could see that a man was trying to filter some water out of the muck below. However, it wasn't until he looked up that I realized who it was.

"Raptor!"

"Odyssa?"

We didn't hug, because he would have dropped his filter or fallen off the boardwalk. But we smiled and laughed, and then I sat on the boardwalk beside him as he filtered some tea-colored water into my bottle for me.

I hadn't seen Raptor since Pennsylvania, and so much had happened since then. As we continued hiking, we talked about the past couple hundred miles, but most of all we complained about the bloodsuckers in Massachusetts.

We spent several hours defaming the buzzing black-winged pests until there were no insults left, and then we started recycling ones we had already used.

One thing I was learning to love about the trail was the sense of community. I hadn't seen Raptor for hundreds of miles, but now we were together again and it felt like we were family. And if I hadn't run into Raptor, then I probably would have found another familiar face, or someone who knew someone I knew.

Trail community is a strange concept, because it's always in flux. Sometimes, mostly down South, I would find myself in a brood of hikers. Other times I would be happy for the company of just one or two, and a lot of the time, especially up North, I was content to be alone and know that there were other hikers ahead of me and behind me. There was never a time, even if I was alone, when I didn't feel part of a larger community.

In Massachusetts, I was more than happy to spend a few days hiking with Raptor. We needed one another for moral support. The flying, buzzing, biting pests were never as bad as the first morning in Massachusetts, but they were still bad, even with the one hundred percent DEET bug spray that I bought.

I don't know much about DEET, but after reading the many Poison Control warnings on the outside of the bottle, I was careful to apply it sparingly to my skin, not on my clothes, and nowhere near my face.

I was careful for about two hours, until I discovered that "sparingly" did little to disperse the flying vampires. And even with the spray on my skin, they still bit me through my clothes.

"Argggg!"

I took out the DEET again, and this time I bathed in it. I used half the bottle on my exposed skin, and most of the rest on my clothes and hair.

After dousing myself in the pungent liquid, the bugs backed away immediately. I now had a good four inches of space between the swarming mosquitoes and my body. It was like an invisible force field. But because it was such a hot and humid day, after a few hours I had sweated off much of the solution, and the insects started landing on me again.

I became so frustrated that when I came to Upper Goose Pond, I dropped my pack and ran into the cold blue water, submerging myself until only my nose and eyes remained above water.

I stayed like that for several minutes, and most likely would have remained there indefinitely if it hadn't been for a small motorboat approaching along the perimeter of the lake. Not wanting to frighten the passengers or risk being run over, I sprang out of the water and waved my arms. I heard a shriek, and the boat rocked so hard it almost capsized, but once the man and woman inside had settled down, they slowly steered toward me.

With my head above water, I introduced myself and explained my predicament.

With great sympathy, Sarah and Rob generously offered to let me join them on their cruise to a local marina. And from there, they said, they could drive me into town.

If there was ever a time on the trail that I was tempted to skip a section, this was it. I wanted nothing more than to enjoy a breezy, bug-free boat ride to a car that would transport me to a protected hotel room. But alas, I declined.

"I can't," I said. "I'm waiting for a friend who's behind me, and even if we do go to town, we'll need to hike to the next road because going in the boat would mean that we'd skip three miles. And we can't miss three miles. I know it sounds weird, but it's really important to us that we hike the whole trail, even the miserable sections."

"Well, we can meet you at the road in an hour and a half if you want," they suggested.

I was out of the water and hiking almost immediately. I knew Raptor was right behind me, and I felt certain that he would be more than willing to ride into town and split a hotel room with me.

I was right, and five minutes after Raptor arrived at the road, Rob and Sarah pulled up in their Jeep. I didn't even know the name of the town where we stayed that evening, I just knew it was off the trail and away from the bugs.

When I had spent the day with Heather in Banner Elk, she asked if I would want to spend a night with her brother and his family in Massachusetts. At the time, Massachusetts seemed like a far-off dream, but after one more full day of hiking with Raptor, I found myself off the trail visiting the Millers.

Maybe it's related to the lack of women on the trail, but throughout all my home stays along the trail, I felt myself connecting very intensely with the women I encountered. They were individually and collectively redefining what I thought a woman could or should be.

Heather taught me that stay-at-home moms were much more than "just" moms. Pastor Leslie showed me that you didn't have to be a man to tell people about God, and that you didn't have to be married to have a family. Wendy helped me realize that my body was important and that I needed to value and take care of it. Magic Momma let me know that it was okay to accept love from strangers. And Emily, well, she blew my idea of a traditional family right out the window.

Emily was married, with two daughters and a son. She was brilliant, articulate, hospitable, and charming, and she was also the primary breadwinner of the family. Emily was a pediatrician, while her husband Isaiah was a stay-at-home dad. I don't know why that shocked me, because I'd heard of it and seen it on television, but I had never seen it while I was living in the South.

I think the perception in the South is that if a man stays home with the kids, then he is somehow weak, but Isaiah was anything but weak. He had basically built their entire house by himself and molded it around the preserved remains of two gigantic oak trees. If you want to assert your masculinity, building a house with two tree trunks shooting out of the living room is an excellent way to do it.

Emily, on the other hand, was as maternal and affectionate as any mother that I had ever met, and she was also a medical doctor. Which was good, because some of my bug bites were the size of a quarter and had become infected. She kindly offered to help me with that.

Whatever system Emily and Isaiah had, however they decided to divide their responsibilities, it was working, because they had some of the most amazing children that I have ever met.

The three kids were bright like their mom and handy like their dad. They helped around the house, they were kind to each other, and instead of playing video games or watching TV (I'm not even sure if there was a TV in the house), they spent time outside or played board games with one another.

For twenty-four hours, the Millers made me feel like family. They opened their home to me, they cooked for me on their woodstove, and taught me their favorite games. On top of that, the next morning, Isaiah offered to shuttle my pack to the lodge atop Mount Greylock so that I could slackpack the section of trail past their house and pick up my things that evening.

I couldn't wait to reach the summit of Mount Greylock, because on the other side of the mountain was Vermont. It was hard for me to believe that I only had three states left.

Back on the trail, it was a beautiful day, and before I knew it, I was standing at the base of Greylock, the tallest mountain in Massachusetts. The first part of the ascent was pretty easy, since the grade was gradual. I was surrounded by towering pines and lost in a world of dense, pleasant thoughts about how one day I wanted a woodstove in my kitchen and a tree trunk supporting my living room ceiling. It took me awhile to notice the wind picking up and the sky growing darker.

However, even if I had noticed the initial signs, it wouldn't have mattered. The storm hit so quickly that, five minutes after I thought it might rain, I was running through one of the worst thunderstorms of my life.

The sky was so dark that it looked like dusk in the forest, and the deafening thunder seemed to shake the ground. At one point, I ran with my hands covering my ears to muffle the harrowing blasts. The lightning flashes lit the dim forest with a blinding brilliance.

As if the lightning and thunder weren't bad enough, next came the hail.

This was my first hailstorm on the trail, and the marble-sized beads of ice stung me and left raised red welts on my skin. It felt like someone was pelting me with stones. To make matters worse, the slick rocks and icy footing made the path treacherous. I slid over the small balls of ice that collected at my feet, like a child trying to roller-skate for the first time.

There were no shelters nearby, and I didn't have my tent to set up because I was slackpacking. The closest building was the lodge at the top of the mountain. I was worried about climbing to higher elevations in an electrical storm, but it seemed like my only option.

Just when I came within view of the summit, the storm stopped. As quickly as it had started, the lightning and hail vanished. I slowed to a walk and caught my breath as I walked the remaining two hundred yards to the mountaintop lodge.

When I entered the building, I was dripping wet, and I left a stream of water in my wake as I walked through the lobby. I was chilled to the core, but a wave of warmth came over me when I saw Raptor sitting in a chair by the window.

Looking over at me, he smiled and winked. "You almost had me worried," he said. Then he pointed me upstairs, where he had placed my pack on a bunk near his in the hiker loft. I was thankful to be reunited with my pack, my tent, and my raincoat. It was incredibly generous of Isaiah to drive my pack up to the summit, but I swore I would check the weather forecast before I accepted another slackpack.

After taking a shower and warming up, I met Raptor downstairs for a lasagna dinner. When we finished eating, we left the lodge and walked over to the lighthouse monument that crowned the summit. Sitting on the gray stone benches nearby, we watched the sun change shapes: from a globe, to a semicircle, to a line, to a dot . . . and then it was gone.

To the south, the large white plume of a thunderhead changed from pink to purple in the dimming sky. Above our heads, there were golden jet streams that pointed away from the farmlands of Massachusetts toward the Green Mountains of Vermont.

Staring off at the green ridgeline, I wondered briefly what awaited me in those mountains. But in that instant, it didn't seem to matter, and neither did the memories of bugs and hail in Massachusetts. I didn't want to think about the past or the future. I was on top of a mountain at sunset with a friend. The moment was too full for any other thoughts.

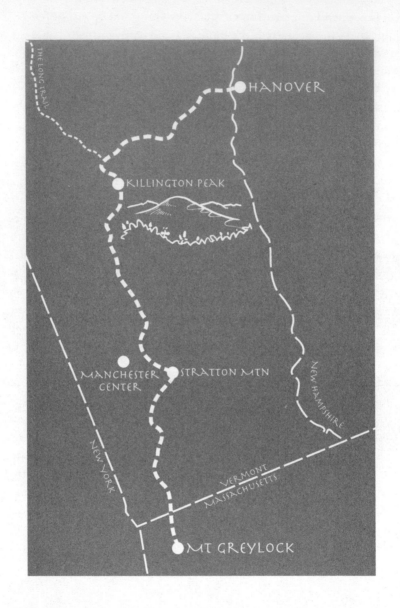

THE LONG TRAIL

HANOVER

KILLINGTON PEAK

MANCHESTER CENTER

STRATTON MTN

NEW HAMPSHIRE

NEW YORK

VERMONT
MASSACHUSETTS

MT GREYLOCK

17

OPTIMISM

MOUNT GREYLOCK, MA, TO HANOVER, NH—160 MILES

In Vermont, everything is green—really green—and the trail is often choked by lush, verdant plants. The narrow path leads to an increasing number of mountain lakes, which offer refreshment and recreation in the summertime. The mountains of Vermont grow taller than their southern New England neighbors and double as well-known New England ski slopes. The region is dotted with quaint towns that cater to skiers, leaf-peepers, and thru-hikers. They pride themselves on serving delicious maple syrup and local dairy products to all their guests.

A warning to future thru-hikers: When you arrive in Vermont, you will think that you are close to the end—you're not. At the Massachusetts/Vermont border, there are still 590 miles between you and Katahdin. That's over a quarter of the trail, and the fourth quarter is the hardest.

Raptor and I parted ways after spending the night together on Mount Greylock. His wife was coming for a visit, and he planned to take several days off the trail. That meant I entered Vermont alone. And as fate would have it, I didn't see another thru-hiker until New Hampshire.

Being by myself again was hard. Because I didn't have any company, I started to focus solely on my relationship with the trail, and that wasn't going so well either. At this point, I expected some reward from the trail: a gold star, or a medal of honor . . . or something.

I spent my first day in Vermont mulling over why I was entitled to walk a red carpet to Katahdin. I had been struck by lightning, caught in a snowstorm, stalked by Moot, offended by an exhibitionist, scared by a religious fanatic, and deeply shaken by a suicide. It seemed to me that I deserved sunshine and wildflowers all the way to the end.

So when the trail remained buggy and humid, when the terrain became increasingly difficult, and when the most exciting discovery in southern Vermont was a big pile of moose poop, I began to feel mistreated.

The first half of the AT had been an adventure. I met new people every day, and I was learning how to backpack, how to be a thru-hiker. The mid-Atlantic was also an adventure, in its own scary way. But Vermont was just kind of boring.

I had figured out how to backpack, so those details no longer occupied my time. I knew most of the people in front of and behind me, and there really weren't any thru-hikers nearby whom I hadn't met yet. My diet, my routine, where I slept, what I saw . . . it had all become commonplace. I hadn't planned on getting off the trail and hitching to Manchester Center, Vermont, but when I came to the road, I just didn't want to keep hiking. So I went to town.

Manchester Center was a cute town. Unfortunately, it was so cute that all the lodging options cost over one hundred dollars. It was a ski town in the winter, a mountain resort in the summer, and a leaf-peeper destination in the fall. They had great coffee shops, expensive restaurants, and very few locals. When I realized that staying inside Manchester Center was out of my budget, I got a ride back down the highway and found a motel several miles from town.

Getting a motel room by yourself on the trail is kind of like drinking alone. It's supposed to be a social tradition, so doing it by yourself often means you're ashamed, or trying to hide it, or else you're just really depressed. I told myself that wasn't it—that I just liked the taste.

The sad thing was, the motel room didn't make things better. At first it felt good—the shower, the warm bed. But once I was clean and dry, I didn't have anything to do and it was only 5:00 PM. I turned on the TV and just lay there for four hours, mindlessly watching a rerun of the MTV Music Awards. I hated it.

Somewhere amid the evening gowns and makeup, the loud music and provocative performances, I was overcome with a sense of fakeness. Nothing about the awards show seemed real. I was stuck in a motel room, listening to overinflated performers sing bad music and watching them receive funny-looking awards. I didn't care how hard, miserable, boring, or scary the woods were. They were better than this.

I realized that I didn't miss the lifestyle I'd left when I started the trail. I missed my family and friends, I missed my warm bed and clean clothes, but I would rather watch a sunset than watch TV, I would rather walk than sit in an office all day, and I would rather sing out loud to myself on the trail than watch the MTV Music Awards.

The next few days were much better. The trail didn't change, but I did.

Suddenly, I loved hiking. I loved the trail, and I loved Vermont. I made a vow that I would only hike twenty to twenty-five miles a day, that I would swim in every lake I passed, and that at night I would find a place where I could watch the sunset.

I also tried to find a resting spot each afternoon where I could sit still for an hour and watch the world around me. I'd stop and get to know a stream or watch the trees dance in the breeze. I marveled at spiders building webs, squirrels gathering nuts, and birds calling to each other. Sometimes it would rain during my breaks, but that was okay because I had my raincoat. Other times I would find myself surrounded by a cloud of bugs, but I would just apply DEET and stare past the swarm.

I learned that I didn't need much to be entertained. I didn't need loud music, bright lights, or TV. I just needed to be still.

Being still was a relatively new concept for me. I couldn't remember much stillness in my pre-trail life. And the times I do remember were highly uncomfortable. My whole life had been filled with activity and movement.

Until now, I hadn't been okay just *being*, I had to be *doing*. Everything was part of a schedule, a routine, a constantly flowing series of commitments. I never stopped after I finished an activity, I just looked ahead and prepared for whatever came next. I started to think about how many different things I used to do in a day. I would schedule myself to the max, and the only free time I would leave was taken up with getting from one commitment to the next.

On the trail, all I had to do was walk. It was up to me how far I wanted to walk and where I wanted to end up. I could stop when I wanted, I could eat when I wanted, I could take naps at any point during the day. The trail allowed me to feel a strong sense of freedom. And it helped me to see the oppression of a busy schedule and the way we multitask in civilization. I no longer saw what was civil about filling my life with commitments if I couldn't stop to watch the sunset or listen to the birds sing.

Because I wasn't in the company of thru-hikers in Vermont, I would sometimes talk with the animals. If I found myself alone in a shelter, I would share conversation and a few crumbs with the resident mice. I knew I shouldn't give them my food, but they were cute and furry, and

I figured if they were full then maybe they wouldn't try to eat a hole through my food bag in the middle of the night.

On the path, I was delighted to once again find the bright orange salamanders that had dotted central Virginia; the fact that they were so lethargic made them really good listeners. I would pick up the lizards, tell them about my day, mention how lucky they were to live in such a beautiful place, then I would put them back down right where I'd found them.

There was another animal in Vermont that I hadn't seen before. It had the coloring and size of a chipmunk, but it looked like a squirrel, so I called it a chaquirrel. I liked the chaquirrels, because it was fun to say their name and because they were mischievous. They skirted around tree trunks and jumped from branch to branch to keep an eye on me. And their noise didn't sound like a chirp or a tweet, but like a laughing child.

When I did come across people, I would talk to them too. Not just "Hi" and "Bye" and "Have a good day"; I wanted to know where they were from, what they were doing on the trail, if they liked it or didn't like it, and why.

I spent one full afternoon on the rocks of Clarendon Gorge talking with the locals who had retreated to the cool rapids of Mill River to escape the summer heat. They shared their food and their stories with me. And as I sat and listened to them talk about interests ranging from car parts to pottery and football to farming, it struck me that every person I had ever met and would ever meet knew something I didn't and could do something I couldn't. It was a simple truth, but I finally realized that the more people I invested in, the smarter and better equipped I would be.

That night at Governor Clement Shelter, I spent the last hour of daylight at a nearby creek, sitting on a rock with my feet in the water, my journal in my lap, and a pen in my hand.

June 12, 2005

Before I started hiking the trail, two of my biggest concerns were that I would be bored or lonely. Aside from the first two days in Vermont, I haven't been bored, and even without thru-hikers around, this trail certainly doesn't seem lonely. I think I actually experience loneliness and boredom more at home than on the trail.

I stopped writing and looked into the water to think, to find my answers in the cold current that swirled around my sore, swollen feet.

Maybe the fact that I wasn't lonely had more to do with the quality of relationships than the quantity. In college, I remember sitting in a packed classroom or cheering at a football game in the midst of a crowd, but still feeling alone. I had also spent the last three years loathing social mixers. Traveling around the room and having the same meaningless conversations with different people left me feeling empty inside.

The problem in college, and in life, was that there were a lot of people who knew *what* I was, but they didn't know *who* I was. No wonder there was so much pressure to look a certain way, when usually the only thing people got to know was someone's outer image.

When I spent time with someone on the trail, it could be for a few minutes or a few days, but the time was focused. There were no distractions and fewer inhibitions. When we parted ways, they didn't just know my profile, they knew my person. They knew what I liked and didn't like, how I felt, what I wanted to be, and what mattered to me. And just as importantly, I knew them.

I picked up my pen and journal again.

One of my favorite things about the trail is that you don't see your face. I mean, I guess you can see it in the reflection of the water, but there are no mirrors, no vanities, and no places to check yourself out. I used to think that people perceived me based on how I looked, but now that I don't see my face, I feel like people perceive me by how I treat them—that is, by what I say to them and how well I listen. Now I feel beautiful when I make other people smile.

My last full day in Vermont was saturated with heavy rain, but that was okay, because rain was nature's DEET. I walked all morning and all afternoon in a steady downpour. It was warm out, so instead of putting my raincoat on, I just let my t-shirt get wet. In the past, I usually tried to avoid rain puddles, but today I was purposely splashing in them and laughing. And instead of reaching for my water bottle when I was thirsty, I would just tilt my chin up and open my mouth toward the sky. The whole day was like combining hiking and a summer swim.

That evening, I was wrinkly from the rain, and since I wasn't near a shelter, I stopped to set up camp at a flat spot just off the trail. As soon as I pulled out my wadded tent, the rain penetrated the fabric, and in the five minutes it took me to set it up, the tent floor became completely soaked by the saturated undergrowth. By the time I put the ground cloth underneath the tent, there were already puddles covering the tent floor. Then when I crawled inside, the day's rain dripped off my body and made the puddles more of a pool. Finally, I unrolled my sopping wet foam sleeping pad and laughed at the idea of putting a perfectly dry sleeping bag on top of a wet sleeping pad in the the middle of a puddle. Finally, I just pulled off my wet clothes and climbed inside.

The next morning I woke up, packed up my soaking wet gear, and hiked—fast. I hiked fast because I wanted to hike fast. Back in March when I started the trail, there was no way I could have comfortably hiked eighteen miles in under six hours with a pack on my back, but now I could. That's part of what made it fun, the fact that I could now do something that I couldn't before, something that most people couldn't dream of doing.

It was also fun because even though it felt like I was going fast, I really wasn't. I was hiking barely over three miles per hour, which meant I was still well aware of my surroundings and could see and appreciate everything as I passed.

I think life would be much better if the speed limit were three miles-per-hour. Traveling by trains, planes, and cars seemed too fast. It's difficult to notice details when you zip past things at sixty-five miles-per-hour. I appreciate mass transportation because it allows me to see friends and family who live far away, but part of me wished that everything and everyone I wanted to see was in walking distance. But then again, after the trail, there was going to be a lot more that I considered "within walking distance."

After six hours of fast hiking, I crossed the Connecticut River and said good-bye to Vermont. I had reached Hanover, New Hampshire.

New Hampshire—my penultimate state.

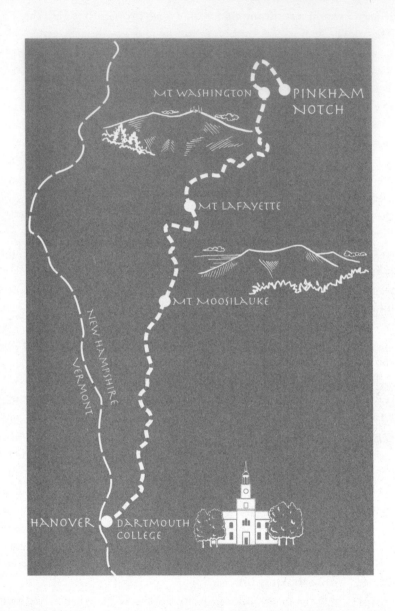

18

REGROUPING

HANOVER, NH, TO
PINKHAM NOTCH, NH—123 MILES

New Hampshire is difficult, but not remote. It feels remote to the tourists who stay at the huts in the White Mountains, visit the rest areas in the notches, and drive their cars or take the Cog Train to the top of Mount Washington. But to thru-hikers it feels scenic, challenging, and populated. Despite the people with daypacks and video cameras lining the ridges and mountaintops, the strenuous climbs are worth the effort because of the stunning views, and the many tourists mean there is lots of potential trail magic.

anover is home to Dartmouth College. After asking a few students for directions, I soon found my way to a brick building that housed the Dartmouth Outing Club. The DOC was a campus organization that facilitated skiing, hiking, backpacking, climbing, water sports, and anything outdoors for the college community. The club also maintained part of the Appalachian Trail and served as a resource for thru-hikers.

Inside the DOC headquarters, I asked a student volunteer about lodging options near Hanover. He presented me with several hotels within walking distance, all with prices over three digits, and then he said there was a bus line if I was hoping to get something in the seventy to eighty dollar range.

I was hoping for *free*. This was a college campus and I was twenty-one and it was the summer. There had to be thousands of empty rooms and beds in this town. I was pretty sure that if I made a sign and stood on a curb, a kind student would share her room. All I wanted was a shower and a place to put my sleeping bag.

"I really don't have that much money to spend on lodging, especially if I can't split the fee with any other hikers," I told him, looking as pitiful as possible. "I was hoping to spend the night and take a shower here, but I guess I'll just keep hiking. By the way, I heard that it was supposed to rain tonight, do you know if that's true?"

The young man took a minute to run his fingers through his hair and then replied, "Look, I'm not supposed to do this without checking with my roommates, but I live in a house just down the road, and I'm sure you could take a shower there and spend the night on our couch if you want."

"Really? Thank you so much! I'll be gone first thing in the morning. Promise."

The student gave me directions to his building, which sounded pretty much like a coed fraternity house. But I didn't care as long as it had a shower and a roof. Along the way, I stopped to pick up brownies so I would have an offering to present when I arrived. The gift was well received by the DOC housemates, and in exchange, I was offered a clean towel and a twenty-year-old couch on the front porch.

I had everything I needed for the night, and I planned to head back to the trail the next morning to begin New Hampshire. But then I checked my cell phone messages and discovered that Nightwalker and Mooch would be arriving in Hanover the next morning.

That was a problem.

It shouldn't have been a problem, because Mooch and Nightwalker were my two favorite people on the trail, and I knew that hiking with them would be fun. But then there was this feeling that I hadn't really dealt with that I had been trying to leave back in Connecticut. You see, I kind of liked Nightwalker. And the worst part was that I was pretty sure he liked me too.

If I stayed and we started hiking together, the feelings would be unavoidable. But if I kept hiking, it would be an obvious and potentially hurtful dismissal of two good friends who had been there when I needed them the most.

I didn't know if I was ready to have permanent hiking partners, because that's what they would be. It was an unwritten rule that you don't start hiking with people in Hanover and leave them somewhere in the middle of Maine. This was the last and the hardest part of the trail, and hikers either teamed up and finished as a pack or continued solo to the end.

I didn't sleep well that night, partly because the twenty-year-old couch smelled like mold and partly because drunk college students walked past the house all night long, but mostly because I was nervous. I wished Nightwalker had never called me, because if we had happened to meet up on the trail it would have felt natural. Now it was a decision that I didn't want to make. When dawn broke, I pulled out my journal, sat up on the couch, and started writing. I felt like if I wrote out my feelings then maybe the solution would reveal itself, like on a Ouija board. But the answer didn't come. I went back and forth, I made columns listing the pros and cons, but I still didn't come to a decision.

This journal had been my hiking partner, and every day, every rainstorm, every person I had met, it was all inside. In ten years, if I wanted to remember my hike on the Appalachian Trail, I could pull it out, look inside, and read about my adventures. I would be the only one who understood, the only one who could relate, and probably the only one who could read my handwriting.

But I wanted more than that. I wanted to share my journey. I wanted to call someone on the phone in ten years and talk about how much fun we had hiking through New Hampshire and Maine together. I wanted to store memories in people, not pages. I wanted friends, and I wanted hiking partners.

When I met Mooch and Nightwalker at the post office, Mooch gave me a hug and Nightwalker gave me an extra-long hug. They made me feel warm, wanted, and welcome, and that was important, because I was trading in my solo-hiker status for these two.

After a brief town resupply, the boys were ready to leave, and together we walked out of Hanover and back to the trail. It was raining so hard when we left that the trail resembled a creek. When the trail was this wet, you could either try to rock-hop, and place your feet on top of large slick stones rising above the current, or you could submerge your feet in four inches of water with every step. Usually, I would try to rock-hop until one foot slipped and my shoe and sock became soaked, then I would hike in the stream for the rest of the day. The boys called this the "freedom step," because once your feet were that wet and muddy, you were free to step wherever you liked without further consequence.

I had already been liberated and was wading through ankle-deep water behind Mooch, when I looked up and started laughing. I hadn't noticed it before, but I could now clearly see a tear in the backside of his shorts. Every time he stepped with his right foot, I could see his pale white butt cheek.

"What's so funny?" he demanded.

I was laughing so hard that I couldn't talk, but I could point, and that's when Nightwalker erupted in laughter as well.

Mooch tried to look over his left shoulder, then his right, but he still couldn't see the tear. He reached back and felt near his shorts pocket. His finger slid through the hole, and a look of shock came over his face.

Nightwalker and I doubled over. I was laughing so hard I cried. For the rest of the day, Mooch hiked behind us.

At Smarts Mountain Cabin Shelter that evening, I sewed up Mooch's shorts with the needle and thread that he carried in his pack. I thought it was ironic that he carried a needle and thread but didn't know how to sew, or at least said that he didn't. Either way, I felt like I owed him after laughing at him for most of the day. Also I didn't want to see his butt anymore, so I was happy to do it.

The next day, we set out and all started hiking separately. I liked that. I liked that we could be hiking together, yet spend the majority of the day walking on our own, at our own pace.

It wasn't rainy, but the trail had become so saturated with spring snowmelt and rainfall that it was a legitimate mud pit. Twice during the day I stepped in the brown sludge, only to lift up my foot without my shoe. That meant I had to hop around on one foot with a pack on my back, trying to dislodge my sneaker from the muck without getting my sock any messier than it already was.

And as if the mud weren't enough of an obstacle, any pause allowed the bugs to attack. In Massachusetts and Vermont, there had been plenty of mosquitoes, but in New Hampshire, they had reinforcements.

Black flies, although not as large as mosquitoes, were now just as prevalent. Unlike the bites of their larger, blood-sucking cousins, black fly bites did not leave itching, burning welts. But a black fly bite was more painful initially, and it left a small dot of blood on my skin, as if I had been pricked by a needle. Plus, the black flies' minute size allowed them easy access under my clothing and through my hair. If I kept moving, the black flies were tolerable, but whenever I stopped, I was assaulted.

I was trying to keep my pace up through the soupy mud and swat mosquitoes away from my face at the same time when my thumb caught my necklace and ripped it off my throat. I watched the silver chain launch off my neck and sink into the murky depths.

I immediately squatted near the surface and began feeling in the sludge for my lost jewelry. I stayed there for five minutes, feeling and groping for it. The necklace had been a present from my best friend, a reminder of her support and encouragement while I was on the trail, and now it was gone, lost in the mud of New Hampshire.

I dug around until the black flies became overwhelming. I had tears in my eyes and mud all over my body from smacking the black flies with brown gloppy hands. Finally I stood up and left the necklace behind.

After losing my necklace, my expensive, uncomfortable new pack came apart. A stabilizing strap that helped balance the pack weight fell off. I couldn't figure out how to replace the strap, and although I tied it on where I thought it should go, it remained ineffective. As a result, my sternum strap, which was supposed to ride across my breastplate, now more closely resembled a choker and caused the pack to pull back on my collarbone instead of my chest.

In its new form, the pack was even more cumbersome than before, and I decided to take it off for a moment to rest my neck and hips. As I removed the pack, a clasp from my pack caught my watch and pulled the face away from the wristband. It fell on semi-solid ground, and when I picked it up, it was in two pieces. I put it in my pack and kept hiking.

Apparently, all my gear was only built for eighteen hundred miles.

I was in a sour mood when I rejoined Nightwalker and Mooch at Jeffers Brook Shelter that evening. Mooch tried to make things better by building a small fire and putting our shoes beside it so that they could dry out. We sat in silence as we ate dinner. At the end of our meal, Mooch returned to the flames, and as he bent down to inspect our sneakers, he looked up from them, directly at me.

"What?" I called from the shelter. "What is it?"

He didn't say anything, just stared at me apologetically, as if he had run over my pet. Then he slowly picked up one of my shoes and turned it so I could see the side that had been facing the fire. It had melted!

The back half of my shoe was brown, and a quarter of my sole had melted away. Mooch expected me to explode in anger and frustration, but after I sat silently for a minute, I surprised everyone—even myself—when I started to laugh. I rolled over on the floorboards of the shelter, stared at the ceiling, and guffawed. The boys looked at each other for confirmation, and when they felt it was safe, they began laughing as well.

I was falling apart. What else could I do?

New Hampshire is rumored to be the toughest state on the trail, and after a hard climb up Mount Moosilauke, and an even more difficult descent that involved ladders, metal bars, and wooden steps, I understood why.

But my shoe had held up. Even missing a quarter of its original foam cushion, it saw me safely down the ladders. My legs were worn out from the jarring descent, my arms were tired from clinging to branches, and my nerves were unsettled by the imposing heights, but my shoe was fine.

I had made it up and down Mount Moosilauke with only one good shoe and a broken pack, and I had covered a third of New Hampshire in just two and a half days. Everyone had told me how hard New Hampshire would be, and I had spent twelve states terrified of it. But standing at the base of Moosilauke, I was no longer intimidated. New Hampshire might be the toughest state on the trail, but I could do this.

What I didn't realize was that Mount Moosilauke was a gateway, a portal to the hardest, most strenuous climbs on the trail. After scaling it, I faced an even more difficult and technical climb up Mount Kinsman. It is an understatement to say that the mountain caught me off guard. Mount Moosilauke was one of the most difficult climbs on the trail, and now I had an even harder climb to end the day. Up until Mount Kinsman, New Hampshire had been challenging, but now it seemed impossible.

I had not been this demoralized or felt this weak since hiking up Mount Unaka in Tennessee. I thought back to how hard that day had been, how miserable I had felt, and then I remembered something I had said that helped me up that mountain.

Every step I take is a step closer to Maine.

I said it aloud: "Every step I take is a step closer to Maine."

I smiled. "Every step I take *really is* a step closer to Maine."

That's what I had said in Tennessee. That's what got me to the top of Mount Unaka on that dismal, wretched, rainy day. I forced myself to believe it then, but now it seemed impossible to deny. I was in New Hampshire, and every step I took, no matter how small, truly was one step closer to Maine.

When I reached the top of Mount Kinsman, the boys were waiting for me. The sun was setting, and the blue sky met the purple mountains in an interlocking puzzle piece. Mooch and Nightwalker were focused on how pretty it was, but I was focused on how the mountains ahead were increasingly taller than Mount Kinsman. I could see them lined up, one after another, taunting me with their jagged profiles.

The boys left the summit and hiked ahead to reach the next shelter before nightfall, but I stayed behind.

Nightwalker had a theory that when the trail got hard, or when there were difficult climbs, it helped to talk trash to the trail. You know, tell it who was boss.

I decided to tell the mountains how it was going to be.

"You don't scare me," I said. "I've come a long way, and you are not going to stop me from making it to Maine! You don't even look that big. Ya ever heard of Clingmans Dome, huh? Yeah, well Clingmans Dome is the tallest mountain on this trail. That means it's taller than you guys . . . and I've already climbed it. You call yourself mountains? You barely even look like hills! I'll be through you in five days, tops. Just wait, you'll see."

Nightwalker was right. I felt better already.

I started to hike down the mountain, and about thirty seconds after my tirade, my mop stick broke in two, and I slid three feet down the trail on my hands and knees.

The mountains—they had done this to me!

I had been hiking with my yellow mop stick for over twelve hundred miles. It had offered me support, it had protected me from dogs and rocks, and it had set a daring new fashion trend on the trail.

I could handle the necklace, the watch, the pack, and the shoe, but the mop stick? It was my friend, my calling card, the object of my right hand, and it was gone.

I sat down and cried.

I loved my mop stick. I felt like a child who had just had her favorite toy taken away, or a teenager who had to turn in her keys after breaking curfew. I had been prideful, and now I was paying for it. I looked back over my shoulder at the towering mountains.

"I'm sorry," I said. "I didn't mean it."

Then I stumbled to Kinsman Pond Campsite in the dark, with a dim headlamp and a broken plastic shaft in each hand.

At the point when I felt completely broken, things started to get better.

The next day, we hiked up and over Franconia Ridge, and although I missed my yellow pole, I realized that, more and more, hiking in New Hampshire required using both hands. And the climbing was a lot simpler now that I didn't have to boulder uphill with my mop stick or javelin it off the side of the mountain as I scrambled down.

The climbing that afternoon was really hard, but I tried not to look up, and that kept me from becoming too discouraged. And since I no longer wore a watch, I didn't know how long it was taking, so that helped too.

The boys were great. Now that the terrain was so difficult, we ended up hiking together for most of the day. There was no longer a "fast" or "slow" pace; we had all been reduced to a crawl.

Nightwalker and I spent much of the day talking. We talked about our families, our friends, high school, college, childhood memories; we talked about what we wanted to do and where we wanted to go after the trail. We would talk until we were talked out, and then there would be a long silence until one of us thought of something else, and then we would talk some more. Hiking with Nightwalker made the climbs seem less steep and the trail seem less difficult.

Unlike Nightwalker, Mooch actually made the mountains seem bigger and the climbs feel harder. It's very difficult to hike when you're doubled over laughing. No matter how dire the circumstances, Mooch could always make me laugh. He had an endless supply of jokes and self-deprecating stories.

When my stomach muscles ached from laughing and my face was sore from smiling, I would ask Mooch to sing a song. My musical taste consisted of whatever pop songs were overplayed on the radio, but Mooch didn't sing those. He sang folk songs. I didn't recognize most of the tunes or artists, except for occasional ballads by James Taylor or Bob Dylan, but that made the words even more magical.

Mooch's voice was beautiful, pure, and earthy. For someone who constantly told very crude jokes, I was amazed at how sweet and innocent his melodies sounded. Mooch would sing me over mountains, along ridgelines, beside lakes, and at night he would always have one last tune to share before we went to bed.

I was missing proper support in my shoe, on my pack, and in my hand. But now I had two other hikers to lean on, and that was more important than having the right gear.

When the boys and I reached the top of the stair-stepper climb up to Franconia Ridge, the unprotected ridgeline provided spectacular views of New Hampshire. There were tall mountains in every direction, and although they were called the White Mountains, they appeared in dark shades of blue, green, and purple. The sky was cloudless, and the rocky outcroppings of the ridge made everything feel rugged and primitive.

There were several day- and section-hikers on top of the mountain as well. They seemed to be enjoying the view too, but something about coming all the way from Georgia gave me a sense of ownership. I felt connected to these mountains in a way that the other tourists could not understand. They were looking out over the same vista that I was, but I was certain that it struck me with a beauty and significance that they were unable to appreciate. I had worked really hard for these views, and the feeling of accomplishment I had on top of Franconia Ridge was more stunning than the scenery.

That night, at our campsite beneath Franconia Ridge, Nightwalker asked me on a date. I knew that our feelings were mounting, but I didn't realize they would come to such a formal head. I said yes, and together we left Mooch in Garfield Ridge Shelter and walked to a nearby boulder, climbed on top, and watched the full moon light up the distant mountains.

I was still uncertain about my feelings for Nightwalker. I knew that I liked him, but I didn't know how much. I wondered how starting a relationship now, toward the end of the trail, would impact our lives off the trail. I worried about the perception of being like most female thru-hikers, who couldn't stay out of relationships along the trail. I thought I had come out here to be independent, not to find a boyfriend.

Despite my indecision and mixed emotions, the one thing I was sure of was that sitting on the boulder with Nightwalker was the best date I had ever been on. I didn't have to dress up, I didn't have to worry about appearance or impressions. The air was filled with the songs of crickets and insects, and we were in the one of the most beautiful places I had ever been, under a full moon, on a warm summer night. In the end I gave in to the setting and my feelings, and confirmed what my heart felt with my lips.

I thought the kiss would make things different the next day, but it didn't. For Nightwalker and me, there was no awkwardness, no expectations, no change in demeanor, just the same respect and conversation that we had always shared. But I wanted to make sure that things hadn't changed with Mooch either.

While Nightwalker was up ahead and I was hiking at a crawl behind Mooch, listening to him bemoan the current mountain, I decided to broach the subject.

"I couldn't hike up this mountain any slower if I were a hobbit," said Mooch.

"Hehe . . . Um, Mooch?"

"My trail name should be Bilbo Baggins."

"Okay, whatever, but Mooch?"

"Yes, my precious?"

"Um, we kissed."

"What?"

"Yeah, well, I didn't mean to. I mean, I didn't *not* mean to . . . but the moon was out, and we could see the mountains, and there were crickets. Well, it just happened. And I'm sorry!"

"You mean you and Nightwalker kissed?"

"Uh-huh."

"Haha. First of all, that's gross, because you stink and Nightwalker stinks, but you smell worse, and anyone who would kiss either one of you when you smell that bad is just gross. Secondly, it's none of my business what you and Nightwalker do. And thirdly, if you guys are happy, then I'm happy for you."

"So you're not mad?"

"Odyssa, why would I be mad?"

"Well, you guys kinda had this thing going. You've been partners since Georgia, and it's just been guys, and now, well, I'm kind of a third wheel."

"Are you kidding? Odyssa, you saved us! Nightwalker and I were about to kill each other before we started hiking with you. Seriously. We were so sick of each other that we probably would have split up if

we hadn't met you in Hanover. We need you. *I* need you. I need someone to talk to besides Nightwalker. I want you to hike with us, and if
kissing Nightwalker is part of the deal, then so be it."

It was a relief to know that Mooch wasn't hurt or upset. Because the
truth was, I liked Mooch just as much as I liked Nightwalker. I liked
them in different ways, but my attraction toward Nightwalker didn't
outweigh my appreciation of Mooch. Nightwalker was turning into a
trail romance, but Mooch was becoming a real-life friend.

That night, Nightwalker and I went on our second date. We sat by
a pond with clear water. On the sandy bottom, there were little black
worms swimming amid the debris of fallen twigs and leaves. Nightwalker picked up one of the black, eel-like creatures.

"You know what this is?" he asked.

"What?"

"A leech!" he answered, throwing it on me.

"Ahhhhh, sick! Don't ever do that again!"

"Aw, c'mon, they're not that bad." Then he picked another one up
and started playing with it in the palm of his hand. It was about three
inches long, and it could knot itself up into a perfectly round ball that
looked like a black pearl. It was weird, not to mention slimy, but at the
same time it was mesmerizing.

I was poking at the leech, making it contract into a perfect sphere,
when Nightwalker started talking again.

"So . . . " he said. "The kiss. Are you okay with it?"

"Um, I think so. I mean, I like you. But I just don't know. What does it
mean? We're almost done with the trail. What's going to happen after that?"

Nightwalker paused for a minute. "I don't know what's going to
happen after the trail. I don't know where either one of us will be or
what we'll be doing. But I do know that I like you, and I know that
we're together now."

"But we're so different. Our stories are completely different, what we
believe is so different . . . And what I believe is really important to me."

"I know it is. And that's why I want to know about it, because if it's
important to you, then it's important to me. I may not agree with
everything, but I respect what you believe."

"Well, I do like you—Ahhhhh, ouch! Get it off, get it off, get it off!"

The leech had attached itself to my thumb.

The Presidential Range presented an entire day of vertical gain toward Mount Washington, the highest peak in New England. Our plan for the day wasn't to summit Mount Washington, but to climb all the "step mountains" leading up to the peak. I called them "step mountains" because there were never any downhills; instead, hikers would climb up a mountain and then walk straight to the base of another mountain, up a mountain and straight, up and straight—just like stairs, but on a much grander scale.

With the elevation increase came spotty weather. The passing rain showers and thick fog made it a cold day to hike, especially for June. We were excited to reconvene midday at a hut for several rounds of soup.

Huts were a trademark of the White Mountains. They were wooden cabins with running water, electricity, and showers—and they were expensive. Spending the night in a hut usually costs about eighty dollars per person. That was for a wooden bunk in a communal room. Essentially, it was a glamorous shelter for eighty dollars a night. Sometimes hikers were allowed to spend the night in return for manual labor, but the only manual labor I wanted to do was walk to Katahdin. For a hiker, the most appealing part of the hut system is that they offered an unlimited soup bowl at lunch for three dollars. Sure, it was just reconstituted broth, but it was *unlimited* reconstituted broth.

While the three of us sat in silence slurping our lunches, a young male hiker walked into the building. We didn't recognize him. It was now June twenty-second, and the hiker informed us that he had started from Mount Katahdin at the very end of May. He was a southbounder! Our first southbounder.

I immediately thought of Dude, the southbound hiker I had met in the Smokies. Back then, I had envied him for being near the end of his journey while I was just beginning mine. Now the tables—and the miles—had turned, and I was the one who was a few weeks from finishing.

For the first time since leaving Springer Mountain, I felt like the end was within reach, and that left me feeling eager and unsettled at the same time. It was as if the morning's first light was disturbing me from a dream not yet finished: part of me wanted to wake up, eat breakfast, and take a shower, but another part wanted to stay in bed and keep dreaming.

After sharing some of our stories with the southbounder and wishing him well on his journey, the boys and I filtered out of the hut and back to the trail. The rain had stopped for the afternoon, but the wind had picked up significantly; the remaining miles to the base of Mount Washington's cone were entirely above the tree line. When I was able to look up, the panorama of distant mountains was awe-inspiring, but for the most part the wind was so cold and strong that I had to keep looking down or it would bring tears to my eyes.

Hiking alone, I had plenty of time to consider my evening plans. There was no camping allowed on Mount Washington, so we would be forced to stay at Lake of the Clouds Hut, a mile and a half below the summit. I had to decide whether to work for my board and spend the majority of my time scrubbing dishes and washing floors, or whether to pay an eighty dollars guest fee for Spartan amenities.

Nightwalker had already decided to pay the fee and not work. It was his twenty-third birthday, so he could justify the eighty dollars. But I had already had my birthday.

After scaling four mountains all named after dead presidents, I arrived at Lake of the Clouds Hut. I didn't see any sign of Nightwalker or Mooch, so I proceeded to the front desk. Still undecided whether to work or pay, I asked if the attendant had seen any tall, dark, scruffy hikers walking around.

He replied, "Oh, are you with Nightwalker? You must be Odyssa. Nightwalker's mom radioed in and paid for the three of you to spend the night as guests."

My mouth fell open and my eyes began to gleam. They didn't even have telephones at this hut, and how Nightwalker's mom knew we would stop here on his birthday and figured out a way to pay for our rooms was, well, magic. Drifting off to my prepaid room, I felt the warm generosity of Magic Momma as if it were a friend walking beside me.

As I settled into the hut, I put on my extra clothes to combat the cold summer afternoon. Even inside, it was still cold, since the huts lacked heat. In a few minutes, I was joined by Mooch and Nightwalker, who had been delayed when they chose to take a short side trail to the top of Mount Monroe.

They were as excited as I was that we didn't have to pay or work for our lodging, and together we spent the remainder of the afternoon relaxing, reading, and being still. It was the perfect afternoon, and the perfect birthday for Nightwalker—until dinner.

When it was time to eat, we sat at long rectangular tables with the other hut inhabitants and passed food around family style. Usually I like family style because it reminds me of camp, and I love camp. But I didn't like the family-style format that evening because the other guests at our table took more than their fair portion of food. By the time the serving platters reached our end of the table, the portions were fit for a five-year-old, and the kitchen didn't provide any second helpings.

I was livid. These hikers, as they liked to call themselves, were out here for a night or a weekend and had plenty of food in their rooms, their backpacks, and in the cars waiting for them at the bottom of the mountain. And from the looks of them, they really didn't need the extra calories!

My stomach was screaming with hunger pains, which I unsuccessfully tried to quiet with the three bites of pasta that had been left on the platter by the time it reached me. But when dessert came, I felt vindicated. It was a homemade birthday cake that the kitchen staff had made for Nightwalker, and they let him serve it. Since I had some influence over Nightwalker, let's just say that everyone there got his or her just desserts.

The next morning we summited Mount Washington. It was cold and windy, and I was wearing every article of clothing that I carried.

At the top of the mountain, there is a large cement building. I wish they had not put the building there. Sure, the inside of the structure with its weather station, museum, and snack bar was pretty cool, but aside from the weather station everything would have been just as effective at the base of the mountain. I guess they needed the building, though, because otherwise tourists wouldn't pay twenty dollars to drive up to the top of the mountain or sixty dollars to ride up on the Cog Train.

I didn't know what a Cog Train was until we left the top of the mountain and started down the backside. I just thought it was a normal train that took people from the bottom of the mountain to the top. What I learned on the descent was that a Cog Train runs on coal and is twice as loud, stinky, and dirty as a regular train. But I'm sure that the tourists who travel the Cog to the top of Mount Washington must like it. Why else would they subject themselves to breathing in black air, listening to a loud whistle, and traveling up a mountain that is usually cloudy to reach an expensive snack bar on the summit?

The train route parallels the AT before crossing the path near the summit. Although we were still several hundred yards away from the tracks, we could see the train slowly lurching up the mountain, and we could hear it too. The noise was piercing even from a quarter mile away, and the smoke was disgusting. I have never seen so much pollution coming from one machine in my life. As we hiked closer, we started to smell the coal that powered the machine, and it burned my nostrils.

The whistling, smoking, smelly monster contrasted with everything that was lovely about this place. Before hiking the trail, I'm sure that a ride to the top of the mountain on the Cog Train wouldn't have fazed me. But several months of living in the woods made loud noise and pollution on top of a remote mountain seem even more abnormal.

The boys insisted that it is a thru-hiker tradition to moon the Cog. I'm not generally a proponent of mooning or public nudity, but when Nightwalker and Mooch decided to turn around and show their cheeks to the locomotive, I couldn't blame them and I didn't try to stop them.

Nearly an hour later, when the smell and haze from the train had lifted, I saw two young men hiking quickly up the mountain. They didn't have packs or hiking poles like thru-hikers, but they also didn't look like tourists headed to the top of Mount Washington. I watched them hike past Mooch and Nightwalker without stopping.

When they drew close to me, I called out ahead so they wouldn't have to slow down.

"How far are you guys hiking?" I asked.

The man in front replied, "This guy behind me is going all the way to Georgia."

"So you guys are slackpacking?" I asked.

The tall blond hiker in the back laughed and said, "I guess you could say that. My name is Trail Dog. I'm trying to set the record for the fastest hike on the AT. This is my friend JB, and he's helping me. He slackpacks me with a support vehicle and hikes with me some to pace me."

"What's the record?" I asked.

"Right now it's forty-eight days, so I have to do about forty-five miles a day to beat it."

JB added, "We left Katahdin eight days ago and we're on schedule, but we have a long hard day, so we'd better keep going."

"Yeah, yeah, of course. Good luck to you guys."

"You too!" they both yelled back as they continued their charge up the mountain.

I thought trail records were impossible. I just didn't understand how someone could hike the trail in less than two months, even without a full pack. But meeting David Horton, who had set the record in the 1990s, and talking to Trail Dog this morning had struck a chord in me.

There was something about these two, about what they were doing, that captivated me. I knew that some people didn't agree with people trying to set trail records, believing that would-be record setters moved too fast and didn't appreciate their surroundings. But both times I met a trail record holder, they had been smiling and enjoying themselves. They hadn't been too busy to say hello, and they seemed to love the trail. I guess you would have to.

After a full day's descent down the slopes of a few additional Founding Fathers, the boys and I arrived at Pinkham Notch and were met by Mooch's parents.

The boys had been invited to a wedding on Cape Cod months ago, and had planned to take a few days off the trail to attend the event. We had decided several days ago, with permission from the bride, that I would go as their date.

When we arrived at "the Cape," I had only a few hours to get ready—a task that should have taken me way more than a day. Thankfully, I did have Magic Momma, my fairy godmother. She drove me to the nearest mall, where I *had* to find something to wear. Being six feet tall with no bust, it had been hard enough to shop before the trail, but now that my thighs were huge, my waist was emaciated, and my chest was practically concave, finding an outfit was nearly impossible. I must have tried on twenty dresses in eight different stores before I found one that sort of fit. But that only solved part of the problem. Next, I had to find a regular bra (with lots of extra padding), dress shoes, hair clips, a razor, deodorant, shampoo, conditioner, and earrings. The sensory overload at the mall almost sent me into a state of shock. I was still in a daze when I arrived back at my room with only thirty minutes to shower, dress, and primp for the wedding.

Against the odds, I was ready in just under twenty-eight minutes, and I looked pretty nice—which was fortunate, because Nightwalker and Mooch had both evolved from legitimate trail trash into handsome dates. Granted, they still had their long scraggly beards, but they had groomed them to appear rustic rather than raunchy.

The wedding and reception were at a beachfront house with the Atlantic Ocean in the background. The weather and setting were perfect, and the entire event was one I wouldn't soon forget. But I did wonder if the bride noticed that the boys and I received almost as much attention as she and her groom, especially when Mooch stuck five wooden shish kebab spears through his beard.

It was fun to dress up and look pretty, eat nice food, and listen to good music. The process was trying, but the end result was enjoyable. By the end of the night, however, sitting on the beach between Nightwalker and Mooch, listening to the sound of the waves rolling in, I couldn't stop thinking about the trail. I remembered meeting our first southbounder and feeling conflicted about the trail's impending conclusion. My time on Cape Cod heightened that feeling. There was so much I was looking forward to off the trail; my mind said my life was going to be so much better, so much easier once I reached Katahdin. But my heart said that I would miss the trail. As I looked at the tiki torches ablaze on the shoreline, I felt like Mowgli in *The Jungle Book*. I was no longer sure which world I belonged to.

On the long drive back to Pinkham Notch the next morning, we only made one stop: to buy a new mop stick.

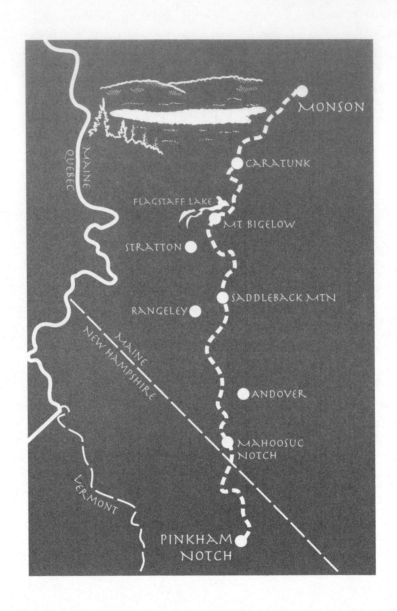

19

TRIBULATION

PINKHAM NOTCH, NH, TO MONSON, ME—199 MILES

Pinkham Notch, New Hampshire to Monson, Maine is the most difficult section of the Appalachian Trail. The rugged terrain and harsh climbs will leave southbounders feeling disheartened and northbounders feeling deflated. It is notorious for its bug-infested summers, river fords, slick bridges, and marshy terrain. The weather is erratic and threatening above the tree line, and there are fewer trail towns and resources than in the neighboring White Mountains. More than any other part of the trail, this section feels like untouched wilderness.

I don't know where New Hampshire came up with the term "notch." I had never heard it used geographically until I came to the White Mountains. In fact, I'm still not entirely sure what a notch really is. To me they seem like gaps or valleys: they're found between mountains and they are very tough to hike out of. Maybe that's the difference. Climbing out of a gap is tough, but climbing out of a notch is excruciating.

The next morning we set out on the trail to try and rise above Pinkham Notch and tame the rugged slopes of Wildcat Mountain. After a few minutes of climbing, we realized that our weekend festivities had left us soft and unprepared for the climb. Unsurprisingly, my body had liked the food and rest it received, and it was not happy about me strapping a heavy, cumbersome pack on my back and climbing up a huge mountain.

My digestive system rebelled against the strain, forcing me to run into the woods every half hour. But the strange thing was, it only *felt* like I had to use the bathroom, and nothing ever happened. Each time, I was convinced that if I didn't make it into the woods within a matter of seconds, something really embarrassing would happen, but after spending several minutes behind leaf cover, I would once again emerge without any results.

I told myself it was probably nothing, but after being on the trail so long and having my body systematically break down, I was starting to become a hypochondriac. I wondered if maybe I had a parasite. Giardia is a common condition on the trail, caused by drinking unfiltered water. Diarrhea is the telltale sign of giardia, and everyone says that if you have it, you'll know. And I wasn't convinced, so I guess that meant I didn't have it.

I put myself in the back of the line as we ascended Wildcat. Mooch was directly in front of me, bear-crawling up the mountain.

"Mooch, do you think I have a parasite?"

"Do you have diarrhea?"

"No."

"Have you shart yourself?"

"Shart?"

"You know, where you think you fart, but more than air comes out?"

"That happens?"

"Oh, believe me, that happens. Think about it. Eating large quantities of food combined with constant physical exertion and a tight pack belt around your bowels. Trust me, it happens."

"Huh. Well, I haven't done that . . . yet."

"Well, then I think you're fine. We've hiked almost two thousand miles. You're exhausted and tired, and your body is just breaking down. We're all breaking down."

What Mooch knew, which I hadn't learned yet, was that Nightwalker was having some embarrassing physical issues as well.

I noticed that Nightwalker seemed cranky and irritable that morning, and he was more eager than usual to hike ahead without company, but because of my condition I hadn't thought much about it; I was just glad that he wasn't hiking with me.

When Mooch and I finally caught up with him, he was stumbling up the trail, gritting his teeth, and squinting his eyes.

"What's wrong?" I asked.

"You wouldn't understand."

"Are you okay?"

"No."

"Is there anything I can do?"

"No. Just keep hiking and let me walk alone."

Mooch heeded Nightwalker's request, but I stayed behind.

"Really, I can help. Just tell me what it is."

Nightwalker flashed me an angry glare and snapped, "My shorts are chafing my manhood."

"What?"

"The humidity and hiking are chafing my penis."

Oh, wow. I guess I really couldn't help.

"I'm sorry," I said. Then I turned so he couldn't see me and smiled. I know this was one of those times when you weren't supposed to laugh, and I didn't, but it was hard.

"Hold on, I have to stop," he said. "I need to duct tape my shorts."

Duct tape has a million uses on the trail, but I didn't know that this was one of them. Nightwalker put a big strip of it on the inside of his shorts to help with the friction, and it worked for a little bit. But after a while the pain came back, and so did his outlandish solutions.

"Odyssa," I heard him call behind me. "Odyssa, hold on."

"What is it?"

"I have to hike without shorts."

"Hah. Riiiiight. That's funny."

"Look at me, Odyssa. I have tears in my eyes. If I don't take off my shorts and hike in my briefs, then I won't be able to keep going."

Why did it have to be briefs? Why couldn't he be a boxer guy?

"Okay, fine, but I'm hiking ahead of you to make sure no southbounders come down the trail."

I hiked several minutes ahead of Nightwalker without incident. *This could actually work*, I thought. *We might be able to make it to the end of the day without seeing anyone else.*

Then a black fly flew into my eye.

It landed right in the corner of my eye and dug its way underneath my eyelid where I couldn't get it out. I batted, I rubbed, but still my vision was blurry and a painful bump remained trapped beneath my eyelid. I needed help. I turned around and started hiking in the opposite direction.

When I saw Nightwalker with my one good eye, he looked naked. I knew he wasn't, but his shirt hung just low enough that it looked like he wasn't wearing anything underneath.

"Stop fidgeting," Nightwalker said as he examined my eye.

"I can't help it. I'm nervous." It was taking him forever to work the insect out, and I was quite sure that I would soon see a hiker coming in the opposite direction, while a man who looked like he wasn't wearing underwear held my face and poked at my eye.

"Got it," he said triumphantly.

Finally I could see clearly, and there was still no one around. I had been spared. And so had Nightwalker.

He walked without shorts for the remainder of the day, and the only person he had to explain himself to was Mooch. But Mooch didn't want to hear it.

"No, really, whatever you two decide to do in the woods is up to you. You don't have to tell me about it."

"Mooch, come on. You know we wouldn't—"

"Seriously, how far you take your relationship is none of my business. But next time I would remember to put your shorts back on."

Mooch was cracking himself up. He thought he was *so* funny.

He was.

The next day, Nightwalker was able to wear his shorts again, so he walked fully clothed into Maine.

We had made it! Granted, I had developed a rash on my upper body, my pack was heavy, my legs were tired, it rained that day, and my stomach was a mass of cramping, air bubbles, and foul gases. But that made entering Maine all the more uplifting.

At a blue sign that read WELCOME TO MAINE, the three of us rejoiced: we took funny pictures, we hummed the *Rocky* theme song, and Mooch did a ridiculous celebration dance.

And then we did what we always do: we kept moving forward.

So much of the trail had been about hiking from Georgia to Maine, and so much of my mental encouragement and positive self-talk had suggested that making it to Maine would mark success. And now I was here.

After crossing the state line, I hiked in front of the group. I mostly looked at the ground, because looking up was demoralizing, but at one point I lifted my head to gauge my progress, and there it was.

"Hor . . . hors . . . moose!" I gasped.

It was a moose, a moose without antlers, a female moose! Her head was sticking through the thick brush, and at first I couldn't figure out what a horse was doing in the bushes beside the trail. Then I realized this was where all the huge pellets of poop were coming from!

I tried to repeat myself quietly so that Nightwalker and Mooch, who were coming up behind me, would understand the situation. I pointed and once again whispered, "Moose!" But seeing that she was about to turn and trample into the forest, I called out louder, "Moose, moose, moose!" Then I watched her gigantic backside disappear in the distant hedges.

The boys never saw the moose. They were disappointed, and I felt bad they had missed her, but then again, they had seen a bear back in Virginia. Now that I was in Maine, I resigned myself to the fact that I probably wasn't going to see a bear on this trip. And although I hadn't really thought about seeing a moose, the five seconds that passed between recognizing the four-legged creature and watching her bound through the thick forest immediately became a highlight of my hike.

The descent down Carlo Col demands hugging the mountain as if it were a rock-climbing wall and slowly inching down the serrated incline. It was hard, time consuming, and exhausting. Nightwalker and I were both six feet tall, and Mooch could look down at both of us, yet there were several places where even our long legs and extended bodies couldn't reach the next ledge. We had to jump, slide, and spot each other coming off the rocky grade.

After that, I thought the trail would get better. I thought it *had* to get better.

I was wrong. The unwieldy traverse that led into Maine was only a taste of what we encountered the next day at Mahoosuc Notch.

Mahoosuc Notch was a mile-long stretch of gnarly, jagged, oddly shaped boulders in a gulch that was sandwiched in between two imposing sheer cliffs. There wasn't any walking through Mahoosuc Notch. The only way through was to squeeze, slip, and slither on top, in between, and beneath the rocks.

It was late June, but we still saw snow on the ground in some places, and we could feel cold air from ice trapped in crevasses beneath the boulders.

There were several points where I felt like a wrong step could lead to serious injury, and I was thankful not to be hiking alone. But as a group, we were discouraged at how long it was taking us to move forward. I kept thinking about world-class track stars who could run a mile in under four minutes. I was pushing myself as hard as I could, and I was lucky to make it a hundred feet in four minutes.

"This sucks," said Mooch.

"I'm so tired," I complained.

"C'mon guys," said Nightwalker. "It's not that bad. Just think of it as Mother Nature's jungle gym."

The fact that Nightwalker wasn't struggling as much as Mooch and me made me a little resentful, but the playground analogy did flip a switch in my head. I finally accepted that there was nothing we could do to increase our speed. At that point, I stopped trying to hurry and just started to enjoy the rock scrambles.

Suddenly the hardest mile of the entire trail became one of the most enjoyable. We stopped trying to fight the elements and began to embrace them. We laughed as we threw our packs off large boulders and pushed them between small cracks before trying to squeeze our bodies through to the other side. We played an adapted version of hide-and-seek as we rounded each turn, and threw our hiking sticks to each other in a skilled game of catch.

It took us an hour and a half to traverse the one-mile Mahoosuc Notch, and when we finally came out at the east end, we were exhausted, proud, and happy. We had completed the hardest mile of the entire trail.

Unfortunately, we were unaware that it was directly followed by the second-hardest mile on the trail.

I might have had a clue if the words "Mahoosuc Mountain" appeared in the Data Book after Mahoosuc Notch, but instead it read "Mahoosuc Arm." Arm? Why can't New England call things what they really are? Instead of "arm," they should have called it a vertical rock wall.

Mahoosuc Arm battered our already fatigued bodies. Traversing the ascent took everything out of us that hadn't already been extracted by the rocks below. There was no walking; instead I placed two palms out on the trail and pawed my way to the top. The incline was torturous, my quads and calves were screaming, and my arms were sore from pulling myself up on the roots and rocks. The only thing that kept me moving was the ominous dark clouds that were beginning to gather above us.

We made it up the arm and to Speck Pond Shelter just before the rain started. I collapsed on the floorboards.

"Well, guys, you want to wait out the storm here and then keep hiking?" asked Nightwalker.

Mooch and I just looked at each other. I knew by the look in his eyes that we were on the same page.

"I can't hike anymore today," I said.

"Neither can I," Mooch echoed.

"But we've only come nine miles," Nightwalker said.

It was true—demoralizing but true. It was 3:00 PM, and we had been hiking for eight hours, but we had only covered nine miles. However, those nine miles were more difficult than most of the thirty-mile days I had done in Virginia.

"Nightwalker, you can go ahead, but I'm done."

"Toast," Mooch agreed.

"Well, let's just see how we feel after the rain passes."

I was more exhausted than I had ever been in my life, and Nightwalker wasn't making it any better. Without any further conversation, I pulled out my sleeping bag and curled up inside it for a three-hour nap. When I awoke, I heard the boys eating dinner. It had stopped raining, but there was still thunder rumbling in the distance. I pulled out my food bag, made myself a cheese burrito, then after finishing the meal with cookies and water, I went back to sleep for another two hours.

It was twilight when I woke up again, and the boys were both reading. I took out my journal, scribbled a quick entry, brushed my teeth, then went back to bed. I woke up at 7:00 the next morning, and I was still exhausted. I had gotten fifteen hours of sleep, and I felt like I could sleep fifteen more. Getting out of my sleeping bag and starting to hike was the last thing I wanted to do.

Out of the three of us, I felt the worst and was having the hardest time. Or so I thought.

"I'm quitting," Mooch told me, as the two of us descended Old Speck Mountain together.

"You're *what?*" I asked.

"I'm getting a ride at the next road and going home."

"Mooch, we're in Maine. We are almost there. What are you thinking?"

"Almost there? There are two hundred and eighty miles of trail in Maine, and so far they've been harder than New Hampshire. I can't do it anymore; my body physically cannot do it. I can't keep up with Nightwalker, and I feel like I'm holding you up. I just want to quit."

With Mooch it was sometimes hard to tell whether he was joking or being serious, because he was almost always joking. But at that moment his tone wasn't sarcastic; he sounded pitiful, and I was ninety percent sure he was serious. The worst part was, we were approaching Grafton Notch, and there was a road there. I tried to buy some time.

"You can't quit," I said. "Nightwalker is several miles ahead of us; you can't quit without talking to him first."

"Nightwalker has you, he'll be fine."

"No he won't. And neither will I. I need you to stay."

I did need Mooch. I needed him to make me laugh, to sing to me, and to hike with me. I probably spent twice as much time hiking with Mooch as I did with Nightwalker. Things between Nightwalker and me were great, I liked him more and more every day, but they were also uncertain. Mooch was my rock. I never worried about our friendship.

We came to the parking lot beside the road. Mooch hiked toward a pickup truck with a white-haired man standing beside it. I grabbed the back of his pack to try and stop him, but he managed to drag both of us closer to the truck.

"Hey, you guys want to slackpack?" asked the white-haired man.

"Slackpack?" Mooch was so intent on asking for a ride that the offer clearly caught him off guard.

"Yeah, I own a hostel. I can slackpack you two the next ten miles and then you can come to my place to eat, sleep, take showers, and rest for the night. I can slackpack you tomorrow too, if you want."

"We would love to!" I exclaimed.

Then I pulled Mooch aside. "Listen, we can both slackpack the next few miles, and tonight at the hostel you can decide what to do when all three of us are there."

Mooch reluctantly agreed.

We put our packs in the back of the truck and set off into the woods with food, water, and raincoats.

After a few hours we came across Nightwalker, who was jealous and a little mad when we saw us without our packs. That made Mooch happy.

As promised, we were met at the next road crossing by the white-haired man, who drove us to The Cabin. The Cabin was much like any other home, except that the basement had been converted into a hiker lounge and bunkroom. We showered, did laundry, checked the internet, watched TV, and ate a huge dinner. That made Mooch happy, too. But I still wondered whether he was going to go back to the trail the next morning.

That night the three of us lounged around in non-synthetic clothes, talking and eating ice cream—a lot of ice cream. My favorite part of The Cabin was the closet full of comfy clothes for hikers to wear while washing their clothes. I loved having the soft, breathable feel of cotton against my clean, warm skin. After hiking through thirteen states, I hated my smelly, clingy hiker clothes. No matter how many times I washed them, they still didn't look clean. And even if my t-shirt smelled good coming out of the washing machine, as soon as I put it on and started sweating, the locked-in smell of nineteen hundred miles leaked out. The heat-activated stench was especially bad under my armpits and made me wish that I had chosen to hike in a tank-top for added ventilation.

The three of us weren't the only hikers lounging around in clean cotton clothes at The Cabin that night. We were joined by Snowstepper, a hiker I had never met in person but whose trail journal entries I had been following since Georgia.

Snowstepper had decided to start his northbound thru-hike from Springer Mountain last fall. He had hiked by himself through the dead of winter, in snow and ice, often without any sense of whether he was even on the trail. His refuge and release became the shelter registers; they were the only form of communication he had.

In the South, his entries about inclement weather and loneliness were expressive yet good-humored, but the farther north he hiked, the more suicidal the entries became. He started to hate hiking, hate snow, hate loneliness, and hate life. Toward the end of Vermont, I had stopped finding entries written by him. I was convinced he was either dead or taking time off to recover from depression.

Mooch was especially intrigued by Snowstepper, and began to ask him about his hike.

"What happened?" he asked.

"I got off the trail," Snowstepper said.

"Why?"

"Because I hated hiking and I thought I was going to die."

"So what are you doing back here?"

"I never thought I would come back. When I got off, I swore that I was done with the trail. I'm glad I quit when I did, because if I had kept hiking, then I probably would have died or gone crazy. But to quit in Vermont—that just felt wrong. I put in so much time and effort to get there. I had overcome so much and then I just quit? Getting off was horrible. Nothing felt right. For three months the trail haunted me, so finally I decided I needed to come back and finish what I started."

I looked at Mooch, but he refused to make eye contact.

That night before bed, the three of us were brushing our teeth over the kitchen sink.

"Mooch, is there anything we need to discuss?" I asked.

"Nope," he replied.

"What are you guys talking about?" asked Nightwalker.

"Nothing," said Mooch. "Absolutely nothing."

Our two days of slackpacking from The Cabin gave us the boost we needed to make it through southern Maine. I can't believe people think that New Hampshire is the toughest part of the trail. Maybe it was because I wasn't expecting it, but western Maine seemed far more difficult than anything else we had hiked. There were very few roads, no huts, and the mountains didn't have snack bars on top.

The peak that changed everything was Sugarloaf Mountain. There weren't any other hikers, but there was a great view. And there, in the distance, we saw her—Katahdin. She was just a speck on the horizon, but we could see the end, and that affected us all in different ways.

Nightwalker was so excited that he talked nonstop for the rest of the day. He had a huge smile on his face and his voice was filled with excitement.

I was stoic. There were so many emotions flooding through me that it was hard to know what to say. I had planned to have it all figured out by the time I got to Katahdin, and instead everything seemed more complicated than when I had started.

Mooch seemed to be the most affected by seeing Katahdin. As soon as the mountain came into view, he took off. Up until this point we had been the two bringing up the rear, but from that point forward, Nightwalker and I struggled to keep up with Mooch. Not only was he a stronger hiker, but he also stopped complaining, even jokingly. I guess now that he could see the finish line, he knew that he could make it.

Our proximity to Katahdin didn't make the daily task of hiking any easier. The trail continued to test us in ways we didn't expect.

Descending off the Bigelow Mountains, I arrived at Little Bigelow Lean-To and found Nightwalker buried in his sleeping bag and knotted into a ball. It was only 6:00 PM. Usually he would be reading, or eating, or searching for a spot to take me on a date, but tonight all I could see was his curly black locks sticking out the end of his maroon sleeping bag.

I heard a noise behind me and turned to see Mooch walking toward the shelter with Nightwalker's cell phone in his hands. As he approached, he put his finger to his lips, signaling me to be quiet.

"He needs to sleep," he whispered.

"Why? What's wrong?"

"I think he has giardia. He just spent an hour in the privy, and he had to dash off the trail fifteen times today. I was with him for most of the afternoon, and he just kept getting worse. He's really dehydrated and I think he has a fever. I tried to call for help, but I couldn't get service on his cell phone."

"What are we going to do?"

"I don't think we can do anything tonight, but tomorrow we can hike to a dirt road a mile down the trail. There's not supposed to be much traffic on it, but I think it's our best shot at getting him out of here."

Mooch and I silently ate dinner. Then, as we prepared our sleeping bags and foam pads, we saw Nightwalker's cocoon stir.

"Nightwalker?" I whispered.

"*Uuuuunnnnnnhhhhh.*" It was one of the most pain-filled moans I have ever heard.

"Hey, can I make you some dinner or get you some water?"

He pulled his sleeping bag below his eyes and then, ever so slightly, shook his head no. He looked horrible. His face was beet red and his eyes looked lifeless. He was struggling to keep his eyelids open, and I could see him shivering despite the sweat rolling down his face. I spent the rest of the evening wetting his bandana and applying it as a cold compress to his forehead.

The next morning, Mooch and I helped Nightwalker down the trail. He had his left arm slung over Mooch's pack and his right arm over my shoulders. We carried him to the road like a wounded soldier.

The guidebook said that only one or two cars would travel this road per day, so after situating Nightwalker in the shade, Mooch and I sat down in the middle of the road. This was not the time for selective hitching; this called for a roadblock.

After about forty-five minutes, we heard a noise coming down the gravel road; standing up, we saw a car quickly approaching in a cloud of dust.

We stood in the road and waved our arms. The driver had no option but to stop. She was on her way back from a Fourth of July campout at a nearby lake, and although she didn't have much room in her vehicle, she offered to cram us in and drive us to the nearest pay phone.

The "nearest pay phone" ended up being thirty minutes away on bumpy back roads. Scrunched on Mooch's lap in the very back of a station wagon with my chest to my knees, it felt like a lot longer.

She dropped us at the first gas station we saw. There, we called a hiker hostel in nearby Stratton, Maine. It took several hours for the owner to come and pick us up, but then he drove us directly to the hospital, where Nightwalker was diagnosed with giardia and given a prescription. From the hospital we returned to Stratton, where we spent two days resting so Nightwalker could regain his strength.

It was hard to stop when we were so close to the end. Katahdin had just come into view, and now it felt like it was taking us forever to get there. But it also made me realize how strong my ties to Mooch and Nightwalker had become. I knew that the boys would have stopped and waited for me if I had been sick. After hiking eighty percent of the trail alone, now it wouldn't have felt right to summit Katahdin without those two by my side.

We didn't do much at the hostel except sleep, watch TV, and stare at the southbounders. There were over a dozen southbounders at the hostel, and they were all so pretty. They looked like models out of an outdoor magazine. They smelled good, their clothes were clean, their hair wasn't in knots, they didn't have tacky hiker tans, and they were full of energy and laughter.

On the other hand, they looked at us in horror. Even after two days of rest, we were still gaunt, sunburned, and covered in bug bites and scars.

Our last night at the hostel, after taking a shower, I spent several minutes looking in the mirror. I combed through my nappy hair with my hands, ran a finger over the scratches on my arms, and picked the loose scabs off my old bug bites. I wasn't pretty—at least, not the way the southbounders were pretty. I didn't look groomed, and I wouldn't be chosen to be in an outdoor magazine. But I did feel beautiful, probably more beautiful than I had ever felt.

I felt beautiful because my body was toned, my legs could hike thirty miles a day, and my arms could pull up on branches or brace my fall when I needed them to. I felt beautiful because my body was capable of hiking over two thousand miles. I felt beautiful because I was part of nature, part of a creation that was expansive and awe-inspiring. I might not have been considered pretty by society's standards, but what society thought mattered less and less to me.

After two nights at the Stratton hostel, Nightwalker felt well enough to return to the trail. We were all eager to resume our journey. Thankfully, the trail leveled out a bit after the Bigelow Mountains, so the next obstacle we came to wasn't a mountain but a river.

Right before Caratunk, Maine, the trail crosses the Kennebec River. Although it's not very deep, the river is extremely wide and can rise rapidly. Thousands of successful fords, or river crossings, had been completed here in the past, but unfortunately, one year, a sixty-one-year-old hiker lost her life when she slipped in the river and stayed submerged due to her pack. After that incident, the Appalachian Trail Conservancy decided to offer a summer ferry service. The service consists of a small canoe that shuttles people across the river early in the morning and again in the late afternoon.

I wanted to ford the river, but the boys didn't.

They told me that the official route of the Appalachian Trail was on the ferry, and that if I didn't cross in the canoe, I wouldn't be on the official trail and it would compromise the integrity of my hike. The ATC had even included a blaze on the bottom of the boat to support that logic.

I didn't see how walking by foot instead of riding in a canoe would compromise my hike.

Then Mooch, determined to get to Katahdin as soon as possible, bluntly stated, "Listen, Odyssa, Nightwalker is still weak. He needs to take the ferry and I want to take the ferry, so if you ford, you ford alone. I know you'll probably be fine fording the river, but what if something does happen? What if you get injured or step on a rock wrong or whatever? We're a week away from Katahdin; it's not worth the risk."

Mooch made a good point, and sometimes the worst thing about being part of a group is having to accept sound advice. The three of us crossed the river in the canoe, and it was actually kind of fun. We may not have been walking, but at least we got to paddle.

Safe, dry, and on the opposite shore, the three of us decided that we would try to catch a quick hitch into Caratunk for an ice cream break before returning to the trail for an afternoon of hiking.

I assumed the position by the side of the road with my right arm out, my thumb in the air, and the boys several feet behind me. As we hoped, the first car to drive by slowed down and pulled over. But as the middle-aged man passed us, I caught a glimpse of far more than I expected to see.

"He's naked!" I whispered to the boys.

"That's ridiculous," said Mooch. "I bet he's just not wearing a shirt."

"I promise you, there is more missing than his shirt," I said.

Still unconvinced, Mooch walked up to the car window. He was there for less than a second before he had to look away.

"Um, no thanks, we changed our minds," said Mooch.

"Are you sure about that?" asked the driver.

"Yep, pretty sure," said Mooch.

The driver laughed and drove off. The boys couldn't believe what had just happened.

"I mean, really? Did a naked guy really just pull over and offer us a ride?" Mooch asked in disbelief.

"I never thought I'd see anything like that on the trail," said Nightwalker.

"Get used to it," I said, smiling. "You're hiking with me now, remember?"

The next day we had to try to hitch again. It was our last hitch of the entire trail, and it was our hardest.

It rained hard all day. It was cold and my gear was no longer waterproof, so I was chilled and soaked to the bone. I also had two hard falls that morning. Both times, I remember looking down at my feet speeding over the slick wet rocks, and then the next thing I remember I was looking up at the sky, trying to figure out how I had gotten there.

I beat Mooch and Nightwalker to the road, because it was cold and, no matter how tired I am, I always hike fast when it's cold. When I arrived at the road, not only was I shivering and wet, but I was covered in mud. I even tried to get a ride before the boys arrived because I knew that if they looked anything like me then no one would stop to pick up the three of us as a group. I stood alone in the downpour getting splashed by cars as they sped through the runoff for twenty minutes without success. Then the boys came out of the woods, and as I expected, they were dripping wet, slathered in clay, and sprinkled with pine needles.

We stood there for another forty minutes, and still no one stopped. Aside from evacuating Nightwalker, the longest I'd ever had to wait for a hitch was ten minutes. But on this, the last hitch, when I barely had the strength to stand by the road and stick out my thumb, I was stuck in a cold downpour for an hour. I started hoping that the naked man from the day before would drive by again. If the boys had agreed to go with me, I would have been more than willing to get in his car.

I was consumed with fatigue and irritability. I began cursing the vehicles that passed us. Not all of them, because there's no way that *I* would have picked us up either, but I did yell at the pickup trucks that passed with empty truck beds.

When a car finally pulled over, my bitterness melted, and I was filled with gratitude. In the end, it was not a truck with an empty bed that pulled over to help us; it was a family of four in a clean, crowded SUV. The mother and father were sitting in the front and two young children were strapped into car seats in the back, and between the seats were layers of boxes and household goods that they were delivering to friends.

The car was filled to capacity without our presence, but the young couple insisted that we could not stay on the side of the road in this weather, so the mother climbed in between the two car seats in the back. Nightwalker sat in the front with his pack at his feet, I sat on him with my pack on my lap, and Mooch somehow contorted himself around the equipment in the back. The mother held some of their belongings to give us more room, and even put light boxes on her toddler's lap.

Unlike other resupply towns along the trail, Monson was not a quick jaunt down the road. The ride lasted nearly ten minutes, and throughout the drive, the mother apologized for the lack of room in the vehicle.

And did I mention that the SUV was not only clean, but it also smelled new? I prayed the scent was coming from some unseen air freshener, because God only knows what we did to that car. As much as I tried to contain myself, the limited space meant that parts of my body were plastered against the window and dashboard. And even without putting any weight on my feet, the mud and water on the bottom of my shoes left clear sneaker prints on the clean floor mat.

The family's willingness to give of their time and to sacrifice their car for us was humbling and completely out of the ordinary. I'm still not convinced that they weren't angels, but I like to think they were human . . . it's more impressive that way.

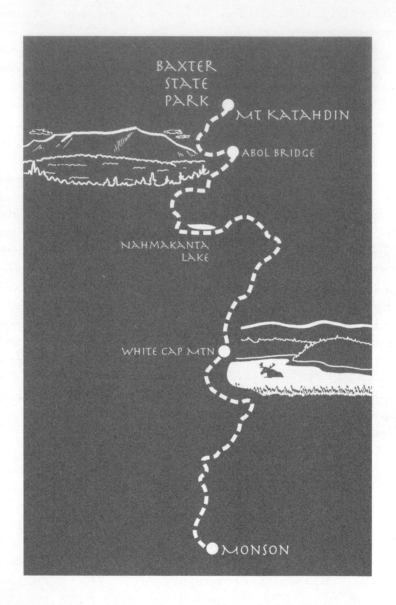

20

TRIUMPH

MONSON, ME, TO MOUNT KATAHDIN, ME,—118 MILES

The Hundred Mile Wilderness is filled with large lakes that are surrounded by warm white boulders. The plentiful water sources provide nice resting spots and a refreshing place to swim. After climbing over White Cap Mountain, the Wilderness flattens out and becomes a victory road leading to Katahdin. The trail is still strewn with roots, rocks, and streams, but views of the big mountain help hikers step lightly over any obstacles. The Hundred Mile Wilderness ends at Abol Bridge. From the bridge, you are ten miles from Katahdin Stream Campground, and fifteen miles from the end of the trail.

You would think that on the last stop of the trail I would have been ready to celebrate. But after a brief stop at the post office in Monson and a bite to eat, the only thing I wanted to celebrate was my bed at the nearby hostel. At the beginning, I had been hiking on the trail to get to towns. Towns had been the reward, but now, at the end of the trail, towns felt more like interruptions.

The next morning, the three of us headed back to the trail and entered the Hundred Mile Wilderness leading to Katahdin. At the start of the Wilderness, there's a sign warning hikers that they should be prepared with food for at least ten days when entering the section. The boys and I carried four days' worth of provisions. We were ready, no matter the conditions, to climb Katahdin five days later. I had no doubt that we would face challenges every day on our way to the mountain, but I also knew that, somehow, we would find ways to overcome them.

One would imagine that our team morale would be at an all-time high as we approached our ultimate goal, but this was not the case.

Nightwalker was in a foul mood because his camera had broken, and he would not be able to capture our finale. He decided to take out his frustration by giving Mooch and me the silent treatment and hiking especially fast. I couldn't fault him for being annoyed with the two of us, since Mooch and I had stopped carrying our cameras long ago with the intention of getting doubles from Nightwalker.

Mooch was irritated because part of his food source (and his trail name) came from mooching off other hikers—including Nightwalker and myself. And by this point, due to our own hunger and waning compassion, we were no longer inclined to share. When we stopped to have lunch together, I took out a bag of dried apricots that I had picked up in Monson. Mooch thought that I had bought them to share, but that was not the case. When I gave him just one, he became indignant. Nightwalker, still bitter about his broken camera, snapped at Mooch for always wanting handouts. That hurt Mooch, so he stopped talking too.

I was feeling antisocial as well, not because I was upset, but because I was more tired than I had ever been. We encountered three tough river crossings that day. The current was especially strong due to the past twenty-four hours of rain, and one crossing was located several yards above descending whitewater. With each ford, I thought the river might wash me away because I was too weak to wade through it.

Toward the end of the day, my vision literally became blurred from fatigue. I tripped and fell on a well-groomed section of trail simply because I was having trouble keeping my eyes open.

When I arrived at Cloud Pond Lean-To that evening, Nightwalker was there, but Mooch was nowhere to be seen.

"Where's Mooch?" I asked.

"He decided to hike ahead."

"Hike ahead?"

"Yeah, he said he wanted to spend a night or two on his own."

I could certainly understand the desire to be alone. But I was mad that Mooch had split up the group so close to the end. At least, I tried to be mad, but even my emotions were watered down with fatigue. I was too tired to care. I was too tired to eat. I was too tired to talk. I just wanted to sleep. If I had become a good hiker on the Appalachian Trail, I had become a great sleeper. It was still bright outside, but I was unconscious by 7:30 PM.

The next morning, when Nightwalker gently nudged me awake, my eyes were still gluey. I could have easily fallen back asleep and slept for the rest of the day. Struggling to pack up my gear, I asked Nightwalker to hike with me for the first half of the day; I needed his conversation to stay awake.

When it was time for lunch, we decided to venture down a short side trail to enjoy our meal by a waterfall. After I finished my meal, I packed up my belongings to head back to the trail.

"That wasn't a very long lunch break," said Nightwalker.

"I know, but I feel like I need the extra time to make it to the shelter this evening. I'm so tired, I feel like I'm barely hiking two miles per hour."

"Okay," he said. "I'm going to enjoy the waterfall a little longer, and then I'll catch up with you."

After about thirty minutes of hiking, I began to wonder why I hadn't yet seen Nightwalker. I hiked for another half hour, and still no Nightwalker. I started to worry. He was a fast hiker and I had barely been going at a shuffle for the past hour. He should have caught up to me by now. Where was he? Was he lost?

I saw a sign up ahead, and much to my confusion, it implied that after an hour of hiking, I was now three miles south of where I had eaten lunch. I pulled out my guidebook and began to survey my surroundings. It looked familiar, but NO . . . I *couldn't* have.

I was hiking in the wrong direction!

The whole point of this trail, the one thing that kept me going, was the knowledge that every step was taking me closer to my goal. All I had to do was follow the white blazes and hike north, and I couldn't even do that anymore.

On the verge of tears, I turned around and shamefully walked back in the direction I had come. My delay put me directly on top of the exposed White Cap Mountain for a late-afternoon thunderstorm. And when I arrived at Logan Brook Lean-To soaking wet to find a completely dry Nightwalker sitting there smiling, I was jealous and also hurt that he didn't seem more concerned.

"What happened?" he asked lackadaisically.

"I went in the wrong direction."

He started to laugh, and I shot him an irritated look, struggling to hold back tears of frustration.

"I'm sorry," he said, trying to back-peddle as quickly as possible.

"I just want to go to bed," I said. And ten minutes later, I was asleep.

As soon as I woke up the next morning, I found myself blinking, batting at, and blowing away the bugs that hovered above my sleeping bag. I packed my belongings and started hiking very quickly, hoping to outrun them. As I jogged through the cloud of insects, I noticed a strange burning sensation in my legs. I looked down and discovered that I had a rash all over the bottom half of my body. My legs were covered with small, painful red dots. In some places, the rash was so concentrated that it looked like hives.

The burning was the worst at my hips where my pack and clothes rubbed. I tried not buckling my waist belt, but the added strain killed my shoulders. Every piece of clothing or plant that grazed my leg felt as if it were cutting through my skin. All of a sudden, I completely empathized with Nightwalker's half-naked hiking strategy.

I tried to wipe away my welling tears, but I ended up rubbing sweat and DEET into my eyes. Now it burned to open them, and I couldn't see the trail. I was a mess, and the only thing that kept me going was the thought of White House Landing. I knew that if I could make it through the afternoon, that evening I could take a side trail to a rural resort known as White House Landing where I would be able to shower and soothe my fiery skin.

Thinking positive thoughts of friends, food, and running water, I managed to disassociate from the excruciating pain in my lower body long enough to reach the lake and small wooden platform that served as the pickup point for the resort. At the dock, Nightwalker and I discovered posted directions that instructed us to blow on the dock's air horn just once. (A bold warning beneath stated that blowing the horn a second time would forfeit the hiker's right to any help from the other side.)

I covered my ears, Nightwalker blew the horn, and together we sat and waited for any sign of life from the opposite shore. We waited fifteen minutes and nothing happened. After thirty minutes, I decided that the lodge hadn't heard the noise and begged Nightwalker to try the horn again. He reminded me that one blow too many would mean no help at all, and suggested we wait a full hour before trying again. Miserable, I spent the next five minutes bathing myself in every last ounce of a rancid bug-repellant that I had.

Finally, after forty minutes, we saw someone descend from the far landing and crank up a motorboat. Considering the quantity and tenacity of the bugs, our chauffeur was lucky to find anything left of us when he finally pulled up to the dock.

For me, the climb up Katahdin started at White House Landing. As the motorboat sped toward the distant dock, the wind blew away the bugs and cooled my rash. But, more significantly, it also blew away the hardships and challenges of the past four months. Before now, I could *see* the end, but this is where I started to *experience* it.

When I stepped out of the boat, Mooch was waiting on the dock to give me a hug. I didn't care that he had left us, I was just glad we were back together again. He helped Nightwalker and me with our packs and walked with us to the lodge where Snowstepper and Texas Ranger were eating dinner. Nightwalker and I ordered our meals, and then the five of us, five thru-hikers who had started in Georgia and walked to Maine, sat and laughed together.

After dinner, I retreated to the shower house. After a long, hot rinse, I covered myself with a soothing balm that the owner of White House Landing had given me to treat my rash. As soon as I put on the clear, silky ointment, I could see the hives start to shrink and the red dots disappear.

As I approached the bunkhouse, I could hear the four boys laughing before I entered the wooden cabin. When I walked in the door, I saw them sitting in a circle, talking about the trail and laughing at the memories, both good and bad. Mostly, they laughed at mishaps and failures, mistakes and misconceptions; what had made them miserable and angry a few weeks ago now seemed very funny. They could look back and laugh because they had overcome the pain and the frustration. They had grown, they were stronger and wiser, and they had almost completed what they set out to accomplish.

I didn't join in their conversation. I just lay in my bed and listened to the guys carry on late into the night. This was the first time in weeks that I didn't fall asleep as soon as I crawled in my sleeping bag. I was still tired, but it was a peaceful exhaustion, and I wanted to keep my eyes open for as long as I could. Even the air in the room felt different. It was as if I could breathe in the joy of fellowship, the contentment of a job well done, and the strength of an intangible bond.

After White House Landing, we had one last full day on the trail before reaching the base of Katahdin. Nightwalker, Mooch, and I were on the morning's first ferry back to the trail. We hiked separately for most of the day, which gave me plenty of time to reflect on the past four months.

Questions ran continuously through my head: *Would I miss the trail?*

Would it be hard leaving the boys? Was Nightwalker my boyfriend? What would happen once the trail was over? Where would I go? What would I do?

When people had asked why I wanted to hike the Appalachian Trail, one of the answers I had given was that I wanted time to think about where I wanted to live and what I wanted to do for a living, and the trail would give me plenty of time to do that. But now that I was at the end, I didn't feel any closer to knowing the answers than when I started. Hiking the trail had proved too difficult to let me look ahead and make future decisions; it had demanded my entire focus.

The only thing I felt more certain of at the end of this journey was myself. I was no longer defined by my résumé or my activities, and I didn't give answers based on what I thought other people wanted to hear. For the first time in my life, I knew who I was—and I was okay with who I was.

I definitely believed in God—that probably stood out the most after twenty-one hundred miles. Every day on the trail I felt God's presence, His promise never to leave me, and His power in all creation. And for the first time in my life, I didn't feel like I needed to hide that or apologize for it. My affection for Mooch and Nightwalker, and their acceptance of me, helped me realize that regardless of faith and background, if you get to know people—not *what* they are, but *who* they are—then you will experience love and friendship you might otherwise have missed.

I also knew that something deep within me connected with nature, hard work, and simplicity. I learned that I was both stubborn and tough, a lot tougher than I thought I was, especially when I let other people help me. I knew that I was beautiful, despite what other people said, and I appreciated my body based on what it could do instead of how it looked. I also knew that I was truly blessed, blessed with a wonderful family and wonderful friends.

Another thing I knew for certain: after four months in the woods, I knew exactly what, or rather who, I was going back to. I was going back to my family.

Even on good days, my family often experienced strained relations. My mother and I in particular, despite being the same height, had rarely seen eye to eye. Yet there were some aspects of this trip that made me miss my mom, my dad, and my brothers more than ever. I had certainly gone longer periods of time without seeing them before, but there was something different about this experience. In a strange way, the challenges and miles of this trip did not distance me from my family, but made me feel closer to them.

I knew that right then, my dad and brother were driving up from North Carolina to meet me at Katahdin, and that knowledge, even in my tired, rugged, dirty state, left me glowing with anticipation.

Lost in thoughts of seeing my family and searching for answers, I hardly noticed the tall, dark creature grazing next to the trail. I heard a twig snap, and I looked up to spot a hairy brown moose twenty yards off the trail. I was elated—another moose! And this time he had antlers.

The animal was so preoccupied with eating the low-lying leaves that despite my proximity, he didn't even notice me. Not wanting to approach too quickly or appear threatening, I kicked a rock to get his attention. Looking up at me, he trotted a few yards farther into the forest and stood at attention. I kept walking down the trail, but my gaze remained focused on his antlers. And as I drew nearly even with him, his antlers began to move and he began to walk—not farther into the woods, but parallel to me and the trail.

We must have traveled about a quarter of a mile together, as side-by-side as a wild moose and hiker can be, before he turned and veered away into the thick brush behind him. I was never scared or worried about having the moose walk so close. It took until the end of my journey, but I was no longer walking *in* nature, I was walking *with* it.

That night we camped at Rainbow Lake, a large translucent mountain lake bordered with white boulders. The boys and I had set up our campsite by mid-afternoon, and we spent the rest of the day playing and talking at the edge of the water.

We started by skipping flat pebbles against the lake's still surface. Once most of the smooth rocks from the beach had sunk to the bottom of the lake, we threw handfuls of round pebbles into the air and listened to the noise they made as they broke the surface. Those notes turned into music, and we became a band. We timed our throws to control the chorus of percussion hitting the water. The surrounding pines provided an echo that allowed the sound of each individual splash to resonate long after the rocks had disappeared.

Our concert was interrupted when we found a small crawfish in the nearby sand. I don't know if it was really a crawfish, because I thought crawfish just lived in the South, but we caught the animal and sequestered it in a small rocky entrapment. Then we added a leech to the aquarium so he would have a friend, but it turns out that leeches and crawfish don't make great friends.

While I was watching the crawfish tug and poke at the leech, and the leech in turn balling up into an impenetrable black pearl, Mooch thought it would be funny to take my new mop stick and javelin it into the lake as far as he could. I was furious with him, until I realized what Mooch knew from the beginning—mop sticks float. The wind pushed the yellow plastic tube back to shore in a few minutes. Its journey was so peaceful and therapeutic that we ended up throwing it back in a few more times just to watch it gracefully sway up to the shoreline.

After a few hours, the boys left the shore to start cooking their dinners. Since I didn't cook, I stayed by the water.

With Nightwalker and Mooch preoccupied and out of sight, I crept along the shoreline to a large white boulder. I climbed on top of the rock where no one could see me and took off my clothes, laying them on the warm granite beside me. Then, after taking one last minute to absorb the warmth of the rock and look into the sun's dwindling rays, I dove into the clear cool waters below.

Totally submerged, with my hair floating toward the surface and my limbs weightless around me, I embraced the unencumbered sensation of being surrounded by water. Rising back to the surface, I looked at my half-white, half-brown body beneath the water. I was amazed at the physical transformation that had taken place since Georgia. I never knew that I could be this strong and fit.

I looked up into the blue sky toward Katahdin. It was like a dream, too far away to touch but too close to be a mirage. I dipped down below the surface and came back up, but the mountain was still there. I laughed and looked up to the sky. I had done it.

Abol Stream Campground was home to an RV park and the first public road in over a hundred miles. The campground separated the Hundred Mile Wilderness from Katahdin's Baxter State Park, and featured simple amenities like restrooms and a small store.

The store had a pay phone, where four quarters bought me two minutes of talk time and one minute of the operator telling me that my time was almost up, first in English and then in Spanish. My first attempt to reach my dad was unsuccessful, so I left a message and went inside the store to scrounge up some lunch.

After trying to occupy myself with food and people-watching inside the RV park, I tried calling my father again. This time he picked up.

"Jen, hello?" *Crackle.* "Is that you?" *Snap.* "We're getting close to Kata—" *Pop, pop, pop.* "Where do you—" *buzzz* "—meet us?"

The phone line was filled with static, but I could gather that he was close and wanted to know where to meet me.

"Katahdin Stream!" I said.

"Otter Creek?" he asked.

I repeated myself slowly and clearly, "Kah-tah-din Stream."

Again: "Otter Creek?"

I was so frustrated, I yelled into the pay-phone receiver, "KATAH-DIN STREAM, KATAHDIN STREAM, KATAHDIN STREAM, KATAHDIN STREAM, KATAHDIN STREAM!!"

Then I heard the operator say, "I'm sorry, your time has expired."

I don't know how he got Otter Creek from Katahdin Stream, but it took another eight dollars in quarters before he repeated Katahdin Stream into the phone.

Katahdin Stream Campground was still several miles from Abol Bridge. Not wanting my brother and father to arrive at an empty campground and go looking for Otter Creek (God forbid there really was an Otter Creek), I told Mooch and Nightwalker, who had just arrived at the store, that I would see them later on. Then I sped down the trail toward Katahdin Stream.

Out of all my previous sprints on the trail—in thunderstorms, through mosquitoes, and away from Moot—this was by far my fastest. With hardly anything in my pack, I raced down the path, skipping roots, hurdling fallen trees, and dancing over river crossings.

Arriving at Katahdin Stream Campground, I was heartbroken to discover that my family had yet to arrive. And I was a little worried that they were waiting for me at a place named Otter Creek.

Sitting anxiously beside the entrance road, I was overjoyed to finally see them pull up the gravel drive. I left my belongings, dashed to the car, and flung open the driver-side door just as it stopped. Instantly, I had my arms wrapped around my dad's neck. He held me tight, except when he had to use his hand to wipe the tears away from his eyes. It felt like an eternity had passed since he dropped me off in Helen, Georgia. And there could be no greater reward than to have him here to greet me at the end.

After embracing my dad, I ran over to my brother. I was happy and somewhat surprised that he had decided to come. Before the trail, he had not been excited about the thought of his little sister thru-hiking by herself, and I don't think he ever changed his mind. But being here at the end proved that he loved me and wanted to support me despite his objections. Or maybe he was just glad that it was over and I was safe. Either way, he was here, and that meant a lot.

My dad and brother stayed in the park long enough to meet Mooch and Nightwalker. Then, after setting a time to return in the morning, they headed off to spend the night in a hotel. Mooch, Nightwalker, and I prepared to spend our final night in the woods.

At the base of Katahdin, Baxter State Park has a shelter designated solely for thru-hikers. I guess if you walk 2,170 miles, you no longer have to share.

We were the only ones at the Birches Lean-To, and over dinner the boys began trying to recite from memory the name of every shelter they had stayed in along the trail. I struggled to remember the name of the shelter I stayed in three nights ago, let alone back in Georgia.

"Okay, let's see," Mooch started. "We stayed at Stover Creek, Gooch Mountain, then we took a night at Neels Gap Hostel. The next night was that one night we didn't spend together. Remember?"

"Yeah," said Nightwalker. "That was the night I stayed at Blue Mountain Shelter. Man, it was packed. I just remember that it was really cold and there were four really cute girls from Georgia."

My ears perked up. "You mean the Georgia Peaches?" I asked.

"Yeah, did you meet them?" he asked.

"Yeah, I met them along with a guy from Alaska and another hiker who was a diabetic."

"Wait," Nightwalker said, surprised. "All those people were in that shelter."

"So was I." It took me a minute to process, but I suddenly realized that I had met Nightwalker before Virginia. I had met him my very first night on the trail in Georgia, and I had slept right beside him. His name hadn't been Nightwalker then, it was Matthew, and his face hadn't been covered in a blanket of hair. I knew he had seemed familiar and that I felt strangely connected to him, but I just thought that was because I liked him.

It was hard to believe that we just now remembered our first meeting, but it had been a long time ago, and we had both changed a lot since then. After the shock wore off, we all started to laugh. I spent my last night on the trail the same way I spent my first: in a shelter right beside Matthew.

After fighting through rain, snow, fog, cold temperatures, high winds, oppressive humidity, and blazing heat, the weather for our climb up Katahdin was perfect. The sky was blue, the air was warm, the wind was calm, and there weren't even any bugs. We started up the mountain at daylight with my brother. My dad remained at the campground and prepared a picnic for our return.

The trail up Katahdin is mostly, well, up. The path follows the rocky spine of the mountain for most of the way, but then, about a mile from the summit, it flattens out and follows a gradual, exposed slope toward the beckoning brown sign on top of the mountain. That sign, that rickety piece of painted wood that marked the mountain summit—that was the end of the Appalachian Trail.

Nightwalker touched it first, followed by Mooch, but it didn't feel like any of us had really finished until all three of us laid hands on the sign and raised our poles, hands, and mop stick into the air with a conquering yell. We hadn't conquered the mountain or the trail. We had conquered our doubts, fears, and weaknesses.

After a few minutes of hugs, shouting, and celebrating, the boys and I started the traditional photo shoot by the sign. It was great to have my brother there, not only for moral support, but also as a photographer with a digital camera—especially since Nightwalker had broken his.

We took solo shots, group shots, silly shots, and triumphant shots. Before leaving, my brother let me scroll through the dozens of photos to make sure that we didn't want to retake any. I laughed at the pictures; I didn't know my smile could stretch that far. To an outsider, the images of dirty sun-worn travelers by a brown mountain sign would mean very little. But those who could appreciate the hard and trying story preceding those photos would understand that the pictures are worth more to me than anything I have ever owned.

When the photo shoot was over, we turned around and started to hike back down the mountain. I don't want to say that climbing Katahdin was a letdown, because it wasn't. But I thought I was going to have an epiphany once I reached the top. I thought I would feel different at the brown sign marking the mountain summit.

But when I was there, I was just happy.

Driving back home to North Carolina with my dad and brother, I had a lot of time to think. I thought about how strange and somewhat demoralizing it was that the same journey through a mountain range that had taken me four months to hike through could be completed in two days by car.

I also thought a lot about Homer's *Odyssey* and its hero, Odysseus, my namesake. In college we had a class discussion about whether the tale of Odysseus taking ten years to return home in the midst of magic, gods, distraction, and disaster could be a real story. I was the only one in the class who thought it was possible.

Now it all made sense. I had just spent the past four months traveling a 2,175-mile footpath. And during that time, I had been struck by lightning and caught in a blizzard. I met a pirate, escaped a stalker, and encountered illegal drugs. I walked with a moose, avoided serpents of supernatural size, and fought with dark armies (of bugs). I suffered unexplained ailments, underwent spells of fatigue, and was rescued countless times by complete strangers. My best friend was a traveling comedian and minstrel, and I happily took part in a romantic subplot with a mysterious and handsome man. I had been met by a higher power Who guided me along the path, and even when I came face to face with death, I continued to seek out life.

But now that it was all over, I wondered: what did Odysseus do once he was back home?

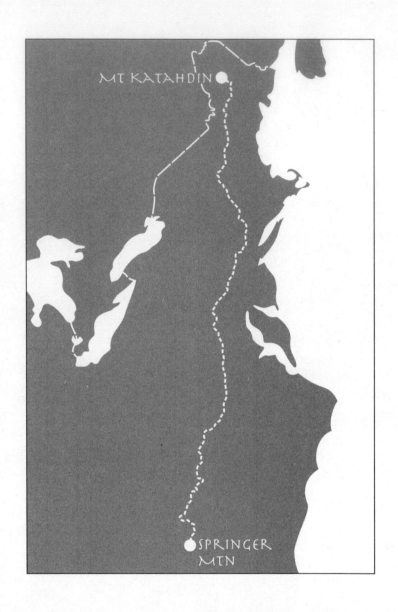

21

HOMECOMING

SUMMER 2005 TO SUMMER 2008—3 YEARS

*"You need to know that the trail can and will change you.
Once you finish the trail, your life might not look the same as
it did when you started. If you don't want things to change,
then you need to rethink thru-hiking."*

The words Warren Doyle had spoken at the Appalachian
Trail Institute haunted me. I was looking forward to going
home, but I didn't realize how hard it would be to reconcile
the last four months with the rest of my life. The world was
the same, but I was different. I had connected on a deep level
to my existence in the woods, and civilization wouldn't be
able to satisfy the parts of me that I had discovered on the
trail.

T he full impact of my thru-hike didn't set in all at once, but revealed itself through my thoughts and interactions over the next weeks, months, and years. Post-trail, I fearlessly set out to find a new home and career, and I quickly found a position at a museum in Virginia. I loved my job and my coworkers, but I didn't love my window. I should have been thankful for the window—with an office in the basement of a two-hundred-year-old house, I was one of the only employees who could look outside. And while I was happy to have the view, I became covetous of what I saw. From behind the glass pane, I watched the seasons change gradually, I observed the rain and snow as an onlooker and not as a participant, and worst of all, I saw feet, lots of feet, walking by my desk. I couldn't see past anyone's kneecaps because the window was above me and the view was limited, but all day every day I saw the shoes of museum visitors walk by, while my feet spent most of the day hidden underneath my desk in uncomfortable dress shoes.

My home life was good. I loved the apartment I lived in with my friend Alice. I loved the cold fruit that came from the refrigerator, the hot water that came from the spigots, and the warm and cool air that came from the vents. For the first few weeks after the trail, I was thankful for every meal, every clean piece of clothing, and every hot shower. But then my gratitude began to fade, and one winter night, standing under the forceful, steaming water shooting out of the showerhead, I realized how commonplace it had become. I remembered my joy at the jailhouse in Palmerton where I'd turned on every showerhead and run through the hot water like a child through a sprinkler, smiling and laughing out loud. My appreciation was now being washed away daily, and I no longer felt thankful for modern conveniences. Instead, I once again felt entitled to them.

It was easy for me to meet people in a new city, but most of my relationships stopped after the introduction. There were people around me all the time, but I didn't feel like any of us really knew one another.

Without seeking depth, I once again began to categorize people: church friend, work friend, good-looking friend, successful friend. And I once again felt alone.

I missed being by myself with my thoughts, and thinking things through to completion. I missed being able to sing out loud. I missed being serenaded to sleep by Mooch. And I much preferred my mountaintop and lakeside dates with Nightwalker to our frequent phone calls and e-mails.

A year after starting my hike at Springer Mountain, I felt like everything around me should have made me happy, but it didn't. I had reverted back to a "normal" life, a life where I met everyone else's expectations and not my own, a life that made me feel numb and empty.

I began to long for discomfort, for any pain or struggle that made me feel alive. I wanted to feel wet, tired, sore, hungry, and thirsty. I didn't necessarily want to be cold, but I wanted to appreciate being warm. I missed always spending the night somewhere different, and I started to resent my stationary bed. When I fell asleep at night, I would dream of adventure, and when I woke up in the morning, I would thirst for real fellowship. I would get up, take a shower, put on clean clothes and makeup, but looking in the mirror, I never felt as beautiful as I did when I was a sunburned, bug-bitten hiker in Maine.

I wanted to go back into the woods.

I wanted to be Odyssa again.

I didn't go straight back to the AT; that took several years. Instead, I saved up every penny I earned at work and took long breaks to thruhike the Pacific Crest Trail and the Long Trail in Vermont. I traveled internationally to explore Machu Picchu in Peru, climb Kilimanjaro in Africa, and hike the Bibbulmun Track in Australia. And every time I went into the woods, I came out different, better, more complete. As if instead of being Jen or Odyssa, I was finally melding together into one identity, on and off the trails.

Through all my travels and hiking, I felt certain that someday I would return to the Appalachian Trail. I knew I would come back, because for me there were more lessons embedded in that ancient mountain chain than anywhere else.

I always assumed that I would return alone. I was wrong.

My love life was pretty uneventful after finishing my first Appalachian Trail thru-hike. I stayed with Nightwalker for a while, but then we decided to become friends, and after that I became more interested in hiking than dating.

In August of 2007, I went for a short car ride with my brother's friend Brew. Brew was six feet tall, with icy blue eyes and dirty blond hair. He was funny, sweet, and attractive, but he was my brother's friend, so I thought our relationship would remain as platonic as they come. During our twenty-minute drive across town, I informed Brew that I would be hiking the Appalachian Trail the next summer. Neither one of us could have guessed that we'd be married before then.

Falling in love, and doing it so quickly, changed my life and my hiking plans. By January, Brew and I were engaged, and while I still wanted to go back to the Appalachian Trail, I didn't want to do it without Brew. As a schoolteacher, he had the summer free, so we decided that I would attempt a supported hike, with Brew providing a 2,175-mile slackpack, so that I could try to set the women's speed record for the Appalachian Trail.

When I first met David Horton and Trail Dog, I never thought that I would one day try to join their ranks as a record-holder. But the thought of flowing down the trail as quickly as possible first intrigued me, and then captivated me. I thought about it every day and dreamed about it at night. It was never really about being a record-holder or hiking the trail in a specific number of days; it was about doing something amazing with my body that in the past had only been attempted by men. It was as simple as doing what I loved, in a place I loved, with the man I loved.

On June 8th, Brew and I were married. We honeymooned for twelve days in New England, then we set out from Katahdin on June 20th to try to set the women's record on the Appalachian Trail.

I averaged thirty-eight miles a day that summer, which still surprises me, especially since I never felt rushed. I just let my body loose.

For me, hiking quickly down the trail was like a free-form dance. It hurt and it was hard, but it never felt oppressive; it felt liberating and full of grace.

I also learned a lot from traveling down the trail so efficiently. Hiking for a record refined my understanding of simplicity and focus, and taught me lessons in communication and trust. There was no way that I could have traveled 2,175 miles in record time without Brew, and after finishing the adventure it felt like we had been married for two years instead of two months—in a good way.

On August 16th, after hiking for fifty-seven days and after seeing thirty bears, I arrived at Springer Mountain. I walked the short one-mile climb from the parking lot, holding hands with my husband and followed closely by my friends Warren Doyle, David Horton, and my family. I touched the rock on top of Springer Mountain amid cheers and the sound of cameras clicking.

"You're probably gonna cry, or yell, or laugh when you get to Springer," David Horton had said.

"It is going to be a profoundly meaningful and deeply moving moment," countered Warren.

But now that I was there, it was Horton who was cheering and yelling and tearing up, and Warren who was reflecting upon the deeper significance of the moment. I felt much as I did the first time I summited Mount Katahdin: I felt happy.

We stood on the mountaintop and took pictures for several minutes. After taking photos, I knew right where to find the hidden journal. The last time I signed this register, I didn't know who I was going to be, but this time I concluded my entry without hesitation.

Since setting the Appalachian Trail record, I have continued to work and I have continued to hike. In 2009, my husband and I thru-hiked the five-hundred-mile Colorado Trail together. It was Brew's first thru-hike and my first time having a hiking partner for an entire trail. We both loved it.

At our home in Asheville, North Carolina, there is a list of potential hikes posted on our refrigerator. It includes local trails for day-hikes, trails that I would love to set a record on, trails reserved for Brew and me to do together, and—if one day we are blessed with children—we have a column for family-friendly hikes too.

For most people, I am defined by my 2008 Appalachian Trail record, which is strange to me, because it was my first thru-hike in 2005 that defined me. People often ask how I prepared for hiking the trail in fifty-seven days, how I developed the stamina and the mental toughness to keep pushing my limits day after day, and why I would even want to attempt such an endeavor. The problem is that most of the time the people who ask the questions are expecting a short response, an easy response, and that's not possible. As a twenty-one-year-old, it took me four and a half months and 2,175 miles to find the answers.

2008 ITINERARY

DAY 0	Mount Katahdin to Nahmakanta Lake (south end)—40.8 miles
DAY 1	Nahmakanta Lake to Rural Logging Rd—43.8 miles
DAY 2	Rural Logging Rd to Maine 15—29.9 miles
DAY 3	Maine 15 to Caratunk (US 201)—36.7 miles
DAY 4	Caratunk (US 201) to Horns Pond Lean-To—31.5 miles
DAY 5	Horns Pond Lean-To to Maine 4 (Rangeley)—37.3 miles
DAY 6	Maine 4 (Rangeley) to South Arm Road—26.4 miles
DAY 7	South Arm Road to Speck Pond Campsite—25 miles
DAY 8	Speck Pond Campsite to Gorham (US 2)—26.5 miles
DAY 9	Gorham (US 2) to West Branch, Peabody River—25.1 miles
DAY 10	West Branch, Peabody River to Ethan Pond—24.9 miles
DAY 11	Ethan Pond to North Kinsman Mountain—30.2 miles
DAY 12	North Kinsman Mountain to Mount Cube—33.5 miles
DAY 13	Mount Cube to New Hampshire–Vermont Line—30.8 miles
DAY 14	New Hampshire–Vermont Line to Chateauguay Road—30.9 miles
DAY 15	Chateauguay Road to VT 103—32.1 miles
DAY 16	VT 103 to Spruce Peak Shelter—35.2 miles
DAY 17	Spruce Peak Shelter to VT 9—37.3 miles
DAY 18	VT 9 to Hoosic River—33 miles
DAY 19	Hoosic River to Tyringham, MA—36.3 miles
DAY 20	Tyringham, MA to Conn 41—41.9 miles
DAY 21	Conn 41 to Schaghticoke Rd—40.5 miles
DAY 22	Schaghticoke Rd to NY 301—37.9 miles
DAY 23	NY 301 to Orange Turnpike—38.6 miles

DAY 24   Orange Turnpike to Gemmer Rd—40.2 miles

DAY 25   Gemmer Rd to beyond Camp Rd—40.2 miles

DAY 26   Beyond Camp Rd to Lehigh Gap (PA 873)—45 miles

DAY 27   Lehigh Gap (PA 873) to Port Clinton, PA—40 miles

DAY 28   Port Clinton, PA to Rausch Gap—41.1 miles

DAY 29   Rausch Gap to beyond Scott Farm—42.4 miles

DAY 30   Beyond Scott Farm to Sandy Sod Junction—47.3 miles

DAY 31   Sandy Sod Junction to Dahlgren Campground—45.7 miles

DAY 32   Dahlgren Campground to Bears Den Rocks—37.8 miles

DAY 33   Bears Den Rocks to US 522—33.4 miles

DAY 34   US 552 to Skyland Service Rd—37.2 miles

DAY 35   Skyland Service Rd to Pinefield Hut—36.7 miles

DAY 36   Pinefield Hut to Rockfish Gap (US 250)—33.2 miles

DAY 37   Rockfish Gap (US 250) to Porters Field—40.2 miles

DAY 38   Porters Field to Matts Creek Shelter—39.1 miles

DAY 39   Matts Creek Shelter to Black Horse Gap—40.9 miles

DAY 40   Black Horse Gap to VA 624—39.3 miles

DAY 41   VA 624 to VA 635—46.3 miles

DAY 42   VA 635 to VA 606—46 miles

DAY 43   VA 606 to VA 623—37.7 miles

DAY 44   VA 623 to VA 16—40.7 miles

DAY 45   VA 16 to VA 600—40 miles

DAY 46   VA 600 to Low Gap (US 421)—38.6 miles

DAY 47   Low Gap (US 421) to White Rocks Mountain—40.1 miles

DAY 48   White Rocks Mountain to Carvers Gap (Tenn 143)—33.3 miles

DAY 49   Carvers Gap (Tenn 143) to Nolichucky River Valley—31.8 miles

DAY 50   Nolichucky River Valley to Flint Mountain Shelter—37.1 miles

DAY 51   Flint Mountain Shelter to Deer Park Mountain Shelter—35.5 miles

DAY 52   Deer Park Mountain Shelter to Davenport Gap (Tenn 32)—32.6 miles

DAY 53   Davenport Gap (Tenn 32) to Buckeye Gap—46.5 miles

DAY 54   Buckeye Gap to Cheoah Bald—46.4 miles

DAY 55   Cheoah Bald to Mooney Gap—46.7

DAY 56   Mooney Gap to Neels Gap (US 19/129)—65.6 miles

DAY 57   Neels Gap (US 19/129) to Springer Mountain—30.7 miles

ACKNOWLEDGMENTS

The trails are such an amazing resource, and I want to thank the organizations, volunteers, and trail maintainers who work so hard to keep the trail open and accessible to the public. I especially want to thank the Appalachian Trail Conservancy and the AT Trail Crews who help to protect and preserve the 2,175-mile miracle in the mountains.

I would not have been able to complete any of my long-distance hikes if it were not for the help of trail angels and the serendipitous trail magic that lined the path. I am especially grateful to Steve, J, the Cruzans, Katie, the Trocki family, the Smiths, Kathy, Julianne, the Randolphs, and the McCargo family for helping me through my first 2,175 miles. A special nod goes out to companies like Diamond Brand Outdoors, Mountain Techs, Lolë, Whole Foods, Blue Ridge Mountain Sports, INOV-8 shoes, and *Blue Ridge Outdoors Magazine* that have been a part of subsequent hikes. Most of all, I want to thank my father, husband, and good friends Warren Doyle and David Horton—it is amazing what a girl can do with four great guys supporting her.

To the team that helped me with this book, thank you! I thought that thru-hiking was hard until I tried to publish a book. Thank you to my dad, Warren, Sarah, Jeff, Isaiah, James, and Horton for your edits and initial feedback. James, I know it took a lot of time and effort to illustrate this book, but I couldn't trust it to anyone else—I am forever grateful. Big Mo, thank you for the beautiful ways that you have captured my heart and the trail in your photographs. And to Eric, Margot, and the crew at Beaufort Books, you guys are the best. Thank you for believing in me and making the book the best it could be without manipulating me as an author or as a character. It is so nice to think of my publisher and editor as friends—constructive friends, but friends nonetheless.

As an author, hiker, and woman, I am indebted to Camp Greystone, Samford University, Ash Lawn-Highland, and Camp Joy for providing environments where I was free to learn and grow. These places made me feel like anything was possible—even the Appalachian Trail. I also owe a special debt to my mom, who taught me the importance of an active outdoor lifestyle as a child, and to my two older brothers, who made me "tough" and taught me how to keep up with the boys. Finally, I want to thank my husband, family, and close friends for walking through the valleys, enjoying the mountain views, and traveling the trail of life beside me. It is so nice to have hiking partners.

ABOUT THE AUTHOR

Jennifer Pharr Davis grew up in the North Carolina Mountains, where she developed a love for hiking at a young age. At age twenty-one, Jennifer hiked the entire Appalachian Trail as a solo female and fell in love with long-distance backpacking.

Since then, Jennifer has hiked more than 11,000 miles of trails in North America, including the Pacific Crest Trail, Vermont's Long Trail, and the Colorado Trail, and completed three thru-hikes on the Appalachian Trail. She has hiked and traveled on six continents; some of the highlights include Mount Kilimanjaro, the Inca Trail to Machu Picchu, and the 600-mile Bibbulmun Track in Australia.

Jennifer holds endurance records on three long-distance trails. In 2008, she became the fastest woman to hike the Appalachian Trail, averaging thirty-eight miles a day and completing the trail in fifty-seven days. In 2011, she became the overall Appalachian Trail record holder, completing the trail in forty-six days.

In 2011, Jennifer won *Ultrarunning Magazine*'s award for Female Top Performance of the Year. She was also named a *National Geographic* Adventurer of the Year for 2012.

Jennifer has written for *Trail Runner* magazine, Away.com, and is a frequent contributor to *Blue Ridge Outdoors Magazine*. She has appeared on *The 700 Club* and CBS's *The Early Show*, and has also been featured in the *New York Times*. Jennifer has written three guidebooks and is the subject of *46 Days: Keeping Up With Jennifer Pharr Davis on the Appalachian Trail*, written by Brew Davis, her husband. Jennifer lives in Asheville, North Carolina, with her husband and is the owner and founder of Blue Ridge Hiking Co. www.blueridgehikingco.com